Reports from the Zen Wars

For Paul and Cecie,
with thanks.

Steve

reports
from the
zen wars

THE IMPOSSIBLE RIGOR OF A QUESTIONING LIFE

Steve Antinoff

COUNTERPOINT

Library of Congress Cataloging-in-Publication Data

Names: Antinoff, Steve, author.
Title: Reports from the Zen wars : a memoir / Steve Antinoff.
Description: Berkeley : Counterpoint, 2016.
Identifiers: LCCN 2015046443 | ISBN 9781619027312
Subjects: LCSH: Antinoff, Steve. | Spiritual biography. | Zen Buddhism.
Classification: LCC BL73.A595 A3 2016 | DDC 294.3/927--dc23
LC record available at http://lccn.loc.gov/2015046443

ISBN 978-1-61902-731-2

Cover and interior design by Gopa & Ted2, Inc.

COUNTERPOINT
2560 Ninth Street, Suite 318
Berkeley, CA 94710
www.counterpointpress.com

Printed in the United States of America
Distributed by Publishers Group West

10 9 8 7 6 5 4 3 2 1

Contents

For Naomi Maeda
empress of bodhisattvas

For Shun Murakami
who translated my work—
though he didn't know me well—
even while dying

For Urs App
touched by greatness

Introduction

S HEN-KUANG CUT OFF his left arm in expression of his determination to pursue the Zen quest even to the death. I have not. The unused blade hangs over my life like a guillotine.

The author, in consequence, is unimportant to these pages, beyond one fact that brings him considerable joy: In stumbling over himself in America and Japan, he fell into position to witness.

King of Whatever Universe

You couldn't approach the old masters without
fear of being struck by lightning.
—Hakuin (1686–1768)[1]

Round One (1972): Down for the Count

JEWISH MYSTICAL LITERATURE recounts how a Hasid called Lieb chose his spiritual master: "I came . . . not to listen to discourses, nor to learn from his wisdom; I came to watch him tie his shoelaces."[2] The man I have chosen as my teacher has refused my choice. Yet, through his own magnificence, he has forced me up against the meaning of Lieb's words—though he owns no shoelaces and though a pair of high-laced shoes tinged with this magnificence has tripped me up for decades.

I call this monk the Thief, in the Zen sense, for he has stolen the world. He stole it the first time I saw him, 4 a.m. my opening morning in the monastery. He led the monks into the chanting hall; dropped into a sitting posture; chanted with the group of them for half an hour while I watched from the laymen's side of the room; bowed a few times; led the monks back to the meditation hall; and while he was about it reduced the other monks to flat, two-dimensional cutouts by his mere presence. I've been trying to steal back the space about me and within me ever since.

But it was stumbling upon him brushing his teeth that turned him into a living Zen koan. I had stepped out of the meditation hall to find him standing by the water pump, hand on hip gazing into the distance, brushing his teeth before the evening meditation. I thought: "This is ridiculous. What he's doing is trivial. What he is doing is the meaning of life!"

I knew nothing of Zen. I did know that whatever Zen is had something to do with this.

His sublime stillness when sitting, the way he handled a broom when sweeping the garden path, his several speeds and styles of "walking meditation" that made all yield to him silent control of the meditation hall—even when he was no longer head monk—are more beautiful to me, more crucial, than any painting or dancer I have ever seen. Later, in Tokyo, Sylvie Guillem dancing Maurice Bejart's *La Luna* floored me. Tremendous as she was, great as Bach is, I could step around them. Try stepping past the Thief and you are struck down, and exhilarated. Aldous Huxley writes: "There comes a time when one asks even of Shakespeare, even of Beethoven—is that all?" The Thief snatches this question as he ambles past and stuffs it back into your gaping mouth.

How he steals is a question without answer. For it's not simply something he does. It's what life does through him. Daisetz Suzuki writes: "When a finger is lifted, the lifting means, from the viewpoint of satori, far more than the act of lifting. Satori is the knowledge of the individual object and also that of Reality which is, if I may say so, at the back of it." The Thief moves; his body seems a transparent chassis through which the power of the universe surges. Each action, each glance of the eye, sings—cosmically charged. And as a movement dissolves, the surging power that infuses it with life does not dissolve but infuses his next movement, and his next, shooting him full of vibrancy even as he cleans his teeth.

I used to trail behind him like an amazed five-year-old, trying to comprehend how gestures so insignificant could be The Absolute. If he felt my presence, he would turn and look at me as if I were nuts. Yet his actions said what the headless torso of the statue of Apollo demanded of Rilke: "You must change your life."

That he could negate another's existence while brushing his teeth would not have entered his mind. I watched his mop ballet along the monastery corridor, one mop per hand. I watched him veer round and with total nonchalance ax one log after another immaculately down the center, though I later learned he had bad eyes. I watched him in one seamless thrust slip out of his sandals, hoist himself onto the sitting platform, form his legs into the full lotus position without using his hands, and with one flick of his fingers crease his robe and kimono under his knees and descend into meditation. The other monks in the monastery, as they headed toward the daily interviews with the master, leaked subservience, doubt. When *he* struck the mallet against the epicenter of the gong and strode toward the master's chamber, his movements alone said: "I'm coming! Be warned!" I have never gotten over his moving, or his stillness. He made visible, casual as a tossed peel, what I have sought the entirety of my adult life: an act that disclosed, as his did, the beginningless, endless life-death force that is infinity.

———◆———

The Thief is wild about meditation. This is a problem each evening when I enter the meditation hall. All the other meditation hall chiefs I have known arrive last, a minute before they are obliged to ring the bell that begins the evening sittings. The Thief arrives first, sitting alone in the empty hall long before any of the monks enter.

There are rules in the meditation hall—*lots* of rules—and there are customs. That the hall chief is entitled to arrive last, after all the other monks are settled on their cushions, is one of the customs. That everyone who enters the hall, before proceeding to his own cushions, must walk to a specified spot on the floor two meters away from the chief monk's sitting platform and bow before his cushions is one of the rules. This bow is mostly an empty gesture executed before empty cushions, since all the monks who later succeed him as chief do everything possible to reduce the time they have to spend meditating and invariably avail themselves of the prerogative of arriving last. Not the Thief. When I enter the darkening hall, hard rubber sandals slapping against the stone floor as I advance to make my bow, he is already seated, a mighty presence lost to the world.

Well . . . not quite lost, and this is the difficulty. The Thief has the unnerving talent of wearing two faces concurrently while he sits atop his cushions. Face one shows him utterly gone, so remote from the hall he couldn't care less about me and my puny meditation. Face two glowers at me the moment I am in his field of vision and cuts me to shreds. Even when my upper torso is parallel to the floor I feel his glance crushing me with my unfreedom. Any doubts about this are dispelled the instant I raise my trunk and confront his eyes boring without mercy, cool and mocking, into mine. Yet never can I shake the suspicion that this is all a mask, that the Thief is too absorbed with what made him quit teaching school and become a monk to be bothered with the likes of me. The first face says: "You've got *that* right!" The second face, the one I would like to dismiss as a mask, winks (without moving an eye) and says: "You didn't come thousands of miles to a Zen monastery to bullshit yourself, did you?"

The Thief does not care about my love life, or what books I have read, or if my Japanese is coming along. He terminates me at a single point, always the same point, the point where I attempt to live. If our eyes never met again he would not give me another thought. Since they do, he forms himself into a koan that I can avert only by awakening to the Zen Self or by keeping the hell away.

I can, of course, circumvent him by entering the meditation hall before he does, forty-five minutes before the official start. That would lengthen immensely the longest, most excruciating sitting period of the day. The evening sitting begins with close to an hour of meditation to ready the monks for their one-on-one interviews with the master. I do not yet attend this interview because of my rotten Japanese. While the monks bring answers to their koan to their teacher, I remain in the hall, legs and back pleading in pain as they file back one by one. To add fifty minutes to this agony to evade the Thief's face for a few seconds—honestly, it's a toss-up.

———◆———

The Thief would not like it if I divulged his name. He is steep and you do not scale him. You may love and fear him as I do, or dislike him as I have heard some of the other monks do—those who have come to the monastery merely to qualify for the license that will enable them to take over their fathers' temples—but he is a precipice that you do not scale. It is hard to conceive that I am thirty years older now than he was then. The uncontrived manliness, the eternal maturity are one in a billion. Beside him the other monks seemed like green kids. These days he is a master. With no disciples, so far as anyone I know is aware. The last time I saw him, in one of our very rare conversations, he told me: "Being a monastery master wasn't for me."

He is one of those singular persons you can still find in Japan (in America and Europe I have met only one): a man who without use of the slightest physical force can stop your life in its tracks. This is the crux of the whole thing. It has nothing to do with rules and customs or even glances. Line up every other monk in the monastery and force me to bow to them before heading to my cushions in the meditation hall; let them all glare into my bones—it would mean nothing beyond the trouble any boss can cause. By contrast, imagine that the Thief altered his custom and began coming to the meditation hall last. I would already be hoisted onto the sitting platform with legs crossed. He would stride into the hall. I would see only his back. He would hop onto his cushions and ring the opening bell without giving me a look. There'd be no ray of negation from his eyes. There'd be no intimidation. His answer would still be NO!

"No, what?" you will naturally ask. But it is simply no. Absolute no in the foundations of my being, absolute insufficiency for living or dying.

He knows it. And I know it.

———◆———

In *The Gateless Barrier,* when his master tests Keizan's awakening with the koan "What is the Tao?" the latter answers: "A jet-black ball speeding through the dark night." That's the Thief. He explodes out of each step like a thunderclap as he strides toward his cushions across the meditation hall, kimono sleeves cracking the Void. I'm sure he has no idea how.

Palpable threat emanates from his acts. It is cosmic, not moral, energy that pours through him; Zen's Original Face prior to the duality of good and evil. The Thief is an excellent man. But it is clear, as with the great Tang master Lin-chi, that the good is but one ray of his force and cannot exhaust him. The monk Bunko tells me that Zen master Eikido killed two monks accidentally with blows of his staff. It may be a blessing that the Thief has no disciples.

When I say this to my friend Mrs. Maeda years later, she says: "My experience is *completely* different." She assures me that if I were the Thief's disciple (I am always searching for a way) he would not break me. She never denies my assertions of his ferocity, but her experience *is* different.

The Thief, you see, is a playful man. I have known this myself from the outset, when I observed him (I observe him whenever possible) with the monk Jun, his best friend in the monastery. They are never serious together. After the two of them have "graduated" the monastery and Jun joins him for one of the seven-day intensive meditation retreats, they disappear on the sixth night, rumor has it to get drunk. He clowns with Dr. Ebuchi, the sixty-year-old lay Buddhist who lives in the monastery and is the master's only pal. I have heard that he once squirted the master with a hose. My monk friend Saburi-san tells me that when someone told the Thief he had spotted him at some clerical function, he replied: "If it was a bald, middle-aged monk, the ass was me." Saburi-san also described riding with the Thief in a cab to the Silver Pavilion. The latter insisted on tipping the driver, against custom in Japan. When the driver protested, the Thief countered: "It was extremely urgent that I arrive not too early, not too late. You have gotten to the exact spot at the exact time," and he forced the money into his hand.

So it is not surprising that Mrs. Maeda sees an aspect of him that I never will. The first time they met, he came to the Institute for Zen Studies, where she works as an editor and librarian, to track down a book that the founder of his temple had written. When the book could not be found, he said: "Sit down and let's talk." They spoke for the next two hours and have been talking ever since.

The Thief and I will *never* talk two hours. Until the very last time I spoke with him, our direct conversations were three: two lasting a few seconds, one of five minutes when I was about to begin the daily interviews with the master and he decided that it was time to give me some advice. On all other occasions, he spoke to me through other monks.

Unless the nature of their relationship has changed—this could only occur at Mrs. Maeda's request—the Thief hides the negating force and lifts her high. I had told her of the gorgeousness of his movements for years. After their second meeting I received a letter from her: "Last week he came to the Institute. I said: 'It's cold in the library. Do your work in my office by the heater.' We talked over coffee. I have never seen anyone drink coffee so beautifully in my life." The Thief comes to her institute once a month. She says it is the day she most looks forward to, and she marks it on her calendar. "I've seen hundreds of monks enter and leave this place," she tells me. "No one even comes close [to him as a Zen presence]." Our judgment is identical, though we know him at opposite ends of his personality.

When I hear Mrs. Maeda describe her relationship with the Thief,

I think I too would like to be his friend. This is impossible. Once I entered the monastery, however inept, I forfeited the right to be treated as an ordinary civilian. I know this because down to 107 pounds and following a bout of blood poisoning, when it became clear that my living inside the monastery was coming to an end, he began to relate to me in a different way, smiling, referring to me, for the first time, by name—"Mister Steven"—though always speaking to me through a third person even when standing a few feet away.

———◆———

When I arrived at the monastery, the master decided I should live not in the meditation hall but in a tiny room by the kitchen. When I had no duties, I was to stay there. One night there was no meditation. I was in my room when the monk Bunko slid open my door. The Thief had sent him to fetch me. I trailed Bunko to the part of the temple where we had our heads shaved to find a small, elegantly laid-out buffet. The food was set out on newspaper that had been spread over the tatami flooring. The Thief was chatting with Dr. Ebuchi. Neither acknowledged my arrival.

I was happy to be awarded this rare reprieve from what had become my cell. Silently, I sat among the three others: the gentle Bunko (the only monk to consistently seek me out to make sure I was okay); Dr. Ebuchi, who once, near-dead with tuberculosis, saved his own life—he is convinced—by escaping from the clinic where the patients in the surrounding beds had died; the Thief: relaxed, off-duty, even so the majestic mountain barely concealing an infinite crevasse. After several minutes I reached with my chopsticks for my first bite—a neatly cut square of tofu—lifted it, and dropped it. The Thief turned to Bunko, said nonchalantly: "Tell him to return to his room," turned back to Dr. Ebuchi, and resumed their conversation where he'd left off.

This was our first personal exchange. He had said to me, in effect:

"Reality isn't just what *is*. It contains an *ought,* a demand. The Zen world requires you to meet that demand. It's called true Self. Better luck next time."

———————◆———————

Both my failure and his reproof mean little, forgotten by him, no doubt, by the time I exited the room and by me soon after. I'll never learn to use chopsticks well, but even if I'd lifted the tofu neatly into my mouth and been permitted to remain at the "party," the answer would still be "No!" The Thief's power to press me to the wall has at bottom nothing to do with his judgment of me. The real danger he poses he has no control over: an inadvertent murderousness that resides in his core, inextricable from his beauty. Lethality and beauty as a co-presence in more than a few great monks goes to the heart of Zen, and some scholar of religion should study it. Rilke had a sense of it when he wrote in the first *Duino Elegy:* "For beauty is nothing but the beginning of terror, which we are barely able to endure, and it amazes us so, because it serenely disdains to destroy us." Or just look at the painting of the Tang master Lin-chi by Soga Jasoku meditating with a scowl, hand clenched in a fist. Zen people call its severity "grandmotherly compassion." It's that. But it's more than that: the "Great Death" or "total negation" Lin-chi celebrated in his famous proclamation shortly after his enlightenment: "Everywhere else the dead are cremated, but here I bury them alive at once."[3]

The monk Bunko, after fifty years one of the deepest meditators in Japan, tells me: "Zen is to become one with nature." I reply: "Nature kills ten thousand people in thirty seconds in an earthquake." He says: "One must become one with *good* nature." It doesn't work that way. The Thief is the tornado, not just the stilled breeze. This is part of his enigma: He is a figure of extreme power, yet the power is not in the end *his* but that which forms him and which he makes visible with beautiful acts. He isn't simply compassion. The Thief, as was Lin-chi, is a scythe. Sometimes intentionally, sometimes despite himself. Thor creates with a hammer.

———————◆———————

My first night in the monastery an incomprehensible jabbering in Japanese pulled me to my tiny window. The monk indicated with his finger that I was to wait; a minute later he slid open the door to my room and hopped up onto the tatami, closing the door behind him. Muttering repeatedly "Eigo dame"—"My English stinks," he dropped onto his butt and produced from the hanging sleeves of his work clothes two donuts, one of which he shoved in my direction with the utmost warmth. When I shook my head in refusal, he placed it on the floor, biting joyfully into the other donut and dripping jelly all over the tatami. He was so friendly that I couldn't be angry, but I'd been told to keep my room spotless and had no idea where to find a rag or a broom. He chatted away between dripping bites, rubbing his shaved head in perplexity at each of my attempts to communicate. Midway through the first donut, he picked up the second, biting them alternately with delight. As soon as he finished, he sat up on his shins and bowed a full prostration in the formal Zen style, head touching palms that he'd pressed to the floor, leaving fingerprints of jelly on the tatami and departing through the sliding door.

This was Chu-san, a babbling Harpo Marx. Rules were not for him, but he was divested of all ill will. One morning as I emerged from sweeping behind the bell tower, the Thief tore into him in front of the other monks. It was a mighty lashing, and Chu-san began to cry.

Later that day, Bunko, as was his custom during the break between lunch and the afternoon work detail, hid himself in the storage space behind my room. Here he would sneak in extra meditation out of view of the several monks who mocked him for meditating more than he had to, or read from the pile of old Zen journals about the great masters from the past. As always he asked about my sitting. I said: "Seeing the chief monk bawl out Chu-san this morning was hard to endure. If the scolding were out of love, I could accept it." I said this less from empathy than from fear that the Thief would rip me to shreds in the same way.

"The chief loves Chu-san, all right. Before he became a monk, he taught in a school for students who are mentally disabled. Chu-san was one of his students. The chief monk brought him here."

The two top monks (excluding the master) rotate the two top posts—head of the meditation hall and chief administrator of the monastery. The Thief manipulates the rotation, staying on as meditation hall chief for an additional six months while postponing his tenure as monastery administrator, since administration duties make the *sesshin*—arduous stints of weeklong sittings—impossible to attend. The switch enables him to sit six *sesshin* in succession. The monk with whom he rotates likes this setup just fine.

In the meditation hall, the Thief reigns supreme. In meditation he is colossal—austere, sublime, not to be messed with. When he cracks the wooden blocks to initiate the brief recess midway through the sittings, he releases himself from the full lotus position without use of his hands; his legs fly off the meditation platform, and in an exquisite unified movement he descends into his sandals and without a millisecond's pause between landing and walking is exiting the hall. It seems not physically possible. The last inch of vertical descent to the floor is simultaneously the horizontal movement toward the doors, like the old Hertz rent-a-car commercial where the customer floats down into the driver's seat of a suddenly moving car. *My* descents are less entertaining. My legs are killing me; my feet usually asleep and I cannot get my toes into my thongs. Since, to my relief, the monks have left me behind, filing across the long garden to the chanting hall or to the meal,

I cheat, bending over and separating my big and second toe with my hands and then kicking the wall of the meditation platform to drive my toes past the bit of hard rubber that holds the foot onto the sandal. This achieved, I stumble after my brethren.

All of whom see I am a disaster in a Zen monastery. Every one of my talents means nothing here; the skills at which I am inept are constantly required. I cannot execute a single movement or task as the monastery bosses like. Dipping my cleaning rag into the bucket of icy water turns my hand into a paralyzed lobster. Racing to catch up with the monks who are meditating in the garden for the "night sitting," I smash into the astonished master in the pitch black chanting hall, crashing the old fellow to the floor. The constant pain in my back, shoulders, and legs makes concentration in meditation impossible; I shift position constantly atop my cushions. One night the torture gets the better of me and I leave the hall and return to my room. None of this would be permitted any of the others. The Thief says nothing. Because I am beyond hope and he's simply following the master's request: "He's come from far away. Welcome him"? From a faith that I will rise to the Zen demand in time?

———————◆———————

Kafka writes that we are expelled from Paradise not merely because we have eaten of the Tree of Knowledge but because we have not yet eaten from the Tree of Life. The Thief gorges himself on that tree. He loves physical labor. Carpenters coming to the monastery from the outside world to make repairs receive affection and respect denied even the monks. In late July, when many of the monks return to their home temples, the Thief kicks into high gear to make up the slack, mopping, cutting wood, pruning the garden, raking the sand garden on joyous fire. His one break is after lunch, when he naps in a room across the kitchen from mine, elegant on his back, Paul Bunyan in repose. Shin'ichi Hisamatsu writes in *Zen and the Fine Arts* of the

Zen "Self-creative" arts . . . among which may be included even the appearance and gestures of a person who has attainted Awakening—the postures that appear when Zen is expressed in man. These may exist momentarily—at a particular time or on a particular occasion—and may vanish immediately after their appearance. Nevertheless, it seems to me that such postures or gestures are of incomparable interest. Rather than something carved in wood or cast in bronze, rather than the formal poses used in arts such as the theater, these naturally occurring expressions in Zen are far more basic.[4]

An eccentric friend from the sixties who curtailed his law career for bad poetry and psychedelic drugs had one inspired line: "Always honor your father and mother, for they gave you a free ticket to the greatest show on earth." The Thief is the Show of Shows. The free admission comes at a price.

———————◆———————

Zen monks beg in straw sandals that fail to cover my Western-size foot and a straw, cone-shaped lampshade of a hat that obscures enough of the face to ensure anonymity. Three days in ten the monks divide into packs of four and beg through the Kyoto streets. Thus far these groups have been of two types: those who reverse direction after an hour and a half to get back in time for lunch. Those who do not head back at halftime but continue away from the monastery and who tickle me by returning in a taxi out of the money we have just begged.

Today for the first time I have been named to the Thief's ensemble. I follow at the end of the queue like a duck learning how to imprint on its mama, chanting the mandatory "Hooooo! Hooooo!" The Thief halts, telling the monk behind him to inform me that the chant is "Hooooo!" not "Wooooo!" I correct myself, but he stops several with the same reprimand. At the hour and thirty-minute mark, we rest, according to custom. Here the monks usually chat, smoke, and buy soft drinks. The Thief sits silently on a stone bench with his back rigid in meditative silence. His seriousness inhibits the others, who neither drink nor smoke nor talk. We rise, but he does not head back toward the temple, rather farther away. I assume we will return by cab, or at least by trolley. We return by foot, still far from the temple.

Eventually the Thief marches us into a wooded region that stretches along a shrine, for the first time this morning turning his head from face-front concentration to enjoy the blossoms on the trees. None of the other monks has ever walked among the trees; nor have I ever seen one admire a flower. I am happy to be "in nature," especially having heard that the Thief likes to beg among alleys where there are barking dogs, to see if they will cower. Two days later there is a shooting pain in the part of my foot that protruded over the sandal. I writhe in my sleep over the next several days with what I think is a bruised heel. The monk in charge of the chanting hall, a true gentleman of six-foot-four and crazy for Beethoven, hears me groaning in the night and applies a plaster. This seems to ignite my foot in flames, and the following afternoon I am admitted for an emergency operation for blood poisoning—very dangerous, the doctor tells the master by phone—and a ten-day stay in the hospital.

Aside from the fact that it wipes out my savings, the hospital is a vacation: My Japanese improves; a pretty nurse comes to my room every night to confess agony over which of two boys she should choose as her husband; I become friends with the patient in the bed next to mine, who annoys me at first because he wears a woman's stocking on one leg. The nurse tells me that the sickness in his leg has kept him out of work for months and that he cannot support his family. On the day of my discharge, this man supports me with his shoulder into the elevator, through the lobby, then down long flights of stone stairs as I exit the hospital grounds; tears roll down my face at the distance between his troubles and mine, his humanity and mine.

At the monastery I am useless, unable to work or sit. I am losing weight by the week, 107 pounds and counting. I decide to move to a room a hundred meters outside the monastery grounds.

The day before I'm to leave, while raking the sand garden, a monk approaches with a request: For the next three days, the monks will be traveling to the mountains to cut lumber; the Thief would like to know if I'd be willing to postpone my departure so there will be, in their absence, someone to receive visitors to the monastery. Of course I agree. That afternoon when I pass him, the Thief smiles at me for the first time.

Four days later, hearing the monks chanting outside the main gate to mark their return, I hobble to the entrance on my bandaged foot and prostrate myself in thanks for their labors, a ritual I've seen the chief cook, who is exempted from the begging tours in order to prepare lunch, do countless times. The Thief grins broadly, and whenever he sees me through the course of the day (never directly, always through another monk), he thanks, in English, "Mister Steven" for manning the monastery. On the morning of my departure, the door to my room slides open. Never before has the Thief sought me out. His face is deadly determined, and though he says nothing, it is clear that I am to follow. I trail behind him past the monastery gate, the sound of our high wooden sandals crunching the gravel underfoot. Not once does he look behind him. At one of the subtemples within the monastery compound, he steps into the garden, slides open the door, and steps into the temple foyer. An old woman, Mrs. K., whose husband was killed in the war and who has cared for the priest of this small temple the thirty years since, welcomes us with a bow to the floor.[5] This is the temple that sponsors me, an arrangement made by the master while I was still in the States. I have never spoken to this priest. It is explained that I will be leaving the monastery and that I have come to take my formal leave. The old priest nods; he doesn't know me from Adam; the whole thing is a formality, but the Thief regards it as a serious affair. I bow, express my thanks, bow again, and when the priest departs, we return the way we came. Back inside the monastery gate, we veer toward the kitchen and my room. Next to the monks' bathhouse is a toolshed. The Thief slides open the door to the shed and slips from sight; a second later he reappears, his back to me, holding my work shoes by their ankle-high tops in his right hand as he slides shut the door to the shed with his left. These are the shoes I wore the day I arrived. I left them in the foyer when I was first taken to see the master. I had never seen them since and wondered if they'd been discarded. He sets the shoes on the ground, perfectly aligned, and walks off toward the meditation hall. Not one word. Nothing but his back. My hundred pounds are standing alone, in a foreign continent in a Zen monastery where I did not fare well, before these shoes. The Thief's point is clear: "You have chosen to leave. It is famously difficult to stand in another man's shoes. You are finding out it is just as difficult, far more difficult in fact, to stand in one's own."

———————◆———————

One of the monks approached as I was leaving the monastery. "Except for meditation," he warns, "you are not to come to this temple." It was clear from whom this stipulation had come, and it made complete sense.

That evening, when I walked the half block from my newly rented room and entered the meditation hall, the Thief was sitting alone. It was mid-August, many monks were still on summer break, and there was no required sitting for those who remained. Each evening for the next few weeks, the Thief sat "unmovable, like a mountain," as Shin'ichi Hisamatsu's fabulous calligraphy puts it, while I squirmed through the five sitting periods from my new spot on the laymen's side of the meditation hall. When the last sitting ended, before I could slip into my street shoes for the walk back home, the Thief would come charging out of the meditation hall, cushions under his arm, speeding toward the stone veranda overlooking the garden and a solitary bout of night sitting.

A half hour prior to that, each evening at 8:30, there'd be a ten-minute break before a final brief meditation, at the end of which Bunko, presently the cook, gonged the bell from the high tower just outside the monastery walls and sang the closing chant of the day. During one of these recesses, as I returned from trying to walk the pains out of my legs, the Thief was waiting for me as I stepped back into the meditation hall. "You can return home at the break." The entirety of my first stay in Japan, his only direct words to me.

No doubt he thought I was struggling enough and that there was not much to be gained by my sitting out a last fifteen minutes. "I'll sit through to the end," I said. He pressed his palms together, bowed slightly, and proceeded to his cushions. I could tell he was pleased.

But as the cold set in, I knew I had had it. My money was gone; I'd lost thirty-three pounds from an initially skinny frame, and though the Zen saying goes: "When pressed to the extremity, there is a break-through," I was inwardly too young to have the courage not to retreat. I made a plan. I would return to America, regain my health and the illusion of equanimity that familiar circumstances and friends bring, replenish my finances, and come back to Japan.

The day before I flew off on a flight of Christian missionaries, where a young American in the adjoining seat proudly informed me that he spoke in tongues and had just spent a week in Taiwan ascertaining that Christianity was superior to Asian religions, I walked through the monastery gate to say goodbye to the master. He gave me two calligraphies and bid me to take care. When I tied my shoes and stepped out of the foyer, I was intercepted by Do-san, a monk my age who would say to me in English: "Japanese language very easy; even two-year-old child can speak it." I was about to thank him for all his kindness, but he broke in first: "The chief monk says to you: 'Please live in this monastery again.'"

ROUND TWO (1976–1979, 1987): SPLIT DECISION

Three years of experiences—including a rifle against my head at 4 a.m. in Hillbilly Land that I thought was the last of me—interrupt my first two stays in Japan. But Richard DeMartino, the great professor who drew me to Zen, says you cannot learn from experience. He means that what is time bound, what has beginning and an end, resolves nothing. That's why I am back in Kyoto. Although when I told DeMartino prior to my first trip that I wanted to study Zen in Japan, he said: "Don't make the problem geographical," and he's right about that too. The problem of being an "I" can be solved neither by moving forward in time nor laterally in space but by casting off time and space.

The Thief sits, hard as marble gone as mist, across the stone floor from my place on the laymen's side of the meditation hall, in the row reserved for monks who have graduated the monastery but wish to continue their training. In other words, he sits alone. He is now chief priest of a temple in the mountains, returning to the monastery only for the weeklong periods of intense meditation—the *sesshin*. He is nonetheless unchallenged king of the hall; thief by nature, he steals the job out from under the current chief monk, though he has no wish to and never utters a word.

During walking meditation, if he walks slowly, the monks, including the chief monk, slow. If he picks up the pace, all pick up the pace. He ignites the meditation hall with a power that he cannot conceal, thunderous in his solitude, the living incarnation of the monk Hsiu, who in Hsueh-Yen's memoir from *Whips for Breaking through the Zen Barrier,*

> kept sitting on his cushion like a solid bar of iron; I wanted to have a talk with him, but he was forbidding. . . . One day I happened to meet Hsiu in the corridor, and for the first time I could have a talk with him. I asked, "Why was it you avoided

me so much last year when I wished to talk to you?" He said: "An earnest student of Zen begrudges even the time to trim his nails; how much more the time wasted in conversation with others!"[6]

I've concocted a new strategy this second time around: renting a room a ten-minute walk from the monastery until my monk friend Saburi-san invites me to live in his temple on the monastery grounds for a pittance; three hours meditation with the monks each evening; living in the monastery one week per month for the *sesshin*. The master agrees.

As usual, I'm stumbling. I can't function in the cold, and the meditation hall—windows open and following rules established in Tang Dynasty China when the technology didn't exist—forbids artificial heat. Two goose down sleeping bags, one inside the other, and still I'm too frozen to conk out. Unable to sleep, I eventually have to pee, and four times in the ensuing years—trying to slide open the paper-paneled door that will take me out of the meditation hall to the outdoor, flushless urinals—my groping hand pierces through the rice paper. Back inside in the pitch dark, I misjudge the location of my futon; climbing up onto the meditation platform, I step on the chest of the layman sleeping in the spot next to mine, who says, in politest Japanese: "It's me." The hard rubber that secures my feet into the sandals the monks have lent me for use in the meditation hall cuts my toes to shreds, making the walking meditation agony. When the cuts become visible, I wrap Band-Aids around my toes to buffer them from the rubber. Invariably one of the laymen, on his way back from the latrine, mistakenly swipes my sandals, since every pair looks identical. Forced into the pair he mistakenly leaves behind, my feet are cut in new places. With socks prohibited, and wearing Western-style trousers, my soles are raw with chilblains. The meditating monks cover their feet with their robes; the half dozen laymen wear *hakama* skirts; Dr. Ebuchi—

the master's best friend and specially privileged because of his age—has me salivating over his thick woolen socks and gloves.

One of the laymen, a young medical student, suggests that I buy a *hakama* skirt. "You can buy a used one cheap at the monthly flea market at the Kitano shrine." I'm thrilled at the bargain—a paltry five hundred yen (and five hundred more for a kimono). The first time I put it to use, in the January *sesshin,* lowering into a bow behind my sitting cushions before the opening sitting period, I stand on the hem and hear it rip the length of my rear. Saburi-san, the master's attendant and thus exempt from the *sesshin,* kindly sews it. I hasten back to the meditation hall and at the next bow promptly tear it again, have it sewn again, and tear it again and am forced back into my jeans.

The medical student advises me to buy a *hakama* like his: used for *kendō* (the Way of the Sword) and tear-proof—he swears—no matter how much I trample on it. He writes down the address of the *kendō* supplies shop. The one I purchase differs from the ordinary *hakama* in that it is divided in two, like culottes, one slot for each leg. Next *sesshin,* in my flea market kimono and new *hakama,* I move stiff as the tin man from *The Wizard of Oz,* but my feet are covered and the heat pocket created by the *hakama* enables me to cut down from eight layers, including two sweaters and a down vest, to five. Between the first and second sittings I switch position. Unbeknownst to me, I manage to get both left and right legs into the left slot. I sit fiercely as I can. The smashing of wooden blocks announces the walking meditation. The monks jump from the sitting platform into their sandals. I do the same and fall crashing onto the stone floor, both feet caught in the crotch of my *hakama* in which there is, as the medical student promised, not a tear.

I am the physically delicate one in every monastery I've ever set foot in. All the monks suffer, but insofar as I can tell from every visible sign, not as I suffer. They execute the monastic tasks (apart from the solutions to their koan) with ease; they beg through downpours and occasional snow in thin straw sandals and soaked feet with lightheartedness, even cheer. Each *sesshin* my stomach goes on strike. Each brings me to the brink (though it is never really the brink). Each thrusts me against what in America my big personality, charm filched from my dad, and grace on the dance floor to a considerable degree obscure: that my soul is held together with rubber bands. Yet within this desperation of weaknesses something has congealed, something that compels me to cross my legs night after day, now for more than forty years. Something the Thief cannot steal and, if he is the man I think he is, will be overjoyed that he cannot steal.

———————◆———————

By the bell tower I run into Saburi-san, the master's attendant and the most brilliant of the monks—he speaks English and French fluently and was living in Paris, addicted to French cinema, until his father died of lung cancer and he was forced to return home and enter the monastery to obtain the requisite license to succeed him.

"The Thief's are the most beautiful human acts I have ever seen," I say.

He responds by telling me of a water fight the Thief started in the monastery kitchen when Saburi first came.

"Do you think he's this way because of what he learned from Zen?" I ask.

"Oh, he's just that kind of guy." He adds that the Thief once told him: "Hito no koto kamawahen"—"I pay no mind to what others think and do."

I remember this years later when, taking an American who had somehow gotten hold of my phone number for a tour of the Kyoto sights, I run into Toga-san, director monk of the Institute for Zen Studies, standing contently by the front gate of his temple home on the grounds of Tenryūji Monastery. Warm as ever, he invites us into his beautiful modern kitchen for cakes and tea. "Isn't [the Thief's] temple affiliated with Tenryūji?" I ask.

"Yes. His temple has many buildings." With a mischievous glint he adds: "He likes to burn things."

———◆———

The Thief's handsome looks, it seems, are partly an inheritance from his mother, a wonderful character, from what I've heard. To a monk who accompanied the Thief on a visit back home she is said to have confided: "I was so pretty that I decided to travel to Tokyo to see how I compared to the women there. I walked the Tokyo shops and streets, increasingly cocky that none of them could touch me. I wandered into a department store. A gorgeous woman in a kimono appeared. Furious, I headed toward her and a few feet from the mirror realized: 'Oh, it's me.'"

———◆———

Grueling as they are, after a year, *sesshin* have ceased to press me to the edge of myself. Meditating hours a day brings thrills that are addictive. An American psychologist who had spent a year in the same monastery and was revisiting briefly just as I arrived for my first stay told me: "It's disappointing to endure a week of *sesshin* and not reach a deeper state of meditation than you achieved the *sesshin* before." I know that feeling—it's a trap. All states of meditation are ephemeral. DeMartino warned repeatedly that enlightenment is not a state. What Yung-chia said in the seventh century about meritorious acts as a means to enlightenment applies to states of meditation: "Like shooting an arrow against the sky. When the force is exhausted the arrow falls on the ground."[7]

So failed *sesshin* by failed *sesshin,* I seal off my escape paths: no more naps; sit through the rest periods; all periods to be sat in the full lotus; sit two periods consecutively without moving; *do* try not to talk so much during the breaks. And to my amazement—though it solves nothing—the monks are off begging and I'm sitting in the meditation hall alone with the Thief almost nonstop until lunch. A half dozen monks who sleep upright through the pitch black meditation periods in the predawn are whacked repeatedly for dozing during the evening sittings, while I—bumbling as ever—grin into the night on my cushions, the full moon stuffed into my brain.

At the November *sesshin*, I'm lounging on the cement, hoarding a half hour of the scarce warm sun in front of Dr. Ebuchi's room. Shinsan, a bespectacled young monk who says he can justify being a priest only if he's useful to society—a rare sentiment among the monks I know—bows before me. I jump to my feet and return the bow.

"[The Thief] wants to know: In your meditation, do you reach the point where there is nothing whatsoever?"

"Not yet," I say. Shin-san bows and departs.

Several minutes later he's back: "[The Thief] wants to know: Do you ever feel energy running through your body, in the lower abdomen especially?"

"Most of the time."

He bows and departs. Seven, eight minutes pass and Shin-san is hurrying toward me. He bows. I bow. "[The Thief] wants you never to forget: When you reach the point where there is nothing whatsoever, do not mistake it for enlightenment. It is only the gate."

———◆———

When I return to the monastery for the evening meditation after the three-day break following the *sesshin*, the Thief, who invariably departs for his home temple at its conclusion, is sitting on his cushions. He has moved back into the monastery to finish up his koan training under the master. Dr. Ebuchi has hung a curtain down the length of his closet-size room; he on one side, the Thief on the other—space for a sleeping body and little else in their shared quarters. I marvel at Dr. Ebuchi, a medical doctor and psychiatrist already past sixty. Stricken with nervous and physical disorders earlier in life, he toughs it out in the monastery year after year, reading and writing about his beloved Morita therapy—a psychotherapy for anxiety-based illness loosely influenced by Zen—on the overturned crate that, apart from a small desk lamp, is his sole item of furniture.

Not surprisingly, the imminent completion of the Thief's formal training triggers talk of the master's successor. For me the Thief is a far greater Zen personality than the master, a thought I cannot reveal. I have heard that the master does not like the Thief. Yet the master has given his official sanction to the monk X-san, which bewilders me. For the first months of my second stay, X-san, who has graduated from official monastic positions but has not yet left the monastery, sits alone with me for the five-minute interval that begins when the monks file out of the meditation hall for the daily koan interviews and ends when the current chief monk—the first to bring his answer to the koan before the master—reappears. The instant the monks are gone, X-san quits meditating, cracking his knuckles and neck and stretching his long arms and legs, ever careful to pop back into formal meditation posture as soon as the returning chief monk's footsteps can be heard. Sixty seconds later, when the chief has resumed sitting, X-san jumps down from his cushions for his turn at an interview. Later, through the master's influence, X-san is made master of a monastery in western Japan.

Ko-san, the current top monk, is rumored as possible successor; the master is fond of him, it is said. My strongest impression of Ko-san was during my first tenure at the monastery, when I joined the monks for a day of work at the *honzan*, the building two hundred meters from the monks' training hall in the same temple complex and where important ceremonies are convened. As I carried some red lacquer trays into the kitchen, Ko-san, then still a rookie, flashed the centerfold of a soft porn magazine my way and in enthusiastic Japlish exclaimed: "Nudo!" He was older now, too fond of his authority, and said to be attracted to koan study, though an extra minute of meditation is never to be observed. It's hard not to notice that when one of his co-leaders graduates from the monastery, the monk newly promoted to the number-two spot is made meditation hall chief, while Ko-san, whose turn it is to rotate back to that post, continues for another six months exempted from *sesshin* as chief monastery administrator.

The most striking remark on the topic of the master's successor is from Tanemura-san, my closest friend among the laymen. Sensitive and brilliant, he reads Martin Heidegger in English "because it's clearer than when I read him in Japanese" and can render any single Japanese word into English, though he won't utter an English sentence. He says: "If [the Thief] is passed over, it'll be time to look for another place to train."

———◆———

My friend Saburi-san, having finished the three years of monastic training he needs to qualify to take over from his deceased father as chief priest of the family temple, spends his evenings reading and listening to jazz in his newly reconstructed bedroom-study down the corridor from the three-tatami cell he generously rents me for $15 per month. One night the door to his room slides open just as I return from the monastery meditations. He shows me the book in his hand—by the Japanese philosopher Yanaihara about the author's relationship with Alberto Giacometti. Saburi gives the most wonderful accounts of Japanese books I will never read. Tonight he explains that as part of the artist's obsessive attempts to paint Yanaihara, Giacometti had encouraged him to have an affair with his wife. Saburi then surprises me by asking if I think I've "got something" as a result of all this meditation. I roll my eyes. He adds: "Maybe it's time you began *sanzen* (the daily koan interviews) with the master." He suggests that he approach the master with the request, then mentions that he had recently spent time with the Thief. "We spoke about you. He says you're training with all your strength. I told him: 'Steven-san really respects you.' He said: 'We've never talked.'"

It is decided that I can begin koan interviews with the master if I show I can handle the modern Japanese renditions that are printed alongside the ancient Japanese texts in the koan collection *The Gateless Barrier.* The current chief monk tests me; he does such a good job jumping in for me each time I stumble that he concludes that my reading is superb. There follows a two-man ceremony accompanied by a stick of incense. He shows me how to pound the gong to let the master know I'm on my way. I'm left-handed, and the position of the gong obliges me to strike it with my uncoordinated right. My rehearsal attempt, like all my subsequent real attempts, is feeble, in full accord with the answers to the koan I bring before the master. The chief monk has me trail him down an S-shaped corridor, hands folded against my chest, to the empty interview chamber. He instructs me how to bow: once at the door to the chamber, once before the seated master just before I am to raise my prostrated upper torso from the floor and give my response to the koan, once when I am dismissed by the tinkling of the master's hand bell. I am never to show my butt to the master and must walk backward as I exit and end with a fourth bow. There are no instructions for what happens the night I put all this into practice: Bowing before the master, I step on the hem of my indestructible *hakama* and stand before him in underpants and skewed kimono, skirt fallen to my knees.

The *sesshin* commences the next day. When the meditations end the first morning, I'm hobbling off my cushions into my sandals and I double take: The Thief, rather than making his usual exit past the laymen's row of sitting platforms and out of the meditation hall, is heading toward me.

He bows. I bow. I'm standing next to lightning. "Thanks for the bread. [I sneak a loaf of German bread on top of his cupboard at the start of each *sesshin*.] A gift to a monk is called *kuyō*. But stop. It's wasteful."

I nod.

"*Sanzen* needs no big words," he says. Immediately I recall the previous spring when he'd walked past on his return from the latrine as I was chatting about Nietzsche outside the meditation hall with one of the laymen—a graduate student in philosophy at Kyoto University—during a *sesshin* break. I had had the odd feeling that he was taking note of me for the few seconds before he moved beyond the sound of my voice. I had wondered what he was thinking. Now I knew.

"Zen says: Harmonize the body, harmonize the breath, harmonize the mind," he continues. "You will now appear daily before the master." He slides both hands past the sides of my scalp, then one hand across the top.

"I should shave my head?"

He laughs. "You don't have to overdo it." He sculpts an imaginary head, indicating that I just need to be presentable. By the fourth day of a *sesshin* I look like Beethoven hung over. "I have a kimono I no longer use," he adds. "My gift to you."

Two gifts, actually. He'd also given me my one-and-only glimpse of his central thought. "Harmonize the body; harmonize the breath; harmonize the mind" is part of an ancient instruction on how to meditate. The Thief had elevated it far beyond sitting to a total way of moving through the world. He's so far beyond my reach that I am stunned when he says: "You and I—Steve as Steve, I as I— we're the same." My face betrayed the preposterousness of this claim, but he countered me at once: "The same. The same anguish." And of course, at the fundamental point—the only point that in the end mattered to him—he was right. His continued presence in the monastery proved it.

"I'm concerned the master will start passing me on koan I haven't really solved," I say. "I know it's a common practice. I don't want that to happen."

He seems surprised by my remark. He mulls it over, then says: "Probably you'll be disappointed." Another pause, before adding warmly: "Let us both hope." He bows and exits the meditation hall.

Fourth afternoon of the *sesshin*: The Thief and Dr. Ebuchi head toward one another along the stone walkway bordering the meditation hall and the steps leading to the latrine. Both bow low to the other just before their paths cross. As the Thief straightens, breaking into a twinkle, he toasts Dr. Ebuchi with what looks to be an enema bag in his hand, as if it were a glass of champagne. Some time later, Saburi-san says of the Thief: "He is not so healthy, you know. A congenital illness that, among other things, severely affects his eyes. Before he came here he was living at another monastery. He once wrote his sponsor priest, the one who arranged for him to train there: 'I work with the monks all day and meditate into the night. I apologize for the large size of my Chinese characters. My eyes are so bad that I can scarcely see what I am writing.'"

"I never would have suspected," I say. "Vitality gushes through his moves."

Saburi-san says: "He disciplined himself a long time to be able to move that way."

"It can't just be discipline. Have you ever seen him wake from a nap, stretch his arms above his head, and yawn?"

———◆———

Saburi-san beckons me to follow him into his temple kitchen. He bids me to open the package on the table. It's a deep blue kimono. I unfold it until it hangs full length. The material is beautifully woven, sturdier than I'd imagined a kimono could be, slightly faded from many washings. The Thief has meditated, struggled, been wondrous in this kimono for a long time. There's a note, in calligraphic ink on thin paper: "Here is the promised kimono. Obligations make it impossible to descend from the mountain for a while. Do take care."

But taking care and stepping through the gate into a Zen monastery have always been for me mutually exclusive. Unable to endure having to go before the master with no answer to the koan, I entered the meditation hall each evening as soon after their "medicinal" supper as the monks would allow. The koan would pulverize me as the interview with the master neared. He'd dismiss me from his chamber in seconds. On the rare evenings when instead of the far-off tinkling of the master's hand bell the chief monk smacked together his wood blocks to begin a new period of meditation—sign that the master was away and that there would be no interview—my heart leapt at the reprieve. But there was no real relief. Zenkei Shibayama says in the Japlish translation that is all that exists of the account of his awakening: "The novice is compelled to have no other alternatives; he had either to flee from the [meditation] hall or throw himself headlong into the world of Zen meditation."[8] I was compelled to do both. It was still *me* within the Thief's kimono: a kid from the neighborhood daunted and inept in alien clothes, unable to suppress the urge to run away fast yet stumbling somehow into an effort not wholly remote from heroic.

When I tore my meniscus during a *sesshin* and was forced for three months to absent myself from the monastery, I was frustrated, alarmed, happy. I made my comeback at a *sesshin* in Yamanashi prefecture; my knee buckled whenever I bent, an ominous popping noise each time I forced it into the lotus position. Completing the November *sesshin,* I showed up for the Wednesday afternoon lecture Professor Keiji Nishitani gave gratis in the offices of the *Eastern Buddhist* journal and in response to his inquiry told him that my knee had held but I'd failed. He said: "Yet one scales the wall of each subsequent *sesshin* from a higher point of attack."

For me, this meant breaking custom and moving into the monastery the night before the start of the notorious December *sesshin*—commemorating Gautama's "enlightenment or die" week of struggle before his awakening at age thirty-five—rather than delaying, as non-monks usually did, until the first night. I packed my huge stock of sweaters, long underwear, and T-shirts—along with the two arctic sleeping bags—into the cupboard behind my meditation cushions and went to pee before the first sitting. As I exited the urinals, the Thief, who I'd not seen for months—was walking toward them. He bowed deeply. When he straightened, he broke into a huge grin. His bow, his grin, spoke unmistakably: "The December *sesshin* is as arduous as Everest. You have imposed upon yourself an extra day of striving. I honor your determination." He walked past.

By the fourth day, under relentless pressure from without and within, I began to fear that I would die the next time I was in the master's room. Nothing seemed left to me but to throw myself at his feet and hope for mercy. I was rational enough to tell myself that this was completely irrational. But from the fifth day, I could not face the four daily interviews. On the sixth day, when the bell woke me from the allotted three hours of sleep, my entire body was drenched in sweat. Sweating during sleep was a constant of my *sesshin* life, a consequence of lungs whose X-rays caused doctors on three continents in three languages to utter the identical sentence: "What the hell is that?" Usually the sweating woke me and I had time to change my undergarments—sometimes up to three times a night. On this occasion I was so fatigued that I slept on sopping wet. With no time to change into dry clothes, trembling in the freezing chanting hall, I was so fixated on the destructiveness of the situation—unable to stop the sweating or control the circumstances whereby adhering to rules required doing myself harm—that when the chanting ended I walked in the direction opposite the exit and smashed into the Thief. He absorbed the blow passively and eyed me curiously. Stymied, I about-faced and tailed the line into the even colder meditation hall, shuddering uncontrollably, even during breakfast, for the next three hours. Even my well-tested method of asking to be struck with the patrol stick failed to stops the spasms. DeMartino had told me: "At some point you have to give up the body." I was terrified of that point.

Cold, ground down, I dragged after the monks across the long, roofed walkway that bisected the garden and connected the meditation hall to the rest of the monastery and the master's morning talk. At the sixty-meter mark, the red leaves of a solitary maple tree for some reason brought to mind Viktor Frankl's description of marching on a forced digging detail just outside the grounds of the Turkheim concentration camp: Beaten by a Nazi guard in the freezing morning, he undergoes an ecstatic communion with his wife, ignorant that she'd already been transferred to Bergen-Belsen, where she'd died. His unity with her, says Frankl, transcended whether or not his wife was still alive. For the first time in my life, I, a Jew, truly hated the Nazis, for making humans suffer and cold. The redness of the leaves seemed the sole remaining brightness in the world, parting from them as the queue of monks walked on an unbearable error.

Each subsequent *sanzen*, both that day and the last, I sat glued to my cushions, remembering a story—could it possibly be true?—of a monk who'd resisted being dragged into the interview chamber with such frenzy that he pulled out a young tree from the ground. When the next-to-last interview of the *sesshin* commenced, I clung to my cushions with eyes closed. A whisper boomed through the meditation hall: "*This* sanzen is mandatory." The voice of the Thief. I climbed down from the platform and followed the others.

Pulled into a black magnetizing core of myself, I trudged across the garden, close to tears that in the night blackness I could not find the red leaves of my tree. The monks spread out into their customary five rows in the chanting hall, waiting their turn to strike the gong and present themselves before the master. I dropped onto my place, last spot, last row. The instant my knees hit the floor, the chanting hall opened out and I was laughing joyfully atop a vast tatami sea. The next thing I remember was the head monk shouting at me: not for laughing—but because when the first row of monks had had their turn at the master and the remaining rows had all shifted one row closer to the gong, I had failed to move. I couldn't stop laughing and didn't want to. In the master's room I made my bows but when prostrated before him couldn't remember my koan and when I raised my upper torso to make my response, laughing was all I had. The master studied me, neither displeased nor pleased.

"What about the koan?" he said finally.

I laughed. He rang me out.

Ten days later I entered another *sesshin*—for non-monks. On the final night I learned that the most beautiful thing in the world is a breath. The next morning, while the others sat the final sitting period, as part of the meal crew I leaned over to set an empty plastic bowl on a low bench and injured my back so badly that I could neither stand, sit, walk, nor lie down. For three weeks I could barely move. My upper torso, too heavy for my legs, was bent almost parallel to the floor when I walked, and I had to crawl to the outhouse.

My back couldn't survive the January *sesshin*. February came, the month a half year earlier I had selected to return home, to be followed by my friend Urs App and the monk Bunko. I informed the master that I'd be attending graduate school in America. He presented me with two of his ink paintings. I couldn't bend when I tried to thank him with a bow.

"Something wrong?" the master asked.

"My back." He reached behind him with tremendous speed for an old man and handed me a brown paper bag. I could not imagine what it might be. "Is it medicine?" I asked.

"Candy!"

I knew full well my shortcomings as a Zen student. I knew that my decision to go home was in part a running away. But the sarcastic joy that lit his face as he said this word—the thrill at his own cleverness—surprised me.

———————————•———————————

A few days after returning to the States, I sat in on one of DeMartino's classes. He had some shopping to do when it ended. I helped lug the packages back to his apartment. When we'd dropped the shopping bags on the kitchen table, he asked: "What are you going to do?"

"For now, to try to get enlightened."

"*For now* isn't good enough."

I had no idea why I had said "for now." The ensuing thirty years have confirmed that while I could never stop fleeing Zen, I could never get away from it either. Probably I said it from nervousness. I'm glad I did. In DeMartino's words, I saw that despite all I had endured in Japan, I could never have awakened. My quest bore within it a fatal flaw. *Sesshin* by *sesshin* I had gradually sought to remove all the gaps in my effort. But I had always permitted the most significant gap to remain: the future. It is not a matter of sitting more or sleeping less but of removing one's future. This is what Gautama had done at the Bodhi Tree. Once his rump touched the ground, there was no tomorrow. Whether he sat or reclined is irrelevant. The tree could have been a penthouse with a plush bed. My *sesshin* had always been ruptured by a fundamental ambivalence: From the first sitting period, I struggled to break through but also to get through. Hisamatsu's own master, Ikegami, warned him: "When you go to the *zendō* [meditation hall] go as if your life is at stake. If you go through it with a half-hearted intention of living through it and returning home, then you had better not go at all."[9] Hisamatsu writes that on the day of his awakening he had "no means of escape left in the entirety of his existence, not even one the size of a hole in a needle."[10] I, by contrast, at every minute of every *sesshin*, from day one through seven, had retained the eighth day—the hole in the needle when I would resume civilian life.

"I can't find the determination to cut off my arm like Hui-k'o,"[11] I told DeMartino.

He nodded.

"But I am not unrelated to that act."

He nodded again. "If you're going back for your doctorate, get through your classes, but keep the real concern at the forefront."

"As soon as I finish my course work, I'm going back to Japan."

"No five-year plans! Take up the koan at the next available moment."

———————◆———————

Seven years later I was accosted by Dr. Ebuchi, the master's best friend, in front of Rinko-in Temple. He ordered me to resume training at the monastery. I did not.

My doctoral thesis ate up the next several months. I did attend one *sesshin* at another temple. My legs were so deconditioned that by the second day, every cell in my thighs seemed to have burst. In July I was offered a teaching position in Tokyo.

Before leaving, there was a last *sesshin*. Run by a group of laymen and -women and held, to my surprise, in the same mountain village as the Thief's temple. My monk friend Saburi-san had recently achieved notoriety as one of the Gang of Four, a cohort of priests who had organized a multiyear boycott when the mayor of Kyoto had tried to tax admission fees that local temples received from tourists. He initiated the clever idea of having every Zen temple in the city admit visitors gratis and accept only voluntary—which Japanese politeness translated into obligatory—"donations." Donations, went his argument, were exempt from tax. The city government was furious; Saburi-san was enjoying himself immensely. I asked him to help me get permission to call on the Thief. Within in a few days, he'd received an answer: I could try.

I skipped the noon meal on the *sesshin*'s second day, cut through the rice paddies, and ascended the steps to the temple. An attractive woman in a kimono, very kind, accepted the loaf of German bread I had brought the Thief, explaining that he was not available and that I should try two o'clock the following day. The next morning my friend Tanemura-san, one of the lay practitioners from the monastery, amazed me by saying that he was attending the *sesshin* for the chance to say goodbye before I left Kyoto. Years before he'd given his one-word assessment of the Thief: "Wonderful!"

I asked Tanemura-san and my friend Mark Thomas, who had never seen the Thief in action, to accompany me to the temple. I called out the customary "Onegai itashimasu" from the foyer while my pals waited outside. The same woman appeared, apologizing that the priest had been summoned away but was expected back soon. I suggested I come another day. She cocked an ear, asked me to excuse her, reappearing to happily inform me that the priest had returned and would see me. For ten minutes I waited alone in the foyer, where in all Japanese temples one leaves one's shoes before stepping up onto the *roka*, the wooden corridor that leads into the interior rooms. The door through which the woman had vanished slid open along its rails. The Thief, splendid in a white kimono, dropped his rear onto the *roka*, completely relaxed, his legs dangling down into the foyer where I stood.

"Some friends have come to pay their respects," I said.

He rejected the request with one windshield-wiper swipe of his forearm — of such explosive force that in the years since I have rehearsed it, always unsuccessfully, in ongoing disbelief that a human arm can move with such speed. The gesture said: "You requested a meeting. This is between you and me."

"I wish to do *sanzen* with you."

"*Sanzen* is no joke. Not something to be done by jumping from master to master."

"I know that."

"It's like this. At a certain point I saw that being a monastery master wasn't for me." The guy was live ammunition. "Do you know the word *rijin*?"

I said no.

"*Ri* is *hanareru* [to separate]. *Jin* is *hito* [people].

"You mean you have renounced the world?"

He laughed. "That would be an exaggeration. I exist apart from people." Silence. "Have you looked around the temple grounds?"

"Not yet."

"Take a look around. It's a pretty place." His way of telling me what I had witnessed so often: that *his* Way, conjoined with meditation, was gardening and hard physical work.

"I'm deadlocked," I said.

"To be deadlocked is good. 'When deadlocked there is a change, with the change you break through.'"

"Only if it's the true deadlock. I'm deadlocked from reaching the true deadlock."

His eyes widened. "You understand well!" It was the first time I had expressed to him where I stood in life and why I had sought out Zen. He seemed to want to give it some thought. Finally, he added: "There are a lot of young Zen masters coming onto the scene. Study with one of them."

"I do not believe any of them can help me."

I believe he recognized that what I said was true and that he knew as well as I there was no one among the new generation of masters like him. He waited a good while before adding, with surprising tenderness: "Then I'll have you pursue the Zen quest alone. It's sufficient, you'll find, and it won't matter whether you are in America or Japan . . . Well, I am a bit tired." He shot to his feet like a geyser. He bowed and with a huge smile said: "It was great to see you." And he was gone behind a closing sliding door.

I was not disappointed. He would never accede to my request as long as his master, nominally my master, was still alive.

Thousands of miles block me from Japan right now. A few years ago I asked Mrs. Maeda to remind him that it was my lifelong dream to have him as my teacher.

The Thief replied: "He's too serious."

Zen Man Hidden

> I never say anything but no one pays any
> attention so I keep repeating it.
> —Richard DeMartino

WHEN I FIRST walked—late—into Richard DeMartino's evening class on religion and literature, this chart was written on the board:

- **Real Man**
    - Man's Man
    - Ladies Man
- **Great Man**

And then, under two drawn chalk lines to indicate an ultimate category:

- **True Man**

The first words I ever heard him speak as a teacher were: "A great man is not necessarily a true man." He gave Charles de Gaulle as a case in point.

Students, of course, wanted to know whether DeMartino was a true man, or true Self, in the Zen sense of the term—that is, was he enlightened? Since it takes one to know one, though we had our opinions, we could not with certainty discern. What those drawn to him *did* know was that DeMartino was a *man,* a man first and a teacher second. His manliness—tough and full of charm—was nonetheless rooted in something far more intriguing: his nonchalance, which suffused the classroom with the sense that he taught from a place not ensnared in the problem of existence he set before us and that several students were forced to acknowledge as our own.

He once brought back from one of the rare conferences he attended a quote from one of the presenters: "All philosophy must be political." "What I think the speaker meant," DeMartino added in class, "is that all philosophy must be existential." Whether or not this was the intended meaning of the quote, it was without question DeMartino's own position. He was existential to the core. A man of supreme intellect, he would say, in speaking of Zen: "Intellectual understanding doesn't cut any ice." Those of us who repeatedly took or audited his classes were driven to know because we wanted *to be*. In DeMartino we found someone whose first premise was that academic knowledge in philosophy and religion had to be in the service of the life-and-death struggle to resolve the fundamental problem of living and dying.

DeMartino was never impressed with himself for being a professor. He was pleased by the actor Spencer Tracy's line: "Take your work seriously but don't take yourself seriously." Though he published rarely, he wrote and thought obsessively, often citing a diary entry of the Japanese philosopher Kitarō Nishida: "I was born cursed to think." In faculty meetings, on buses, on trains, over meals, he would revise what he'd written into a yellow legal pad pulled out of the cheap double-handled gym bag that accompanied him everywhere. At least once he was denied promotion for scant publications. But when it came to his writing he said: "I hurry for no one." When the research project he proposed to gain time off from teaching was rejected, and the department chair suggested he reapply in the future and mention that he knew Japanese, DeMartino refused to make the addition, telling me in the most forceful tone: "I cannot promote myself. And I won't."

In the early years, after class ended, he always sat in a front row desk and copied his blackboard notes into his yellow legal pad. The night I approached him for the first time, straggling behind after the other students had left the classroom, I said: "You're the most important man in America."

He put down his pencil and asked: "Why do you say that?"

"Because you're the one elucidating the ultimate problem of human existence and it's solution."

Nothing in DeMartino's brief nod at these words suggested that he received them as a compliment. Nor was there any trace of the false deprecation one often hears from celebrities at the outset of their after-banquet speeches: "Listening to your generous introduction I was sure you must be talking about somebody else." His nod was confirming, in silence: "Whoever is elucidating the fundamental problem of human life and its solution might well be the most important person in America. It's true, that's what I do. But I am not myself."

From then on, without permission, I began walking him back to his $60-per-month apartment at Broad and Dauphin, questioning him till he disappeared behind the door. In response to one inquiry, he pointed across Broad Street up to a third-floor pool hall. A man was visible in the window, chalking his cue. DeMartino said: "See that guy up there. He thinks if he can just hit the seven ball into the side pocket, everything will be all right. It won't be all right." When I once remarked on the difficulty of breaking through to enlightenment, he grasped hold of the high iron railing that fenced off the Hardwick Hall dormitory, hoisted himself chin and chest against the bars, and said: "To step back from the gate and tell yourself 'I haven't broken through' accomplishes nothing. All you can do is press your head back against the gate and keep banging."[12]

DeMartino was my teacher, and friend, for more than four decades—the most significant person in my adult life. I attended his lectures as a university student and for many years after. I was not a disciple. He had none. He once said (not referring to himself): "No master wants a disciple. He wants you to be the master." He quoted Krishnamurti from a radio interview: "Masters and disciples corrupt one another." Early on, at a Temple University event at which he was serving as a panelist with the visiting Japanese Zen philosopher Keiji Nishitani, I smiled at him from my front row seat. He responded with the tersest smile possible and looked away, leaving no doubt as to his warning: "Don't dare try to attach yourself to me. The Self that you are looking for cannot be attached to. I am as elusive as it is." When—in an upsurge of emotion—I tried to embrace him in front of the Temple center-city campus the night before my departure for a Japanese Zen monastery, he got me in a judo hold, spun me 180 degrees, and pushed me in the direction of my home—his way of telling me: "You are alone!"

This hardness was an expression of his warmth. He answered every question I posed to him in all my letters from Japan, every question posed in Philadelphia, on the street and on the phone, however late the hour. In my thousand-plus encounters with him between 1969 and 1999, when his Parkinson's put an end to my post-retirement visits to his Long Island home, he never once denied his help and never once did harm, even when he slammed me, or forced me to slam into him, which was often. He seemed to have trodden each step of my path long before I had. He never lied. I never once knew him to act without integrity or to compromise a principle. He could be fierce, funny, explosive, gentle, cantankerous, stubborn. But if you observed him with care in these alterations, his mood never changed. Since his death in January 2013, my overriding impression is how interesting and entertaining he was, how much fun to be around. How serious when you needed him to be deadly serious about serious things.

Ruthlessly serious with himself too, although, following Chuang Tzu, he hid his universe in the universe, and few noticed. If cursed to think, DeMartino always transcended being a teacher, a garment he easily removed, as though it had never been worn, once he retired. He described himself as a "vagabond student" or a "bum," which he esteemed as a true art form. He said: "Until my forties I never had a penny." Key to his twenties were his two wars. He enlisted in the Naval Reserve and was sent to the navy's Japanese language school in Colorado to learn Japanese—"much better than learning how to fire a cannon." Simultaneously, as he once told me, "I was fighting a war of my own." This second war, the problem of time and its attendant problem of first cause, tore him to shreds. By 1944, stationed at Pearl Harbor, he was volunteering for night duty so that he could attend courses in Eastern philosophy during the day. From University of Hawaii professor Charles Moore he first heard the name of the great Zen personality D. T. Suzuki. He was part of the invasion force at the battle of Tinian Island, serving as a Japanese language interpreter. An episode he recounted from the aftermath of that battle—both the story and the way DeMartino told it—is informative of his character: The US Navy surgeon attached to the invading force was obliged to amputate the leg of a Japanese local wounded in the invasion. He invited DeMartino to be present during the operation. Noting his reluctance, the surgeon heartily added: "It's like slicing a ham!" After the surgery, DeMartino was obliged to break the news of the amputation to the young man's mother. "I explained to her it was the only way of saving her son's life. I'm sure she thought I was lying until her dying day."

He arrived in Japan shortly after the atomic bombings and spent several weeks in their vicinity (so that almost fifty years later, when we were in New Mexico, he passed on a trip to Los Alamos on the grounds that he'd already been exposed to enough radiation for one lifetime). Moving eastward to Tokyo, he was struck by the docile acceptance by the Japanese of the US occupation; at three in the morning he walked the streets among the recent enemy in complete absence of fear. About to be discharged and sent back to the States, he was offered a job as historical consultant to the Defense Panel of the International Military Tribunal for the Far East (the Tokyo War Crimes Tribunal). This enabled him to stay on in Japan, which led to his meeting with D. T. Suzuki in 1947. He told me: "For the first six months I visited him, I didn't know what the hell he was talking about. But I sensed he had the answer I needed, so I kept going back." Years later he added, with wonderment at the way life plays out: "Hundreds of people met Suzuki and moved on. I met him and stopped." For nearly two decades, he studied with him, served as his chauffeur, his assistant, even as his pillow, for the aged Suzuki would slump onto DeMartino and nap, including the night Suzuki pressed him to drive fast from Los Angeles back to Claremont, then conked out on his shoulder while DeMartino negotiated with the cop who had pulled him over for speeding.

In the meantime, DeMartino was going through hell. He said that Suzuki had tears in his eyes when he saw the extent of his suffering. It was Suzuki himself who for years suggested, given DeMartino's temperament, that he study with the more severe Zen personality Shin'ichi Hisamatsu, the critical figure in DeMartino's life. "The talk that I abandoned Suzuki for Hisamatsu was nonsense."

His characterization of his second teacher—"Hisamatsu cuts like a razor. It takes you three days before you realize you've been cut"—was borne out at their first meeting. A delayed reaction to their encounter, a dinner in Kyoto where Hisamatsu swiftly turned DeMartino's struggle with the problem of time into a Zen koan, produced a cough and a fever that lasted more than a year. Back in New York, as Suzuki's assistant at Columbia, he locked the windows of his apartment, fearful he'd jump out the building in his sleep. Soon enough he decided that if he was capable of jumping while asleep, he was equally capable of unlocking the windows, then jumping. Up flew the windows. "I decided if I was going to kill myself, at least I was going to get a good night's sleep." I asked if his parents, also in New York, knew what he was going through. "I concealed it. It wasn't easy. Only [Phillip] Kapleau knew." He said: "Nineteen fifty-two, fifty-three was a helluva year." In his classes, he "was just going through the motions." One day someone approached him and asked with concern: "Are you OK?" At these words, to his utter surprise, he was.

———◆———

DeMartino rarely spoke about his Zen experiences in class and, when he did, only in warning. He rebuffed 1960s advocates of psychotropic drugs as a means to enlightenment by telling of a lecture he'd heard in New York City in the 1950s—in which the speaker had described his mescaline trip—and concluded with a dismissive: "I'd experienced all that in a Zen monastery in 1948." I'm uncertain if his description to me of an experience that occurred the same year—also intended as a warning—referred to the same event. I had asked him about some odd developments in my meditation. He said: "Not all those pleasurable sensations are desirable." He proceeded to recount how in 1948 he was meditating at Engakuji Monastery in Kamakura, on the same grounds where Suzuki lived. His back was killing him; he'd had enough for the day and decided to go home. A friend said: "Sit one more set." He did and, in even greater physical pain, renewed his plans to leave. His friend kept telling him, "Sit one more set. Sit one more." DeMartino reluctantly continued, exhaustion steadily increasing, when all at once he blew up larger than the meditation hall. The monks exiting and reentering the meditation hall between sitting periods walked right through him. He remained on his cushions in this ecstasy through the afternoon. Afterward, he went to Suzuki and explained what had transpired. Suzuki said: "If it happens again, put a stop to it at once." DeMartino told me: "It was very pleasant stuff. Once it happened, I could bring it on at will. If I hadn't had Suzuki, I might have wasted the next thirty years of my life practicing kundalini yoga."

A decade before he related this, in the first weeks I knew him, I'd heard that he'd had an orgasm in a breakthrough at a Zen monastery. DeMartino never said this in my hearing. But in recounting to me what had occurred in 1948, he did say, minimizing the significance of what he'd experienced: "For what it's worth, I'd figured out what Wilhelm Reich and his orgone were all about."

———————◆———————

The word *satori*, DeMartino felt, was overused, covering such a broad range of experiences that it needed to be scrapped. For him awakening meant one thing: the Great Death of the ordinary I. Everything short of this he relegated to the category of an "insight" or "glimpse" in which the ego structurally still remained. When a student countered: "But such experiences can change one's life," DeMartino said: "Falling down a flight of stairs can change one's life."

It was invariably as admonition against taking a partial experience for genuine enlightenment that he gave this account: He had had a breakthrough during a *sesshin* at Hosshinji, Sogaku Harada's monastery in Obama. At the next *sanzen*, Harada kept him in the interview chamber for forty-five minutes. When DeMartino returned to Kyoto and presented his experience to Hisamatsu, it was rejected. DeMartino "rejected Hisamatsu's rejection." A few days later DeMartino realized that Hisamatsu was right and "the whole thing fell apart."

A long-standing student of DeMartino, knowing that he never spoke untruthfully, one night in class was clever enough to ask: "Were you subsequently able to replace the experience that collapsed?"

It was the only time I saw DeMartino try to dodge a question. He gathered his papers as if he hadn't heard, but when the student asked again, DeMartino looked down, stuffed the papers into his gym bag, and muttered under his breath: "Yes."

What he'd replaced it with, so far as I know, he kept to himself. It was never my style to ask DeMartino whether he was enlightened. I did inquire once about his discovery that Hisamatsu had been right in rejecting him: "You said your experience fell apart. Does that mean you were back in the problem in the same way?"

"Well, I was still a hell of a lot better off than I'd been before."[13]

———◆———

I did a double take when DeMartino, in his last professional appearance in New Mexico, described himself as a "terrible speaker." He was a magnetizing force in class. Chief testament to this was the number of auditors in his classes—one semester as many as 35 percent at the old center-city campus on Walnut Street. Students brought their friends, lovers, and spouses. Former students passing through Philadelphia would drop in for a lecture or for the duration of their stay. He was admonished for this by the Religion Department chair but ignored him. "What am I supposed to do?" he said to me. "Some of these students have been hanging around my classes for years." He also believed in auditing in principle: "It was the way I was educated." When I admiringly reported what I had learned from a documentary—that J. Robert Oppenheimer was such a compelling teacher that a student went on a hunger strike after being refused permission to take his quantum mechanics course a fourth time—DeMartino reacted to Oppenheimer's rejection with distaste.

Armed with references to Sinatra, Humphrey Bogart, New York cab drivers, and comics like Joey Lewis ("You only live once, but if you do it right—once is enough"), DeMartino was a man of the 1940s. Yet he perfectly fit the need of a certain type of student of a 1960s he had no interest in being part of. He appreciated deeply our interest in Eastern thought. But he tore the wheat from the chaff with a hacksaw. To a student who espoused the bohemian freedom of Jack Kerouac's novel *The Dharma Bums,* he replied: "The true dharma bum must be free even at the president's ball in white tie and tails." When a student back from a year in a California Zen center insisted that enlightenment without seated meditation was impossible, DeMartino pressed her: "What if someone has no legs?" The student said that would just be too bad. DeMartino responded: "You'd better go back to California and do more meditation."

He pandered to no one; I know of no beloved professor less concerned with being loved. He was ruthless with our illusions. I recall the night he blasted us free hippies: "Look at yourselves—you're all wearing uniforms!" Virtually every male in the room, myself included, wore blue jeans, a blue work shirt, and a beard. He admired us for our quest. The highest compliment I ever heard him pay a class was: "I can sense your interest is not merely academic." But he also said: "We're not here to make friends" and fought us hard lest our struggle be misguided.

————◆————

On that one kindness rests what mattered in my education, in accordance with DeMartino's distinction between education and propaganda: "Propaganda permits only answers; education wants you to question." He could be gruff, cutting me down mid-sentence as soon as he intuited I was in error. He nailed me frequently: "You're too contemporary!" "You've got to smash that middle-class veneer!" "I've told you before, there's something egotistical in your quest." When I asked about the admonitions to practitioners mentioned in the Ming Dynasty book *Whips for Breaking through the Zen Barrier,* DeMartino exploded: "The hell with their admonitions! Make your own admonitions. At this point, throw yourself into the koan and resolve it!" But he was always encouraging. When I despaired at ever breaking through, he conked me gently on the top of the head and announced: "You'll get there." When I said: "I think my struggle is further advanced than my ability to sit in meditation," he said: "I think so too." When I confessed I was afraid, he said: "Originally there is nothing. From where does the fear come?" When I telephoned to tell him I had abruptly roused from sleep only to die in the middle of the night—an experience that happened so quickly I didn't have time to quake until I woke the next morning, he laughed and said: "If I told you how many times that happened to me . . ."

He was starkly honest about the difficulties of the Zen quest, especially knowing that my body often betrayed me: "The first thing any good Zen master will tell you is to take care of your health." But he also said: "The point comes when you have to give up the body." When, at a seminar in New Mexico, a pregnant woman (husband also in attendance) asked about the costs of the Zen quest—nervous that its demands would negatively affect the raising of her child—she was cheerfully assured by some of the participants that there were none. As soon as the session ended, I walked over to DeMartino. His first words: "Of course there are costs."

I once asked: "The people in Auschwitz were desperate. Why didn't they break through?" He said: "To be in despair is not enough. The despair must be focused." To provide proper focus was his constant concern to anyone who came to him. Usually it was lacking. "Ninety-nine percent of the questions brought to me are psychological, not religious," he told me. And in class: "People stay up all night worrying about everything but the one thing they should be worrying about." Among my few keepsakes is a letter from 1977, when the physical pain of prolonged meditation had me over the cliff. He wrote:

> With regard to your questions about *zazen*, pain, active and passive,[14] etc., I think you are getting too entangled in all these questions. I think the more advisable procedure would be to focus on the root-source of the problem (or motivation) that made you go to Japan. Let the restlessness and untenability of this problem (or motivation)—at its *source*—be the motivating power and directing force of your *kufū*.[15] Above all, *do not rely* on anything—neither *zazen,* koan, pain, your

teachers, Zen, me, or any thing else. I'm sure you know that already.[16]

———————◆———————

Zen Buddhism as "something," as an object or phenomenon to be attached to, meant nothing to DeMartino. In "The Human Situation and Zen Buddhism," he wrote: "For Zen Buddhism, finally, neither is in itself nor does it offer any objective, substantive content to be studied as such psychologically, religiously, philosophically, historically, sociologically, or culturally. The only valid component of Zen Buddhism is one's own concrete life and existence, its basic contradiction and incompleteness, and, in distinction to the mere longing, the actual quest for reconciliation and fulfillment."[17] The sacred cows and traditions of Buddhism and Zen meant equally little. "So much of Buddhism is irrelevant," he would say. Or, "If Gautama said *that,* he was wrong." He questioned every internal contradiction he found in Eastern philosophy and practice. That's what he meant in saying: "If you go to Japan, go as an American." Told socks were not permitted in a monastery during a freezing week of meditation, he countered: "The true Self is formless. Why this attachment to socks? Once I get used to the cold, I'll remove them." Against traditional interpretations of the Four Noble Truths, he said: "To say the cause of the human problem is craving is *very* superficial." He said, discussing compassion: "'Father, forgive them, for they know not what they do' is far more profound than anything in Buddhism." He rejected the epithet of "the Perfect One"—even the designation "wise"—as applicable to Gautama, insisting: "Enlightened people can make mistakes." He held that awakening solves the root problem of human existence but that wisdom in any concrete situation requires insights that awakening does not of itself bring: "Just because you're Jesus Christ doesn't mean you can play the violin."

———————◆———————

No teacher in my experience thought on his feet as well as DeMartino. He *wanted* to be argued with—it helped clarify his thinking. He would order course readings by authors who disagreed with him, challenging: "Read their stuff and shove my analysis back down my throat." In hundreds of debates in class, he was virtually never bested. On the rare occasion a student did land a punch, DeMartino cracked up with delight. Self-deprecation was a permanent feature of his teaching style: "When I walk into a room, it seems like somebody important just walked out." "Once for any man, twice for a fool, no, no—once for any man, twice for a fool, three times for DeMartino." He always insisted, acknowledging that it was difficult when things got hot, that in class we "argue ideas, not persons," and he was starkly impersonal even in criticizing himself. Walking up Thirteenth Street, discussing his revision of "The Human Situation and Zen Buddhism"—which I had just proofread in manuscript—I pointed out that in describing the nature of the Zen resolution to the human problem, the newer rendering contained a sentence stating the exact opposite of what DeMartino had written in the published version twenty years before. He halted on the sidewalk, evidently contrasting in his mind the two long sentences in question. Suddenly he shouted with icy brutality: "I was wrong!"

This impersonal dimension was not just integrity. It was what he called "being without being," the Self that is not itself. Once some students invited DeMartino to a campus showing of Jean Cocteau's film *Orpheus*.

"I have to attend a faculty meeting."

"We'll come and kidnap you."

"I won't even be there."

———◆———

DeMartino's enterprise as a teacher spawned from Gautama's utterance: "I teach two things: suffering, and liberation from suffering." The fundamental problem of the human person, the solution to that problem, and how to existentially arrive at this solution formed the through line of his teaching career. He ceaselessly reminded that intellectual understanding was not to be confused with existential self-actualization. But while warning that the former could get in the way of the latter, he firmly asserted that a clear intellectual understanding could be of real help in avoiding the myriad dead ends and pitfalls lurking in the Zen quest. "If I didn't believe this," he told one class, "I couldn't accept my contract."

The contracts he did accept never earned him much money. He was already forty-one when Bernard Phillips, whom he had known in both New York and Japan, invited him to come to Temple University as a teaching assistant and to take a doctorate at the same time.[18] He played the stock market[19] to pick up the slack, once had a million dollars on paper, and shrugged when the market plummeted: "What would I do with a million dollars?" He lived simply, seldom leaving campus, stunningly self-contained. I recall two women coming up to him at the end of class in 1969, one asking for the both: "Isn't it difficult for you to live alone?" DeMartino replied, stuffing papers in his gym bag: "I'm alone, but I'm not by myself."

The three Philadelphia apartments he lived in ranged from small to tiny, books and photocopies everywhere, with the chairs so cluttered with books that the extremely infrequent guest couldn't sit down. He filled a high cupboard with folded large brown paper shopping bags, ignoring my warnings that these were not just a fire hazard but two hundred bags more than he could ever use, years later chiding me gleefully when the bags ran out before we finished moving him to a new apartment. He was a pack rat, a habit learned furnishing foxholes. (When we bagged the last books from his mantelpiece, what remained was a reflector from a bicycle fender I'd seen him pick off the ground several years before.) Watching DeMartino, I learned that a true eccentric is not someone who simply behaves oddly but someone who does everything according to a strictly thought-through logic that others judge bizarre. It was his Logos, as he called it, that drove him to stock up on identical radios that he liked and to purchase a drawer-full of identical blue dress shirts; that made him go nowhere without a shaker of garlic powder in his gym bag; that drove him to buy the entire stock of a powdered vitamin-protein supplement called Superfood from the health food store at Second and Market because the company might one day cease production. (It did.) It was his Logos, manifest in a cascade of commands, that slowed every attempt to clear the items out of his apartment when two students and myself moved him to his last Philadelphia abode. It was his Logos that prompted him to put on his overcoat in the interval between the inner and outer double doors of the various Temple University buildings, to avoid sweating by donning it one step earlier while still technically inside or catching a chill by waiting until he'd stepped outside.

———————◆———————

I had had, at twenty, a negative satori—a sudden illumination, incontestable in its authority, pinning me to the wall. That concurrent with this event was DeMartino's in-class articulation of the conceptual framework of what had happened to me was the luckiest break of my life. His lectures were the full-orchestra version of what he'd said in an early conversation after class: "You've run up against the problem at a young age. That's good. But the problem is not the final word. There's a solution." How to attain that solution was the core of our discussions for years. I was struck from the outset that rather than suggesting I meditate, he said: "Set an hour aside each night, sit in a chair, struggle with the problem, and take it from there."

Taking it from there, two years later, when I graduated, culminated in my decision to go to Japan. DeMartino warned: "Don't make the problem geographical."

I wrote him no letters from the monastery. Back in Philadelphia after my first stay in Kyoto, twenty minutes late for his evening course the Monday following my return, I walked through his classroom door. DeMartino—discussing the Zen memoir *The Empty Mirror*—said: "Perhaps Mr. Antinoff has something to say from his own empty mirror."

"Don't hitchhike," I replied, and I did not speak again in class. When the last of the students had filed out, I told DeMartino how, arriving in California on a missionary plane from Asia, I'd hitchhiked across the country, gotten in the wrong car on a desolate road in Appalachian Kentucky, and wound up at 4 a.m. with a rifle pointed at my head. My Zen reaction, after my stint in a monastery? I shook from head to foot.

"You should have broken through," DeMartino said softly. "Your self-preservation instinct took over instead."

———————————•———————————

DeMartino's views on meditation surprised, in some instances displeased, the many students who asked him about it. He was never overly impressed with cross-legged sitting, though he'd done a lot of it,[20] including five weeklong *sesshin* his last eight weeks in Japan, because "I knew I was going back to America." He referred to those who saw sitting as the way to enlightenment as mere "meditation masters." For him, meditation *as normally practiced* was trapped in the same difficulties of any method: A method—of necessity—established a duality between seeker and path, between path and goal. Therefore no object-method, path, or means undertaken by the ego-subject could definitively overcome the duality of subject and object that constituted the human problem. But as always with DeMartino, one had to understand the precise nature of his attack. He never discouraged anyone from meditating. When he put to me the question that he often put to meditators—*Why* do you meditate?—and I answered: "To meditate without a meditator," he accepted this with an only slightly grudging: "Well, okay." When I told him I reached a state where my body was inert, he said. "*All right*, but that's not enough." He was fully aware of the physiological and psychological benefits of sitting meditation: "I don't deny that the full lotus posture is a very comfortable position." He said: "Anyone who embarks seriously on the Zen quest will have hundreds of peak experiences." But Zen awakening, he insisted again and again, is not an experience, which is by definition transient.

A leading member of the Philadelphia Zen Center who asked DeMartino at a public lecture at the Ethical Society if he did *zazen* was nonplussed by his reply: "I do it and I don't do it, but the *zazen* I do and do not do has nothing to do with sitting." Against the strongly held view that Dogen's famous expression of his awakening—"Body and mind fallen off"—pertained to sitting meditation, DeMartino said: "You've got to be able to walk down the street without body and mind." When I pressed him in class on the necessity of meditation, he said:

> *Dhyana* ["meditation" in Sanskrit] doesn't mean sitting. It means to start from the "I" (which is where we have to start)—the "I" which is split, dualistic. *Dhyana* as a practice means overcoming the problem of the "I," however you do it. The purpose of *zazen* on the "way to"[21] the resolution is to actualize the great doubt block [the existential deadlock of thinking, feeling, and doing that is the precondition for enlightenment according to the Rinzai school of Zen]. I'm not denying formal sitting may be of help. But how do you actualize the great doubt block? In one sense, it's impossible. The great doubt block can be actualized only by plunging into the problem and sticking with it. But when the problem takes over, you are no longer the active agent. You are grasped by the problem and as such are its recipient.

So long as there was a duality between grasper and grasped, sitter and meditation, cross-legged meditation was of slight religious consequence to him: "To be able to sit in *zazen* for six hours without moving is of little interest. But to suddenly realize you've been sitting in *zazen* for the last six hours [without having been aware of it]—that begins to be interesting."

When I asked: "Hisamatsu said in his conversation with Paul Tillich that true meditation must not only be objectless but subjectless. What relation does this have to those states of sitting meditation in which there is neither subject nor object?" DeMartino said: "I would say none."

A year later I asked: "What is the relation between states of meditation and the great doubt block?"

DeMartino said: "I would say there's no relation."

"But what about reaching the state in which there is neither subject nor object?"

"It's a trance. Or else a temporary self-transcendence, but one that is still within the matrix of the 'I.' Insofar as the subject–object structure is transcended, there is some relation, as in any ecstasis. Looking back later, after awakening, one may see some relation insofar as there was an overcoming of the subject–object scheme. I don't deny that sitting can be of help. You can 'broaden and deepen' koan after koan through sitting. But you'll never break out of the matrix."

He said: "As far as we know Hui-neng never sat *zazen* for even one second. Shen-hsiu [the chief meditation monk at the same monastery in seventh-century China] sat all those years and didn't get it." In class, while critiquing meditation, he would often glance my way. Yet once, at the end of a class in which he attacked the overreliance on sitting, he acknowledged, almost under his breath, "At the beginning, it is probably essential."

But when does the beginning end?

———————◆———————

I had once asked DeMartino if at the crisis point he'd been struggling with a specific koan. "No," he said. "It was a matter of life and death."

A solution to a koan that did not solve the problem of the "I" held little meaning for him. He loved the reply of a certain Kyoto Zen master whom he had run into on the street and asked how it was possible that a Westerner, B—having passed all the koan—was starting over his koan training from the beginning: "B has met all the koan," said the master. "But B has not yet met B."

"You don't get enlightened by solving seventeen hundred koan," DeMartino would say. "The seventeen hundred koan are solved by getting enlightened." For him, the Zen koan is what you *are;* the koan given by a Zen master is secondary and would have no binding power if your existence were not a koan from the moment you became aware that "I am I." The koan *is* your awareness, not an object that your awareness is aware of. The koan cannot be grappled with, worked on, or attacked. In class DeMartino said: "Insofar as one 'works *on*' a koan, one will never solve the koan. Insofar as one 'concentrates *on*' a koan, one will never solve the koan. Insofar as one 'meditates *on*' a koan, one is never going to solve the koan."

There is, he said, no traversable path to enlightenment. Hence DeMartino often quoted the conversation between Bernard Phillips and Hisamatsu, for which he was the interpreter:

Phillips: "If you follow a way, you'll never get there."

Hisamatsu: "That's right."

Phillips: "But if you don't follow a way, you'll never get there."

Hisamatsu: "That's right."

Phillips: "Then it seems you have a dilemma."

Hisamatsu: "That dilemma is the way you must follow."

Since I was ceaselessly asking him about method—"How do I solve the koan?" "How do I actualize the great doubt block?"—DeMartino eventually said: "You keep asking, 'How am I to follow the dilemma?' You keep trying to step out of the dilemma to ask how to get out of the dilemma. But I ask you, how would you improve on Hisamatsu's formulation? 'The dilemma *is* the way you must follow!'" He added:

"All you can do is keep your nose to the grindstone. On the other hand, the nose *is* the grindstone."

That should have shut me up, yet the following week, in the checkout line of the Pantry Pride supermarket, I asked: "Should I try to break through or let go?" DeMartino said: "If your breaking through is different from your letting go, something is wrong." I persisted: "Should I try to break through the koan or do I let it carry me across?"

DeMartino said: "Let it carry you across."

"Like a mantra?"

"No, not like a mantra." (Years later, when I reminded him that he'd once said: "Let it carry you across," he replied: "I shouldn't have said that either." [His implication: You can neither actively break through the koan nor passively let it carry you across. Without being active or passive—if will won't do and grace won't do—now solve it!])

Not long after, walking him back to the Broad Street bus from the downtown Temple campus, I said: "Hisamatsu says in his commentary on the first case of the *Mumonkan* [*The Gateless Barrier*]: 'All routes must be brought to the extremity and extinguished so that not one remains.' But it is impossible for the ego to do that."

DeMartino nodded. "Now you're in the dilemma."

Suddenly, all he had been saying for years about the contradiction of a means to enlightenment became clear. I blurted out: "The great doubt block can only be reached when the contradiction between the impossibility of resolving the problem and the necessity of resolving it is brought to the point of final extremity."

DeMartino said: "Of course."

The semester ended, and he went up to Long Island for six weeks to be with his widowed mom. When he returned to teach an introductory religion course for the second summer session, I was, as always when in the States, seated in the back row. When the opening class ended and the students had fled, we shook hands:

"Well?" he said.

"Trying to intensify my efforts to break through."

He shouted: "*You* [as ego] CAN'T break through!"

"Then it's impossible."

He shouted even louder: "Did Hisamatsu ever say that?"

———————◆———————

Most afternoons or early evenings, DeMartino would walk the grassy slope on the east side of Temple's Paley Library. His exercise route always commenced with a single set of W's across the gently slanted lawn until he reached the one steep point of incline by the rear of the building. This he'd ascend and descend for twenty to thirty minutes, the cardiovascular part of his exercise routine. As an undergraduate, I'd accompany him to the slope whenever I ran into him in the library. In graduate school, each time I spotted him from the window of the Critical Languages office, where I worked as part of my scholarship requirement, I would sneak off from my job and ask him questions.

We had hundreds of conversations walking that slope. One that was indispensable: In intestinal pain for months I said: "The pain is so bad I cannot practice."

"What's your practice?" he demanded.

"*Sesshin* and meditation are my practice."

"That's not your practice. Your illness should be the source of your practice, not its impediment."

Another chat I in part recall because it was punctuated by a neighborhood kid skidding out of control and slamming his roller skates into DeMartino's leg. He continued up the hill as if nothing had occurred, saying: "It's not enough to want enlightenment. You've got to need it. No one gets awakened without sweating blood. Yet effort alone won't get you there either. There's a passive element. The effort of the ego can do nothing to actualize the nonbeing aspect. If you start from the ego, the Zen quest is not only difficult, it's impossible. The moment you start on the Zen quest, you are in the wrong direction. But of course not doing anything won't get you anywhere either."

Only when we'd descended the slope for the final time did DeMartino pull up his trouser leg. His calf was bleeding. I asked if it was painful. He straightened and as we moved to the next stop on his exercise course said: "Those skates aren't made of paper."

A third conversation on the same slope: Upon returning to America after my second stint in Japan, I described to DeMartino my meeting with Hisamatsu. I had prepared the one question I felt essential. I asked Hisamatsu: "Is the life-staking effort that Gautama made at the Bodhi Tree—enlightenment or death—necessary?" Before I could recount Hisamatsu's response, DeMartino exploded: "*Of course* it's necessary."

He was exercising again as I left work the following day. Discussing Hisamatsu's fundamental koan—"Whatever you do will not do. What do you do?"—DeMartino said: "To answer that koan you must change the question mark into an exclamation point."

It was on that day that I asked him to test my breathing. He pressed his index finger against my lower abdomen and then said dismissively as I exhaled: "*That's* not it." Completing another lap up and down the slope, he added: "If you are still aware of your breathing, you are not really working on the koan."

As we parted he said: "To be I yet not I—that's what Hisamatsu means with his fundamental koan."

———◆———

In his apartment, where I sought his advice about a sculptor friend who was in a bad way, DeMartino said: "Sometimes the only thing you can do is to listen with love." He was no doubt influenced by Tillich's beautiful passage on the three ways love tries to be just to a person—through listening, giving, and forgiving—in *Love, Power, and Justice*, a book that DeMartino regretted had no equivalent in Buddhism. Not long after this conversation, as I said goodbye to him in center city after some Sunday academic event, DeMartino said: "I'm off to visit Barrett in the hospital. If you don't have plans, I'd appreciate your coming along." DeMartino was a loner and had been—I once asked him—since his youth. I sought him out or ran into him on campus hundreds of times; when I fell into step, he accepted my company as a matter of course, but he never—prior to or after this request—actively sought my companionship. I of course said yes.

In a Hahnemann Hospital room, tended by his wife, Leonard Barrett was slumped in a wheelchair, face drooping on one side, an obvious stroke victim. I knew him only as my teacher in an undergraduate summer course on African religions fifteen years earlier, and I liked him. I recalled a lively dignified man, explaining that "we Jamaicans are 90 percent Catholic and 120 percent voodoo"; that it was not uncommon for someone to fake eating the communion wafer and secretly slip it into a pocket for subsequent use in a potion; that hair was a spiritual property and if you came home and found the armpits and crotch cut out of your wash hanging on the line, you could expect to be put under a spell. During my sole conversation with him at the end of class, he sporadically plucked imaginary lint from my shirt and slipped it into his blazer pocket, his charming way of implying that he too had a spell in mind.

Looking up and seeing DeMartino at the door, he slurred: "Look what nature is doing to me."

They small-talked. DeMartino was striving—in his own mind unsuccessfully it seemed to me—for something adequate to say. As the half-hour conversation neared its end, Dr. Barrett said, "I'm going back to Jamaica. The sun and sand and sea must be permitted to do their work."

"You're a wise man, Leonard."

"I *cannot* teach!"

"Sometimes you've got to tell the world to go to hell. That too is compassion."

————————◆————————

But DeMartino also used to say: "To turn your back on the world is to turn your back on your Self," though *how* one turned toward the world could never be predetermined: "The bodhisattva can assume any form, even that of a prostitute." In passing illustration he once mentioned a Japanese friend, a Zen-influenced psychiatrist of deep compassion, who, feigning sleep and not wanting to hurt the visitor's feelings, did not resist as his overnight guest sneaked into his bed. The class in which he mentioned this tale I have never forgotten. The summer after my first stay in Japan, I ran into DeMartino on Montgomery Avenue en route to auditing his lecture. I said: "You emphasize the once-and-for-all Great Death of the ego and rebirth as the true Self as the solution to the human problem. Masao Abe [his close friend] told me: 'You must kill yourself at every instant.' Abe's demand has an overt ethical aspect. Is the moment-by-moment killing of the ego related to the Great Death?"

DeMartino started to respond, but class was about to begin. I took a seat in the back of a Curtis Hall room. For the next ninety minutes, his entire lecture was addressed to my question. Only at the end did he look my way and ask: "Did that help?"

One sentence of his lecture struck me above all: "You're not going to get enlightened by giving your worst enemy a bunch of roses."

————————◆————————

In my novel *The Atheists' Monastery,* I stole my description of the composer Misha Karensky from my experience of DeMartino:

> From 1924–1930 I was a student at the Leningrad Conservatoire. In Professor Zaslavsky's opening lecture on counterpoint I never once put down my pencil. By the third lecture

I never once picked it up. Three classes and he was a dried well, spent to the last insight.

There were some professors that kept my pencil busy for half a semester, and in one case a year and a half. Sooner or later I got to the bottom of them all. Maestro Misha Karensky had no bottom. He was the only bottomless man I have ever known. You could take notes on him for a hundred years and not have arrived at the beginning of him, let alone the end.

Walking from Anderson to Gladfelter Hall I said to DeMartino: "You're always on top of your content." DeMartino replied: "I have no content."

On another occasion I said: "Every time I illuminate an aspect of you, I find I've simply exposed an even more illimitable darkness." He said: "You're not making very much progress, are you?"

When I said that in trying to understand him these many years I was just scratching the surface, he said: "I always tried to remove those scratches."

———◆———

DeMartino's devotion to his major writing project—*The Zen Understanding of the Human Person*—was total, though he'd say, "There's a tidal wave of misunderstanding out there, and my work wouldn't stem a trickle." In thinking and writing, he was a perfectionist. In one sense this led him astray. When I inquired upon his return from sabbatical as to the progress he had made, he told me that he had spent the entire summer on a footnote arguing against Bertrand Russell. Too many years were spent revising the first two chapters of this work. Illness came, and the essential last two chapters were never completed. How much this bothered him I cannot say. When the *Eastern Buddhist* rejected the dialogue with D. T. Suzuki that he had edited and revised over a couple of years, he said, indifferently: "So it won't get published." Of his later writing, DeMartino said: "If [his wife] Kathleen likes it, that's enough for me."

He loved Chuang Tzu's advice on the use of being useless in the Taoist sense of the term. Given his years in Japan and the "credentials" these provided, he could have easily employed the 1960s interest in Eastern religion to celebrity status. He quietly chose not to. "No genuine religious teacher has ever charged a penny" was one of his firmer assertions. He did not consider himself a religious teacher of any sort. But he fielded all questions, academic and personal, inside and outside class, from anyone who asked. Always he was his own definition of a Zen koan: "A Zen presentation in the form of a Zen challenge." I never met that challenge, never could get past the cage his words built around me. That I am part of these recollections of him is unavoidable but of no significance at all. The cage is important though—others may fall into it; someone may break out of it—and I'll let DeMartino sing two final bars.

DeMartino had been saying in class, as he often did, that the ego knew itself to be a subject—might even resist to the death the attempt to reduce it to an object—yet could not know itself *as* subject but only as an objectified image of itself. The next day, as we were climbing the library slope, I asked if the true Self (unlike the ego) knows itself as subject. "Of course," he said, and without breaking stride he bent over, picked up a fallen leaf, righted himself, and presented it to me. "Here it is."

I hesitated—then grabbed at it. Still in stride, he held the leaf before me for a few seconds. Then, as I reached for it more aggressively, he said: "Here," letting it drop to the ground, "and not anywhere."

One morning I groggily answered the telephone.

"Did I wake you?" asked DeMartino.

"No."

"Sorry about that."

Cut with No Razor

There are monks who criticize Hisamatsu for not being
on the inside. He's more inside than the inside.
—Richard DeMartino

A WOMAN—A WESTERNER—having come to Kyoto, wanted to meet Shin'ichi Hisamatsu, the lay Zen master adamant that the only master is one's true Self. It was arranged that she would come for dinner at Hisamatsu's home, with his American Zen student, Richard DeMartino, serving as interpreter. Hisamatsu sensed an arrogance to her as he walked into the room. He dropped onto his shins at the low table where his two guests were seated on cushions. He was silent. He stayed silent.

"HISAMATS!" he suddenly roared.

"Yes!" he answered himself.

"HISAMATS!" he boomed.

"Yes!" he replied.

He turned to the woman. "Can you call me as I call myself?" he asked.

She peeped: "Hisamatsu."

Hisamatsu made no response.

"Have I answered you?" he asked finally.

She said yes.

Hisamatsu shook his head no.

Complete silence.

"When you call me as I call myself, I will answer you," he said. He poured tea into her cup, then into DeMartino's. For the next two hours he bantered and inquired, casually, cordially, always the cultured gentleman, through the successive courses of the meal.

The evening ended. No sooner was the woman out the front gate than she said to DeMartino: "I'm so ashamed. I've been in psychotherapy for fifteen years and he got deeper into me in thirty seconds than my therapist has in all that time."

"Don't be ashamed," said DeMartino. "Pick up the pieces and take it from there."

———————◆———————

DeMartino's own first encounter with Hisamatsu was a time bomb. It was months before he realized it. This meeting too was a dinner, in a Kyoto restaurant, 1952, at the invitation of DeMartino's other Zen teacher, D. T. Suzuki, who was also present. Hisamatsu courteously demolished him before the first course had been ordered, dismissing DeMartino's attempt to slide a cup of tea his direction with a terse: "You learned that from a fine person [Suzuki]."

His meeting with Hisamatsu, DeMartino later wrote, "initiated not only the 'shaking' but the total collapse of my 'foundations.'"[22] Seventeen years later, when I first began attending DeMartino's college classes, I was just learning what being shaken might mean. Sitting on the rug of my first apartment, back propped against the side of the bed, three thoughts jumped into my head in rapid succession:

"Are you happy?"

"For that question to arise the answer must be no."

"Were you to write plays greater than Shakepeare, become a better philosopher than Plato, have Casanova's charm, this unhappiness would not diminish because you are ensnared totally, without cause, therefore without remedy."

DeMartino said, when the time came to tell him all this: "You've collided with the problem at a young age. You're fortunate. But the problem is not the final word. There's a solution."

———————◆———————

In DeMartino's many references to his teacher during lectures, what drew me most was Hisamatsu's nonchalant absoluteness in stories like these: A certain Westerner had arrived in Kyoto. Several among those who called themselves Hisamatsu's disciples[23] stated that they could tell by looking at this man's face that he had "gotten something." DeMartino said to Hisamatsu: "I can tell by looking at his face that he hasn't gotten anything." Hisamatsu retorted: "If you've still got to look at the face in order to tell, that's very superficial." Another Westerner seeking Hisamatsu's sanction of his enlightenment received instead: "I'll accept your enlightenment when you can walk out of this room without using your legs."

The English translation of Hisamatsu's eulogy for D. T. Suzuki revealed the same uncompromising ease. "You admirers of Dr. Suzuki," he said, in effect, "have come to his memorial service in order to pay him homage. The only way homage can in fact be paid is for you yourselves to die the Great Death."[24] In this way Hisamatsu took the event of Suzuki's demise and threw it up against his audience as a koan of fundamental import. Yet it was obvious that Hisamatsu could convert—for whomever he happened to be addressing—any random occurrence into the ultimate problem of life and death. Suzuki's death was merely the occasion that presented itself.

Excited, I caught DeMartino dining in the student cafeteria. "I've just finished reading Hisamatsu's essay on Suzuki." DeMartino shot back: "That's no essay. It's a dialogue with a dead man!" I studied everything by Hisamatsu I could find. Yet I liked him more when I heard from DeMartino: "Hisamatsu never had much interest in his own writings." In all I read and heard, Hisamatsu stood always at the same point. He once described that point thus: "The spider stands free of the web it spins."

As he did in the remarkable photograph I saw set on DeMartino's mantelpiece the first time I made it up to his apartment: Hisamatsu meditating in the full lotus position under the Bodhi Tree in Bodhgaya, India, taken on the way home from his trip to America and Europe in 1957–1958. I had never before seen Hisamatsu's face. DeMartino pointed out that some criticized Hisamatsu for his arrogance in sitting under the very tree beneath which Gautama is said to have attained enlightenment. "Arrogance!" DeMartino sneered at the critics. Then, nodding at the photograph, he pressed me: "Is he there or isn't he there? Is he there or isn't he there?"

———————◆———————

In 1971 I decided to go to Japan. DeMartino warned: "Don't make the problem geographical." But while DeMartino had given me an invaluable map, he could not give me the determination to conquer the territory. I thought I could cut my escape routes by placing myself in a formal monastic setting. To this persistence he said: "If you meet Hisamatsu once, it will be worth your whole trip."

I arrived in Kyoto the following spring and was soon being bailed out of one difficulty after the next by another of Hisamatsu's "disciples" of long standing, Masao Abe. Kind and wonderful, Abe bailed and bailed, but I was in over my head. Though intellectually never doubting the necessity of traversing the Zen path to its end, existentially I was not prepared to face on a day-to-day basis the grueling demands of a Zen monastery and the Zen quest. When it looked like I might fall below one hundred pounds, having lost thirty, I elected to retreat. Only once during my stay did I hint at meeting Hisamatsu. Abe responded by saying that Hisamatsu was seriously ill and that whenever he received a visitor he gave so much of himself that he often suffered severe physical consequences for two or three weeks. As a result, even those closest to him refrained from visiting.

I had heard something of the recalcitrance of Hisamatsu's body. At sixteen he had overheard a doctor telling his mother that her pleurisy-ridden son would be dead within six months. Half a century later, when Hisamatsu was once again dangerously ill and his disciples urged him to replace his physician (also a disciple but whose area of expertise had nothing to do with the affliction), Hisamatsu refused, insisting in a letter that he would sooner die than hurt the feelings of another man. In 1958, straight off the arduous flight returning him from his sole trip to the West, he began work on a calligraphy for the cremation casket of a friend who had just died. Repeated attempts through the night left him dissatisfied; by the time he got the calligraphy to his liking, his health was broken. DeMartino was unable to see him for two years. Illness was such a pervasive force that Hisamatsu once told DeMartino that he had spent more days of his life on his back than upright. Add to this his advanced age, and I wasn't surprised when Abe told me that his teacher was not well. In retrospect, I cannot help feeling that had I met Hisamatsu at that time, my immaturity would have vitiated the event.

I returned to America, in a sense with my tail between my legs. Yet from the moment I was back in the United States, I began to ready myself both economically and inwardly for a second stint, and in April 1976 I found myself sitting opposite Masao Abe in his Kyoto study. On that occasion I learned that Hisamatsu's housekeeper had died, and though a female disciple had offered to quit her job as a librarian for the purpose of caring for him, it was finally agreed that he would end a sixty-six-year tenure in Kyoto and retire to his home prefecture of Gifu, where relatives could care for him. He was eighty-seven at the time.

Five *sesshin* later, right after Christmas 1976, Abe informed me that he would be visiting Hisamatsu the first Sunday after the New Year and invited me to accompany him if I were free. We both laughed: He knew quite well I would cancel the world for the occasion. The next few days were spent in anticipation of finally having a face-to-face encounter with the man DeMartino said would in two hundred years be recognized as one of the greatest Zen masters of all time, the man to whom the celebrated philosopher Kitarō Nishida had said: "All my disciples know the road I travel; you know where I arrive." But when I reached Abe's home, he came to the gate to inform me, as I had no phone, that Hisamatsu and his entire family had come down with colds and felt it unwise to receive callers. The visit was postponed. Two Sundays later, however, Abe and I were in a taxi en route to Kyoto Station, where we were to meet some others and head on to Gifu.

At the station was Renny Merritt, an American who in addition to having an interest in Zen was a student of Japanese landscape gardening, and a shy Japanese youth whose name I do not recall. As we chatted, I noticed another member of our group consciously keeping his distance: a Japanese schoolteacher in his late twenties—Toyoshima-san—whose existence both inspires and plagues me to this day. He stood motionlessly, utterly preoccupied. There was what I can describe only as a density to his being, occasioned by his own anguish, which pulled him like a magnet into himself and from which it appeared he could emerge only with difficulty. He spoke only when spoken to. Yet inadvertently, without even a word between us, by virtue of both the instantly recognizable power of his commitment and the frightening though compelling extent to which he was grasped by the Zen problem in a manner quite beyond his control, he thrust into question—or should I say left in shambles?—my whole approach to the religious quest. Standing beside him I felt like a Sunday tourist, a dilettante lacking the seriousness without which awakening is impossible.

Abe would allow us to pay for only our return tickets. His demeanor made it clear that he gave not a thought to laying out what must have come to a considerable sum. I suspect that he was so grateful for our opportunity to meet Hisamatsu—an opportunity for which he himself was responsible—that he wanted no financial setback on our part to tarnish our experience. Within two hours we climbed out of the taxi that had brought us from Gifu Station to Hisamatsu's house. There we were met by Hisamatsu's nephew, who led us to a room where we sat on floor cushions for several minutes. Eventually Hisamatsu appeared, walking shakily with a cane and supported by his nephew. Lowering himself to his knees, he bowed before us in formal Buddhist fashion and then, raising his upper torso to be seated in the *seiza* position, greeted us in English with a single word, "Welcome!"

In that simple utterance, I knew I was in the presence of an unparalleled man. I had never seen anyone so delighted to be living. His "welcome" was an invitation to that delight, to a joyous domain in which every trace of anxiety seemed to have been extinguished. His eyes, whenever he glanced my way, said: "Do you realize how wonderful it all is? Do you?" Yet his was a world I had neither the freedom nor power to enter. Even he could not grant entry—only an invitation. He beckoned and he blocked.

And emitted an uncanny sense of alertness that bespoke the reason an enlightened person is said to be "awake." The room was alive with his existence, yet I had the ridiculous sensation I could put my hand right through him. I thought of the photo of Hisamatsu at the Bodhi Tree and of DeMartino's interrogation: "Is he there or isn't he there? Is he there or isn't he there?"

For the next two hours the conversation proceeded: Hisamatsu making inquiries of Abe and myself about DeMartino, asking Abe questions pertaining to his forthcoming lecture series at Princeton; Abe bringing him up to date on the Zen group—in large part civilian, not clerical—that for decades had centered around Hisamatsu in Kyoto. The discussion did not seem to be tending toward any particularly existential concerns. Unsure as to the protocol, I kept watch for an opening to put forth a question. For I had long before concluded that should I ever have the chance to meet Hisamatsu, I would have to have formulated in advance a single question that penetrated to the core of the human predicament as I experienced it. I had prepared that question, one that laid bare the terror in my heart and threw me up against my own self-destructive cowardice. I was, as the adage has it, a man sitting between two stools. Unable to find any repose in my ego existence, neither could I locate in myself the will to make the total commitment necessary to break through it. My whole life seemed to have been reduced to a contradiction between confronting the Zen problem and evading it. And while the vast majority of my time was spent hovering about the "evasion" pole of that duality, I could never, not for a single day, quiet the ineradicable need to face that dilemma and solve it. Mine was a situation that could be succinctly summed in Jack Spicer's line: "I chicken out at the edges of it."

An increasing dread seized hold of me as the afternoon wore on, a dread that on the surface was linked to my worry that the meeting would be terminated without my having the opportunity to pose my question. In fact, however, the dread stemmed from my fear of plunging into the abyss, the abyss that would negate my existence as ego and yet comprised Hisamatsu's subjectivity and was the source of his infinite delight. Without an explicit challenge, Hisamatsu's very being had nonetheless driven me into a state of acute ambivalence. Before me, I do believe, sat a man who had died the Great Death and attained the "peace that surpasses all understanding." But to achieve this peace, Hisamatsu had had no recourse but to undergo the blackest existential torment. I needed the end but dreaded the means. That life would be no less untenable by continued flight in no way diminished the overwhelming sense of inertia that arose from my fear of wrestling the problem head on.

Yet now the visit appeared to be over. Hisamatsu withdrew from the room. Disconcerted that I had lost my chance at an interview, I asked Abe if it would not still be possible to ask a question. Abe, protective of his aged teacher's health, eyed me with uncharacteristic gravity, then said he'd put the matter to Hisamatsu.

The latter returned and presented to each of us a piece of calligraphy from several he had recently drawn. Abe asked if I could make my inquiry. Hisamatsu, with immense gladness, laughed: "Of course!"

I said that Gautama had subjected himself to six years of extremely torturous ascetic practice before arriving at the foot of the tree where he vowed not to move until he had either awakened or perished. Was it essential, to attain enlightenment, to arrive at a similar determination?

Hisamatsu replied that it was not. What is essential, he said, is to undergo what he termed the "ultimate negation." He then proceeded to explain that the essence of all Zen koan is contained in what he called the fundamental koan: "Whatever you do will not do. What do you do?" To undergo the ultimate negation and to resolve this koan are one and the same.

I felt I understood why Hisamatsu had answered in the negative as to whether it was necessary to make the vow: "either awakening or death." He was not so much concerned with rigorous training, as in the case of Gautama's ascetic ordeal, or even with the vow not to move until the problem was resolved or one died in the attempt. In posing the fundamental koan, in demanding the ultimate negation be gone through, Hisamatsu released the aspirant from any particular form of religious practice yet raised before him or her an even more formidable barrier. Whether one sits (in meditation), stands, walks, or lies; whether one trains relentlessly or relaxes his effort, confronts the problem or tries to escape it—none of this is of any avail as a means of contending with the human dilemma. As DeMartino himself had formulated it in his essay of twenty years earlier: "Nothing [the ego] can do can resolve its contradiction." "The ego, in an existential quandary which it can neither compose, endure, abandon, or escape, is unable to advance, unable to retreat, unable to stand fixed. Nonetheless, it remains under the impelling admonition to move and to resolve."[25] To actualize this contradiction or quandary at its root and break through it—this was Hisamatsu's single charge. Meditation, religious practice, and discipline of any kind were secondary and inessential: valuable insofar as they culminated in the overcoming of the predicament intrinsic to personhood; worthless, from an ultimate standpoint, if they did not.

The intense Japanese schoolteacher—seated to my right and silent the entire afternoon—now bared himself. Pressed to the precipice for years, he was impelled to exertions in meditation that were, as I later witnessed, Promethean. Hisamatsu challenged: "Sitting will not do. What do you do? Why don't you stand? . . . But standing won't do either."

And that was it. Hisamatsu, vibrant as at the first, was not going to be permitted by Abe or his nephew to continue any further. We made our bows and got up to leave. Hisamatsu, without his cane, accompanied us with slow movements toward the vestibule. Beset by a state of distraught vertigo, I was seized by an irresistible urge to touch this beautiful old man. As soon as I took hold of his hand, the anxiety that had been surging within me for much of the afternoon burst. The bottom seemed to drop out of my existence. My guts felt as though they had been ripped apart, and I began wailing in a deluge of mournful, spasmodic sobs. Through my anguished tears came Hisamatsu's demand: "Clasp my hand without using your hands!" Abe, having put on his shoes with his back to us, had begun to turn around to make some parting remarks. But as soon as he completed his turn, he became cognizant of what was taking place and lapsed—mid-sentence—into silence.

My sobbing persisted uncontrollably. Sundered at the core of my ambivalence, I stood nailed to myself in a paroxysm of simultaneous agony and joyous relief. I had in my grasp the living resolution to the problem of human existence. Of this I was in no doubt. But that resolution was Hisamatsu's, not mine, and I was blocked in terrified anticipation of the crucible that loomed before me unless I fled it at *the* cost of a squandered life.

I finally managed to get into my shoes as the others made their farewell. Hisamatsu had his *juzu* (Buddhist prayer beads) in his hands, and he who had an hour before claimed to be thoroughly without piety bowed repeatedly before us, displaying in spite of himself a piety I do not expect to see equaled. Clearly he was deeply honored we had come. The others passed through the gate, but I kept turning around for one more look. He bowed whenever I turned, saying: "Whatever you do will not do; what do you do? . . . Give my regards to DeMartino-san . . . Whatever you do will not do; what do you do?" At last I had no alternative but to step through the gate. Everyone was already seated in a cab that had apparently been called. I entered, and as the taxi headed for the station, I cried without respite. Renny Merritt placed a hand upon my shoulder.

I sat vacantly as the train sped toward Nagoya. We switched to a crowded Kyoto-bound train in which we were forced to stand. At one point Abe began to gaze intently at the Japanese schoolteacher, saying to him after a time: "What's wrong?" The man, who had not uttered a syllable since leaving Hisamatsu's house, replied softly: "I'm thinking." Abe said: "Yes, it's good to consider Dr. Hisamatsu's words carefully." Then, following a moment's pause, and in a tone that revealed Abe's own recognition that he had not yet said words of sufficient value to this suffering individual, he added: "If necessary, you can meet with Dr. Hisamatsu alone."

A tinge of jealousy stole into my heart. I envied not simply the man's opportunity to visit Hisamatsu again but, strangely, the despair that thrust him into a depth from which I was as yet barred, a depth without which I knew my efforts would be in vain. I felt myself as a bar of Ivory soap that, however many times it is pressed to the bottom of the tub, floats—unless completely stuck—inexorably back to the surface. In that brief instant of envy, I was painfully reminded that my ego had in no way been shattered in my exchange with Hisamatsu, merely temporarily bent out of shape. For no object can ever genuinely negate the subject. And Hisamatsu, from the standpoint of my dualistic "I," was still an object, albeit an object of incalculable worth. Consequently, try as I might to prevent it, the significance of my interview was bound to recede. The lessening of the impact had already begun.

More or less my "old self" again, I thought through the day's events. Smiling at how I had been sliced to pieces, I recalled DeMartino telling me: "Hisamatsu cuts like a razor; it takes thirty minutes before you realize you've been slashed." Writing these words now, there comes to mind a conversation I had with William LeFleur the following summer on the veranda of the small temple in which we were both residing. "Have you ever heard Professor Abe's characterization of the difference between Hisamatsu and Suzuki?" he asked. I replied that I had not. "When you collide with Suzuki, you knock him down but he always bounces back up. When you smash into Hisamatsu, it's you that crumbles."

At Kyoto Station, Professor Abe and I took leave of the others and boarded a bus back toward the vicinity where we both lived. Halfway home, Abe commented: "Today you had a great encounter." When I asked him why he thought Hisamatsu had responded to my question in the negative, he suggested: "Initially I was surprised that Dr. Hisamatsu said it was not essential to make the kind of existential commitment Gautama had made when he sat down at the base of the tree. Then I realized that Dr. Hisamatsu was concerned not with the 'occasion' but with the 'ground' of the awakening. Gautama's determination was merely the occasion for his enlightenment. To go through the ultimate negation is the ground, and it is this that Dr. Hisamatsu wished to emphasize."

I told Abe that I could not surmount what Nietzsche had called in his *Origin of Ascetic Ideals* the "horror vacui"—horror of the void. Abe said with a smile: "Yes. I know that passage," in a manner that indicated: "And I *knew* that fear." "But," he went on, "today you met living proof of a man who leapt into that void—and look at the result."

We exited the bus, and I walked Abe to the front gate of his house. The next day I was to enter the monastery where I trained to participate in the January *sesshin*. The knowledge that in addition to the usual backbreaking and leg-breaking pain and sleeplessness, I would be frozen solid twenty hours a day for a week had darkened my heart the past month. For it was significantly colder now than it had been during the December *sesshin*, during which my frozen feet had burned with chilblains and I could not stop my body from quaking.

I grinned at Abe from the peace of the tenuous calm sometimes achieved in the aftermath of an exhausting experience and remarked: "Somehow after today the cold no longer seems much of a factor." Abe slapped me vigorously on the back and with warm firmness commanded: "Do *sesshin*!" With that injunction resounding in my brain, I sped through the night toward my freezing room.

Meditation Prometheus Falling through the Shaft

PART ONE

THE NIGHT BEFORE I left for my second stay in Japan, I stood on a Philadelphia street and wept into the arms of a friend. Those tears found their justification in later sorrows. For the core of my life in Kyoto, as I had already determined prior to my departure, was to be those unparalleled sojourns into the hell known in the Zen tradition as *sesshin*, the weeklong stints of meditation wherein sincerity, dread, and an aspiration for the ultimate somehow combined to hold for a time my ambivalence in check, thus making possible a serious confrontation with what Zen calls "the great matter of life and death" before the will became again dispersed in the seduction of daily concerns.

Before I even began, I encountered a test. The evening preceding my first retreat, the monk second-in-command in the monastery urged me to forgo the rigors of the full *sesshin,* with each day's labors lasting from 3:30 a.m. till 11 p.m., and to come to the Zen hall for the evening meditations only. Though this meant the subversion of my journey in its first critical moment, my will-to-comfort responded instinctively to this gift from an unexpected quarter: my own fear legitimated by a figure at the apex of the monastic hierarchy actively encouraging me to let myself off the hook. But an opposing impulse—as deep-rooted as the desire to sidestep the suffering the *sesshin* would of necessity impose—

would not permit evasion of the fatal truth of Charles Olson's caveat: "The hour of your flight will be the hour of your death." When I held fast, the monk responded with a smile that for one instant—across barriers of language, culture, and monastery walls—brought us together as men. Yet never again would we meet in such sympathy. He briefly admonished me to toughen myself for the morrow, then departed, fading into himself and into his own quest. The paper-paneled door slid shut, leaving me with the consequences of a momentary courage. In this way the black heart, driven to Japan, took upon itself to blacken further in the hope of one day being rid of its blackness.

My knees, swollen so badly from the long hours of sitting that I cried when I tried to walk, would not straighten sufficiently to allow me to sleep. Half-smiling, half-chagrined at the stupidity of being the only person awake at 1 a.m. when the ordeal was to begin anew at 3, I lay exhausted amid a cacophony of snoring monks. Pain after repeated sittings set in after only a few minutes, and in the evening, when a number of lay practitioners joined the monks for the interview with the master—from which I, due to language deficiencies, was initially barred—the resulting period of prohibited movement for two hours was one silent interminable scream.

These trials, in themselves sufficient to at times induce in me a condition of mild shock, were to be compounded by the difficulties concomitant with the winter months. Until the later acquisition of a concentration that produced its own warmth, my trembling body—as I sat through the freezing nights—could be quelled only by the blows of the patrol staff, and I was repeatedly obliged to ask to be struck. Sleep proved impossible unless I was overdressed, and I'd wake in an hour dripping in sweat, change my clothes in the icy darkness, and repeat the cycle. My exposed feet, protected neither by socks, which were not permitted, nor by the heat pocket the monks achieved by tucking their crossed legs under their robes, shriveled away from the bone, so that I was actually stepping on my own sagging flesh, each step causing in my frozen extremities the sensation of walking on burning coals.

At the heart of this trial I sought to place the koan, the fundamental problem of my existence whose solution, I was convinced—however great life's other accomplishments—could alone obviate paying the horrendous cost of a thrown-away life. DeMartino had warned of the danger of becoming so preoccupied with the physical discomfort of long hours of sitting that one became caught up in secondary difficulties at the expense of the more fundamental dilemma of living and dying. My experience, however, was that the two proved generally inextricable, and the conditional physical and emotional distress generated by the structure of the *sesshin* seemed to fuel the struggle for awakening with its needed intensity. Koan and the *sesshin*-induced anguish forged into a grindstone against which the sparks of my existence sputtered uselessly, and I felt myself being ground into a crumbling powder. It appeared plausible, then, that the *sesshin* might prove the occasion for the ultimate negation, or Great Death, of the ego and the simultaneous emerging of the awakened "true Self," which Zen has from its inception taken as its raison d'être.

Nevertheless, the intensity engendered by the *sesshin*, at times seemingly life threatening, showed itself transient. To the extent that it was the consequence of a condition—the rigors of *sesshin* being artificially embossed onto the innate problem of being human that had led me to Zen—it was fated to dissipate as I became habituated to the regime. Sitting one morning among a group of lay practitioners during their spring meditation week, my lips traced into a slight smile with the realization that I had imperceptibly begun to coast. This smile was more than the expression of the relief natural to the easing of a year of extreme hardship. It spoke likewise of a secret joy at my having achieved a much-longed-for refuge through which I could step out from under my burden. The manifestation of a healthy instinct for self-preservation, this smile was also testament of a more dubious instinct of ego preservation. Thus it is that the unawakened "I" stands inherently at cross-purposes with itself, for it seeks its fulfillment through both its preservation and its negation.

Mine, therefore, was the joy of the false reprieve, the happiness of the critically ill patient informed that his doctor is unavailable to operate. I had come to Japan fettered, had willingly imposed a fetter on that fetter in the hope of bursting its grip. Yet the second fetter hurt as did the first, and the decline in its power to bind made the condition of having but one fetter seem pleasant. *Sesshin* would hereafter remain tough but manageable. For a year, I had doubted whether I could survive its tribulations. Now I realized these would be withstood, but I knew simultaneously that they alone would not culminate in my self-overcoming. As I sat through the cool April morning, fear dissolved into a sigh that held laxity in its womb.

Into this complacency obtruded a motionless human form, at first a vague presence in the margin of my consciousness as I half-gazed at the tatami from atop my sitting cushions. When the bell rang and I gratefully pulled my thighs off my legs for the brief respite prior to the onset of the next sitting period, the shape across from me—alone among those in the meditation hall—did not stir. The torso had a look of utter passivity, held erect solely by a force outside itself, yet the strained quiet of the face had the hint of its undergoing slow execution. The sitting recommenced. I snuck several glances, bewitched by an aura of danger in this stillness. Only with the signal for the noonday meal did the body yield to what must have been a ferocious impulse for release, for when it did at last rise it broke into horrendous convulsions. My mind, splashed into witness of this, also convulsed, imploding in shocked, sudden apprehension of the full implications of the Zen quest.

The "I" who animated this body was not unknown to me. I had met him three months earlier, one of a group of four invited by Masao

Abe to visit his Zen teacher Shin'ichi Hisamatsu. His name was Kenzō Toyoshima, and I have elsewhere described my initial impression as we stood in Kyoto Station:

> At the station . . . [Abe and I were greeted by] Renny Merritt, an American who in addition to having an interest in Zen was a student of Japanese landscape gardening, and a shy Japanese youth whose name I do not recall. As we chatted, I noticed another member of our group consciously keeping his distance: a Japanese schoolteacher in his late twenties— Toyoshima-san—whose existence both inspires and plagues me to this day. He stood motionlessly, utterly preoccupied. There was what I can describe only as a density to his being, occasioned by his own anguish, which pulled him like a magnet into himself and from which it appeared he could emerge only with difficulty. He spoke only when spoken to. Yet inadvertently, without even a word between us, by virtue of both the instantly recognizable power of his commitment and the frightening though compelling extent to which he was grasped by the Zen problem in a manner quite beyond his control, he thrust into question—or should I say left in shambles?—my whole approach to the religious quest. Standing beside him I felt like a Sunday tourist, a dilettante lacking the seriousness without which awakening is impossible.

I stared hard at this man, thick with religious seriousness. His spasms continued uncontrollably, and as his trembling hand unsteadied his bowl in the dining hall, he withdrew it from the serving crew filled with a bare lump of rice so as not to be an inconvenience. The meal over, undeniably half-starved, he forswore the afternoon break, proceeding at once to his place in the meditation hall.

There he sat: alone in a way very few are alone, and in a way in which perhaps all are alone. He moved encased in an abyss, and where he moved, the abyss moved with him. He was swallowed up, Jonah in the whale, falling through the shaft of himself. Too many years of loneliness, of isolation and despair, had seared in him two awesome creases from nose to chin, had forged a desolation that drove him, it soon became evident, unremittingly toward his cushions. Others among us, myself included, were marked by similar forces. Still, we hovered outside the meditation hall, in chatter light and serious and in afternoon sleep, repelled from the untended meditation hall to which he alone was propelled, as if that bare room of sitting cushions and a single human figure bore the sign of quarantine.

In this distinction, to my mind, lay his magnificence. Every person who has ever been driven by an ultimate task must surely know the resistance to its completion that lies in the marrow of that calling. There repeatedly emerges the cross formed by the simultaneous repulsion from that to which one is most fundamentally drawn. Later conversations confirmed that he knew the full force of this resistance, that he dreaded those pillows that he saw as critical to his salvation. Still, he never flinched.

This alarming resolve made him, through no desire of his own, the conscience of my own quest. Reflected in his mirror, my efforts seemed doomed. Pulled toward him, the next *sesshin* I presented him my respect in the form of a modern Japanese translation, recently published, of the seventeenth-century Zen master Hakuin's *Orategama*. This he received with modesty, but he left the package unwrapped and its contents unknown, saying simply: "When this is over, perhaps we can talk." We didn't. Months later at another retreat, the evening's sitting ended, he came to where I was casually holding court with a few of the other participants, listened for a moment, then walked away. He gave, as always, no sign of disapproval. Yet with each retreating step, I knew I was wasting myself.

That same *sesshin* he was nailed to his mat. I'd already had the uncomfortable task of passing him with the patrol stick, barely able to suppress the impulse to break the snail-like pace customary to the Zen tradition and speed past him as he sat there, pressed on by an inner mandate far exceeding my puny authority. I'd even contemplated a sign: "Detour, Man at Work." With our usual venue unavailable, the *sesshin* was held in the large meditation hall on the second floor of the Institute for Zen Studies. It was impossible to get to one's gear without traversing the length of the room and walking past him, as he was invariably ensconced—even during the breaks—in his spot to the inside of a partition. He seemed to me Lin-chi, Hakuin, Tzu-ming in their pre-awakened youths, monstrous in their strivings. I was the countless monks and laymen without names, dissolved into death, their sole legacy an after-scent of ambivalence. Secretly I wanted his cushions to be vacant, to be comforted—against all better judgment— that resurrection was possible without crucifixion and that I would not have to intensify my efforts to an unendurable pitch. Once, seeing his place during a rest period at long last unoccupied, I broke into song as I crossed to the small makeshift storage room at the far corner of the meditation hall to grab a sweater from my bag. Sweater in hand and still singing, I reentered the hall, en route to an hour's leisure. The song fled my mouth. Eyes closed, full lotus posture—storage room side of the partition and hence hidden from the entrance side of the meditation hall—sat Toyoshima, potent as death.

When I first came to know him, Toyoshima-san was a primary school teacher. His obligations to his work, and to his elderly parents, with whom he lived, gave him at best three chances a year—twenty-one days total during vacations—to sit with others in a formal structure. The rest of the year he was forced to confront himself alone. From these bouts of lonely struggle he must have been made forcibly aware that his tremendous inner strength was fated, as one bi-pole of an intrinsically dualistic human nature, to be pitted in constant battle with a formidable and ineradicable weakness. Every night in his room he rolled up his bedding, vowing to sit through to morning. Every night he slept. He began to tie his legs into the full lotus with a kimono sash, and when that failed, he chained himself into meditation, tossing the key to the far side of his quarters. Inevitably, however, feet shackled to his thighs, he would crawl after it, the unhitching of the latch bathing him in doomed relief. Alone, he could not ultimately hold out against the power inhering in every episode of sustained temptation: the one way in which weakness is stronger than strength, needing but a single instant to prevail, whereas strength, if it is to dodge defeat, must surmount the forces resisting it continuously. Nevertheless, he forbade this weakness to have the final word, and hoping to keep it at bay just long enough to achieve breakthrough, he sought in *sesshin* the plank from which to plummet from the precipice.

The perpetual regeneration of will entailed in the attempt to prosecute that leap seemed to us superhuman. To him, sitting within temple walls made possible a carefully laid strategy predicated on the incontrovertible recognition of his own frailty. I recall in this regard a story DeMartino told early on about two US GIs in a truck behind enemy lines during the Second World War. "What's the matter, buddy, you scared?" chides the driver, brimming with machismo, to his more delicate sidekick. "If you were half as scared as I am," comes the rejoinder, "you wouldn't even be here."

He was convinced that the awakening for which he so ardently strove could not occur lest he was pressed to the final human limit. Thus, while the value of the *sesshin* resided in its demanding more than he could demand of himself when alone, he in turn demanded more of himself than the *sesshin* structure demanded. Greater exertions still brought failure, and each failed *sesshin* brought greater exertions. In an Osaka coffee shop years later he remarked: "Rather than force my students to study an hour, I let them decide. They elect half an hour, and the result is poor. Gradually they realize on their own they must increase to forty minutes. It is the same with *sesshin*. You realize on your own you must sit more. And more."

To this end he determined to apply an intensified will precisely at the point of his greatest vulnerability: those times he was under no external compulsion to sit. This meant the rest breaks (sixty to ninety minutes after meals), the nightly optional sitting after the conclusion of the evening meditation known as *yaza*,[26] and the five-minute intervals between the end of one sitting period and the next. Other forces would be sure to hold him to his cushions once the formally structured group sittings began. Self-examination inclines me to the belief that, in general, vanity is to be listed among the forces that make possible an endurance of a physical agony hardly withstood for even a few moments when one sits alone. But an episode antecedent to my knowing him suggests that even if a trace of vanity were a motivating element in his struggle as well, then this was an egoistic impulse paradoxically harnessed in the service of a drive to negate the ego even at the cost of his life. In an early *sesshin,* the pain of the full lotus prompted him to wiggle a toe at the very moment when a veteran practitioner passed with the patrol stick. Catching sight of this, the man simply laughed. "That," Toyoshima told me later amid laughter of his own, "was a good way of handling the patrol stick. From that moment on, I vowed I would die rather than move before the period's end."

During *yaza,* and during the allotted breaks after meals, he sat aware that he was free to terminate his sitting and that pain or exhaustion would eventually cause him to succumb to that freedom. What was essential was to rouse his will and resume sitting however often he quit. But there was always the safety valve that the decision of when to stop and start remained at all times his. What precipitated the greatest anguish, therefore, were the brief interludes between the formal, monitored stints of sitting. He without fail—ignoring the bell announcing permission to move the legs and readjust one's position—sat through two periods in succession, in this way increasing the length of a single sitting from thirty to sixty-five minutes. He would usually rise for the ten-minute period of walking, then sit again through the next bell for another sixty-five. It was this that caused the convulsions in the first year I knew him, for it was simply too much for his organism to withstand. He saw this clearly enough. There were ominous pains down his arms and in the area of the heart, and his breathing was at times strained to such rapidity that it barely passed the tip of his nose. Unnatural and unhealthy as he knew this to be, he could not stop. Yet neither could he suppress the desire to stop, and the five minutes between sittings when everyone moved were a repeated and unendurable torture. For in that interval lay the last liberty to retreat from the ledge. He felt compelled to exercise that liberty through its denial, so as to be thrust in the ensuing thirty minutes into the extremity of life and death. "You think to yourself," said Toyoshima-san, "in that gap between the two periods: 'Shall I unbind my legs?' But then the bell rings and you give up."

This staggering effort occasionally broke out into gallows humor. When, one evening, all of the senior practitioners were forced to absent themselves, a younger member, Iki-san, was placed in charge of the meditation hall. He at once proceeded to condense the usual five sitting periods into four, thereby lengthening each by ten minutes. That night, collapsed into his futon, Toyoshima-san uncharacteristically jumped to his feet and in imitation of the overly enthusiastic Iki-san bellowed: "Tonight we shall sit four periods, each period forty minutes"—pressing forearm to forehead in mock despair and flopping backward onto his bedding. It was the first and last time I ever heard him even obliquely hint that he'd like the universe to give him a break, and I, cursing Iki-san in a muttered snarl as I spread out my quilts, was so taken by the lightheartedness with which this plea bargain with destiny was carried through, and by his final indifference to destiny's response, that my mouth fell shut. For the universe had indeed given him a break, only he would not take it. The lengthened periods brought ample justification to move with the bell, but despite the increase from sixty-five to eighty-five minutes that sitting his typical two successive periods would entail, he was not to be budged from his plan of attack.

Nevertheless, the heart and core of Toyoshima-san would be missed if he were grasped solely in terms of an unbending will strategically attacking the problem of his existence. He did not believe he had the power to attack anything. To the contrary, especially in later years, he held that his meditation, like the rest of his unawakened existence, was meaningless. He repeatedly described himself with the phrase "Neuchi ga nai"—"I'm worthless." Whenever I asked during a *sesshin* how he was faring, in one of his tragicomic gestures, he would cross his forearms into an X. Or he would place his hand up to his neck to indicate that he was drowning. Otherwise, in his execrable yet poignant Japanese English he would say, simply, "Mō gibu appu shiteiru"—"I've already given up."

This giving up did not mean, as I had initially misinterpreted, that he was contemplating abandoning the Zen quest. Rather, it was an expression of the profound lucidity of a man who had for years been sundered by a dilemma he could not circumvent, since this dilemma was his very existence in all its aspects, and against which even the most prodigious efforts had been, and had to be by the nature of that dilemma, of no avail. As DeMartino had said: "All you can do is keep your nose to the grindstone. On the other hand, the nose *is* the grindstone." The problem cannot solve itself; the "I" could do nothing to precipitate its own death-rebirth, and Toyoshima-san knew it. Still, he was driven to hold himself at the extremity, driven against his will to exert his will until catapulted by the striking of the meditation bell beyond his will into a Gethsemane to which he year after year resigned himself, and from which again and again he would step away unaltered. Yet a few morsels or a quick stretch later he was back on his cushions.

Only twenty-eight (I learned later) when I met him, he was already possessed of an enormous spiritual maturity. But he must have long been
remarkable. Horrible bouts of motion sickness had haunted him from
early on: "I never saw scenery until I was in middle school. Whenever
there was a class trip, my head was in a bucket. That's when I knew I
was different from other children."

The condition was to plague him for years, until desperate, and following the recommendation of a Zen-influenced author who asserted
"the nonduality of inner and outer" as the basis of the treatment for
seasickness, he ingested his own vomit. This too was regurgitated.
But the pitch of his misery, coupled with the impact of the Zen layman and samurai Yamaoka Tesshū's remark that a true Buddhist in
receiving a donor's offering must be able to eat in welcome a beggar's
vomit, strengthened him to persist until the repeatedly regurgitated
substances were finally held down and the problem to a manageable
degree quelled.

He was torn from his existence for the first time through the shock
of the Buddhist monk Eshin's painting of hell that hung over the altar
of his childhood home. When a few years later, at the funeral of his
grandmother, an ardent Pure Land Buddhist devotee, he saw a bucket
of her bones, terror rent the initial fear into a fissure upon which for
some years he could still contrive to stand. There followed, in 1964, the
Tokyo Olympics. As he watched the athletes on the television screen,
for reasons unknown, superimposed on this sight of maximum and
accomplished human striving was another vision—fundamental and
incontrovertible it would turn out later but at this point still intermit-
tent in its force—the vanity of all human effort and affairs. At sixteen
and thenceforward, the dominating focus of his life was to be, to an
ever-absorbing degree, the problem of nihilism.

With his last year of high school came the hitherto unanticipated
possibility of a way out. During a sweltering intensive summer session
on the reading of classical Chinese texts, his teacher—himself having

practiced at a Kyoto monastery—introduced the well-known exchange where in response to a monk's plea for a means of escape from the torrid heat, the Tang Dynasty Zen master Tung-shan replied: "Go to the place where there is neither summer nor winter." When he read Tung-shan's rejoinder to the monk's subsequent question as to where such a place was to be found—"In summer you sweat to death; in winter you freeze to death"—Toyoshima-san suddenly felt "a new world had opened up for the first time." He at once resolved to center his university studies on classical Japanese to facilitate penetration of Zen texts.

The classical language specialist at his university confessed, however, his inability to comprehend Zen and sent Toyoshima instead to a colleague, a disciple of the lay Zen master Shin'ichi Hisamatsu. Not long after he was informed by this professor that Masao Abe, who had studied and trained under Hisamatsu since the war, would be lecturing at their university; the professor urged Toyoshima to speak with him. Abe heard him out, and in consequence Toyoshima-san began attending the weeklong meditation intensives of the Kyoto-based lay group founded around Hisamatsu during the Second World War and headed since Hisamatsu's retirement largely by Abe himself. It was there, almost a decade later, that I was able to make Toyoshima-san my friend.

In the meantime, political turmoil had broken out on the campus of his university, generated by the increased Americanization of the war in Southeast Asia and the related issues of Japan's role as an international power and the future direction—in light of this—of the Japanese educational system. It became mandatory for each student to take a position: Marxist, nationalist, and existentialist being the predominant choices. Toyoshima-san, alone, held forth his standpoint as Zen. A rare chance at romance gone awry culminated in what he termed simply "the incident," the result of the unleashing within him of an emotion so explosive and unexpected, so personally repellent, that in the aftermath of this event he felt himself stained irrevocably at his very core. The fracture traversing his existence now yielded into an abysmal rupture into which surged a realization, now stripped of every sporadic quality and disclosed rather as an elemental human destiny, of the utter meaninglessness of existence: first, as he was to subsequently put it, "subjectively—the meaninglessness of myself; later, objectively—the meaninglessness of the world." Erotic desire as one fundamental expression of the life force had spawned from its entrails a negation so total as to turn against the very life force that engendered it.

The pressing triad of death, meaninglessness, and guilt now pared itself down to the consuming focal question of how to transform his contaminated "I." But when at an early *sesshin*, during the private interview period especially designed for such encounters, he inquired of Masao Abe as to the means of solving this problem, Abe dryly returned: "How do you think you solve it?" Toyoshima-san, responding—as always in such situations—only because he was asked, replied: "absolute nothingness." To this sheer intellectual rejoinder, Abe at once shot back in the Kansai dialect common to them both: "Sore wa arahen"—"There's no such thing!"

Toyoshima-san returned to the meditation hall and from that point began thrusting himself beyond his limit in the manner that thereafter became characteristic. The effect was climactic. "In that *sesshin* I suddenly was extinguished, entering for the first time the domain where there is nothing whatsoever." He brought this experience to Abe. Abe rejected it. Within that repudiation of even "nothingness—*samadhi*"[27] there whirled and flashed the inescapable koan that at all eight points of the compass blocked the way to the Tree of Life: Shin'ichi Hisamatsu's: "Whatever you do will not do. What do you do?"

———————◆———————

This single phrase was the thick tentacle lashed around both our hearts, and it bound us together in friendship. Toyoshima-san would never have sought me out; he sought out no one. But that we viewed things at their root with the same eye he held in respect, and later affection, even though he was far more resolute in the face of what he saw. For me, his being as an unawakened man who staked everything on the prospect of a realization not guaranteed was as important a gift as the existences of the rare awakened persons I had met. They were living proof of the answer. He was testament of the life-or-death commitment requisite if the answer was ever to obtain. Moreover, he was within my reach. Hisamatsu, in a critical sense, was beyond it. I once asked Toyoshima-san his impression of our visit to Hisamatsu, whose works he had studied extensively and whose thought and existence formed the most critical lines in the cartography of his own quest. In imitation of those Japanese tour guides who keep their clientele in tow when visiting national treasures by means of a ubiquitous yellow pennant, he waved his closed hand back and forth and said: "Kanko mitai"—"Like going sightseeing."

I knew exactly what he meant. My meeting with Hisamatsu had driven me to tears. His personhood was exquisite, unforgettable—his giving easy but total. He cut open the chest and emblazoned it with jewels, which my heart proceeded to smolder. And though he entered my sinews with the glance of an eye, he was, from my side, the inapproachable other shore. Between us stretched an unending chasm, one that had to be bridged if life was to be lived yet that stood refractory to every attempt to traverse it, meditation included. Toyoshima-san crossed his legs and impaled his soul on the razor tip where the impossibility and necessity of awakening intersect, the very point that Zen promised—when the impalement was thoroughgoing and irreversible—would occasion the emergence of the illumined Self. On this infinitely small and vast point, he simultaneously exerted himself to the absolute limit and "gave up."

———◆———

In his silence, he gradually overhauled the nature of my own struggle. The decision to abandon the hard-won relative ease of the half lotus posture for the hell (in my case) of the full lotus tore me to pieces. I would weep on the garden veranda during walking meditation, trying to resolve whether to ease my burden by backing off the cliff's edge for the next thirty minutes with the less demanding position or be plunged anew with the full lotus into what Ta-hui called "the boiling cauldron." I have often heard meditation called the "dharma of tranquility," and ultimately this must be the case. But I could not dislodge myself from the admonition of Hakuin, whose *Orategama* in English translation was pocketed within my cushions:

> If you are not a hero who has truly seen into his own nature, don't think it is something that can be known so easily. If you wish accordance with the true, pure, non-ego, you must be prepared to let go your hold when hanging from a sheer precipice, to die and again return to life.

I went to Masao Abe at his home, sundered by the reality that *sesshin* had again become, and who knew how long would remain, a nightmare—perpetual torment if I retained my position at the edge; perpetual failure, I felt, were I to draw back. I brought up the case of Toyoshima-san and asked Abe if the pain was worth it. "Do you think," he replied calmly, "that Toyoshima-san has the luxury to even ask that question?" Before parting that evening, Abe added in supplement an indelible postscript: "Very few people in this world have the spiritual courage of Toyoshima-san."

Part Two

Once, waiting for a light to turn, I told Professor Abe I felt I was being crushed by the Zen problem. "*If* that is so"—and I know now how right he was to emphasize that *if*—"you must do everything possible to corner yourself." Unleashed within that utterance was the central requisite dynamic of the Rinzai Zen tradition: "Cornered, one passes through." But because for me the incapacity to meet Abe's demand was in great part predicated on an ambivalence of will, I did not apprehend the equal measure in which this inability was predicated on the futility of will. Forced out of a *sesshin,* ill and exhausted on a friend's floor, I opened my eyes to find Toyoshima-san crouched next to me, his day's labor of meditation completed. "To want to do *sesshin* and to be unable—that's *sesshin,*" he said. With my sickness making it difficult for me to focus in Japanese, he repeated the sentence three times until I was able to make the words congeal. Even so, his intent eluded me. I could not then grasp that the distinction between *sesshin* and daily existence had for him largely disappeared. Meditation and *sesshin* had ceased to be a practice. To be stripped of all practice, of all method, was his meditation, his *sesshin.* He saw my despondency at having effort thwarted by infirmity with eyes already inured to the disclosure that he was barred from the final cornering even by maximum effort. "Tell me what he's leaving undone," DeMartino asked in regard to him years afterward. "It's just that [despite himself] he keeps slipping out." Endlessly assaulting the door to no house, he was at the moment of penetration already always on the outside.

You cannot nail yourself into the coffin when the last nail must of necessity be hammered from its exterior. Nonetheless, he had no recourse but to seek to overturn Lin-chi and "drive a stake into an empty sky." Sisyphus without a rock, bowlegged in training pants, towel obtruding from back pocket, increasingly disheveled in conse-quence of more ultimate preoccupations, he'd sit out of view into the night, then sleep in his clothes. Having remained unmoving through the afternoon lecture—often a verbose two hours or more—he'd storm around the veranda to ease his legs, hands folded to chest, in prepa-ration for one last solitary push in the deserted meditation hall before the evening sittings began. But I spotted him one late afternoon on that same veranda, back propped against the paper-paneled sliding door. Surging past fingers instinctively but uselessly pressed to dam it, anguish broke from his face and forehead, which from my angle of vision seemed to ask: How many years of this have yet to be endured before release comes? And is it possible, despite the Zen promise that "beneath the great doubt lies the Great Awakening," despite the innumerable anecdotes of enlightenment pervading Zen literature and the sporadic but unforgettable encounters with those who appeared to be its living confirmation, that there is no satori, only an impenetrable wall?

When a couple of nights later I asked how he was faring, he drew an oversize X in the air, smiled slightly, and walked away. Another evening, the last before the retreat ended, I found him in the inner corridor between the meditation and dining areas. "My meditation is garbage can meditation," he said. "But when I look around at the others, I see the faces of bodhisattvas."

He must have longed for respite, but he would barely permit himself anything short of the sole true respite of awakened peace. I remember him lying atop his bedding, fully clothed as always, as I prepared mine. "Hakuin had a breakthrough in a dream," he said, then he shut his eyes. This was uncharacteristic. He never forwent long bouts of *yaza*, the optional night sitting whose price was sleepless hours. I took my cushions out to the veranda in an effort to push on. It brought nothing, and I soon relinquished. Treading past the sleeping forms, I sought my futon in the now darkened room. His, I noticed, had been abandoned.

He held firm in his isolation, I suppose, because he was convinced that nothing short of illumination could really alter it. Three times a *sesshin*, during the afternoon sittings, it was permitted to leave one's cushions, bow before any of the seated practitioners whom one desired to question or challenge, then go off to a room designated for such encounters. Invariably, the younger participants approached their more experienced seniors. On none of these occasions had I ever seen Toyoshima-san budge.

One afternoon, from a corner of the meditation hall there entered into my field of vision, limited to the tatami by eyes half-closed and cast downward, the silent gliding of a *hakama* skirt. In sudden understanding, I could not resist lifting my head loose from concentration and up past the *hakama* and kimono to confirm the identity of the face. The dry, austere, elegant dignity that had thrust my life so totally in love with Zen now tinctured the form of Masao Abe, then sixty-two, as he approached and then bowed before the motionless frame of Toyoshima-san. He knew too well that it was he who would have to initiate the interview, and his respect impelled him out from an avalanche of pressing affairs and obligations to convey that though submerged in a black abyss, Toyoshima-san was not alone. Later, during Abe's two-year stint at Princeton, I urged Toyoshima to stay in touch with him, for I knew Abe was one of the two or three people he felt could bring insight to his ultimate concern. I asked him if he had written. He replied that he had not. "Why don't you write him?" I prodded. He answered: "I haven't anything to say."

———◆———

The day that Masao Abe had taken us to meet Shin'ichi Hisamatsu, he had introduced Toyoshima-san to his revered Zen teacher in terms a man like Abe would never have uttered lightly: "He has arrived at an extremely critical point." These words were the first I'd heard used to describe him. On the train home, Abe promised a second, private meeting if Toyoshima-san considered it necessary. Difficult as it was to meet the aged and often infirm Hisamatsu even once, Abe's offer was obvious evidence that he held Toyoshima-san in unique regard. When he subsequently sensed my own esteem and affection, and above all the significance of Toyoshima-san's existence in my life, he confided: "Toyoshima-san was already beset by a tremendous religious problem ten years ago. Even then he'd already fallen into a dark hole."

The two had negligible contact, however, once Abe began his long sojourn in America, moving every two years, sometimes more frequently, from one university to the next as a kind of academic itinerant. He generally returned to Japan for part of the summer, and when on one such occasion he solicited my help with the preparation of some work in English, I mentioned that I'd recently been in touch with Toyoshima-san, who—wanting to put a rare week off to use—had expressed interest in doing a *sesshin* at one of the Kyoto monasteries. Abe tried to get him admitted to the temple at which he himself had trained in earlier years and where I currently was practicing. I knew well that the *jikijitsu,* the monk in charge of the meditation hall and the latest in a list of disappointing replacements since the fabulous Thief[28] had vacated the post a few years earlier, had little enthusiasm for the Zen quest; as with so many of his fellow monks, he was there primarily to gain the qualifications necessary to take over a temple. Unlike most of his colleagues, however, he was not of a clerical family and had no temple to go to. Eventually he was to marry into one, a package deal, but by the time this was accomplished he'd achieved sufficient seniority to float to the top of the monastic command. He was subordinate only to the *fūsu*—the monk who essentially ran the monastery—a man whose ambitions to be a monastery master committed him to completion of his koan training but whose resourcefulness in worming his way out of his six-month rotation in charge of the meditation hall made obvious his dislike of meditation. It is said that Zen rests on the exercise of compassion, but in monasteries the exercise of authority for authority's sake often holds sway. Toyoshima-san's petition to participate in the *sesshin* was rejected. The *fūsu* later did gain sanction as a "Zen master." The head of the meditation hall, by his early forties, was dead of cancer of the throat.

Toyoshima's desire to place himself in a traditional monastic setting bespoke a sense of urgency. Though he did subsequently mention that at first he thought the guidance of a traditionally trained Zen master indispensable, he seemed to want little truck with Zen monasteries. He balked at what he perceived as irrational elements in monastic discipline and considered it essential to speak out against them. He thought the violence associated with the Zen tradition was often misapplied. And he disliked the *keisaku*—or patrol stick—an antipathy that might have originated with his inadvertently cracking the rib of an Englishwoman, after which he categorically refused to take it in hand. When the injury was publicly announced by the man who had delegated him the patrol assignment against his will, no names were mentioned. But Toyoshima-san immediately pressed his palms together and bowed.

Beyond this, I had the clear impression that he believed that if Buddhism were justified in claiming itself capable of resolving the problem of the human person, then it had to be soluble by—and he wanted to solve it as—an ordinary man. He had heard the charge that Hisamatsu's group of lay practitioners had never produced a breakthrough except in instances where monastic training had also been concurrent. However, Hisamatsu, the group's now retired central figure, had insisted that the human predicament must have a method of resolution applicable and accessible to all persons in any situation. Whether Toyoshima-san felt so indebted to Hisamatsu as to try to achieve this, I do not know. But he was evidently determined to succeed or fail in settling the problem of being in this world by being in this world. His consequent rejection of the monk/lay distinction, which he considered illusory, was not from pride but from the depths of his own inner reality: "I'm not a layman," he said. "I'm not anything."

Abe persisted, and at length he got Toyoshima-san into the May *sesshin* at a monastery in western Kyoto. The next time I was at his home, I asked if there had been any word. Abe laughed warmly and said: "He says nothing happened." That August, Toyoshima-san said that he needed a vacation and expressed interest in an exceptional monastery in Yamanashi prefecture where no temple licenses were awarded; thus all who trained there, monk and layperson alike, were motivated by an existential concern. Still hobbled by a torn meniscus that had forced me out of the spring and summer *sesshin,* I decided nonetheless to take him. Unable to sit myself, I felt it an honor to help him in any way possible. When I informed Professor Abe that for a few days I would not be available to assist him and why, he affirmed my sentiment with a simple, silent nod.

We decided to hitchhike. Toyoshima-san, who though from Osaka always had an aura of being from the country, showed up in a large straw farmer's hat, flashing our "Bound for Tokyo" sign with such enthusiasm that I am certain it delayed our getting a ride by at least an hour. A truck driver, accompanied by his young son, finally took us on. The child drew out a side of Toyoshima I had not yet seen. They were soon friends, Toyoshima-san asking the boy if he could be of help with his homework.

Perhaps his new comrade was still on his mind that evening as we took the train from Tokyo Station toward Yamanashi. For the first time I learned of his life as a teacher, how he'd awaken every morning at 5:30 to work in solitude on a small patch of land he was cultivating with his students. I learned as well of his anxiety about how to adequately educate the innocent and his sorrow at seeing the hints of an inevitably full-blown *dukkha* in the easy emergence of their many childhood fears.

An hour out of Tokyo, a group of twenty or so women of college age boarded the train in hiking gear. I assumed, given the late hour, they were heading homeward, but Toyoshima-san, directing my gaze to the untainted whiteness of their walking shoes, suggested that they must be just starting out, probably for the night climb up Mount Fuji that would bring them to the summit for the sunrise. For a time he was silent. Then, jutting his chin their way, in an almost inaudible tone he confided: "Sometimes I think I'd like to go in that direction."

My heart ached. There came to mind the July *sesshin* of the previous year; Toyoshima, because of the heat, had dressed not in his usual training attire but in white cotton. His face, hardened in agony, seemed refractory to the possibility of approach. As always, he appeared physically powerful, devoid of the prospect of illness. And yet it looked as though he were dying. I left him to himself, drifting afar on ice long since dwindled to nothing, and set to work.

Four or five days into it, at twilight, I chanced to enter the doorway leading from the temple proper to the garden veranda at the same instant he was entering the doorway from the veranda side. Bringing his palms together, he bowed deeply in the formal Buddhist gesture of pardon. It was a bow, I am certain, tinged with *samadhi*. His frame seemed less substantial than the air. He straightened again, one countenance meeting another. The face before me, unresolved yet transfigured, was overrun with beauty.

Yet here on the train was a different, and indifferent, beauty. The women, oblivious of their own radiance, chattered and laughed in the stunning hopefulness of the young Japanese girl. It was one of several times I've reunderstood Bob Dylan's "I was hungry, and it was your world." In the great ascent of their lives, what use would they have for a man so utterly descendent? Still, despite his isolation and preoccupation, I was convinced that this gentle and modest man, who never allowed his pain to injure even a petal of the existence of others, would make a fine husband and father. But I could not deny that even if he were to adjust his course and "go in that direction," he would likely remain invisible to the women of this earth.

We arrived at the monastery after lights-out. The head monk, Bunko, an old friend, had waited up for us, and we were intercepted at the gate. My injured knee made me useless at a Zen temple and I soon returned to Kyoto. Later I heard from Urs App, who'd spent several days with Toyoshima-san in Yamanashi. After two weeks at the monastery, claiming he needed a vacation from his vacation, he'd gone off to attend a *sesshin* in Chiba, saying he'd be back.

We were together for one last week of hard meditation before my departure for America. Toyoshima-san said that his back was bothering him. The pain must have been considerable, for when the bell rang, for the first time in the years I'd known him, he broke from his regimen of sitting successive periods without interruption. Stiffly, he readjusted his pillows. When I caught his gaze, he made a quick gesture of throwing up his hands. The first six days we spoke only once, and even then he offered but a single sentence. "Fuan no katamari," he told me—"I'm a block of anxiety."

The final morning, as we cleaned the meditation hall, he came over, damp rag in hand, to where I was sweeping the tatami. This was unexpected; he invariably worked in seriousness, methodically, and alone. That he came not to work but to talk and the substance of that talk were even more unanticipated.

"Because of the way I am driven to sit," he said, "in one sense there is no one to push me. That you, a Westerner, sit as hard as you do, this is a great encouragement." He nodded to a calligraphy of the Chinese character for silence fixed by the entrance of the meditation hall, then added: "Silence is extremely critical. You, on the other hand, are a chatterbox."

As ever, he spoke gently, and I was in no doubt as to the intent of his rebuke. This was a man who imposed his view on no one. We had struggled knee to knee for three years, and now was the hour to warn that my efforts, which even I had to recognize as no longer insubstantial, were being undermined by my gregariousness, that I was in the grip of a diversion that if left unchecked would prove lethal.

"When you sit across from someone whose movement disturbs you," he continued, "I notice you shift your spot. Someone else is disruptive and you move again. Choose one place to sit and die into it, regardless of external circumstances.

"Sit *yaza* alone. The sitters inspire one another morning till evening.

In the late night hours confront yourself by yourself, no matter how many times you quit and start."

"You used to be the last to sleep," I interrupted. "Now you're the first."

"I used to sit a couple of hours and go to bed self-satisfied that I'd exerted myself. Now I sleep straightaway. Two hours later the anxiety attacks for not making sufficient effort and I'm up. I sit through the night, and an hour before wake-up try to grab some sleep."

That seemed to end the conversation, as he began wiping down the sitting platforms. Then he walked back to where I was sweeping and said: "Those tea ceremonies [after the meals and lectures] are nothing but tea parties. Keep away from them." With that he walked off a few paces and resumed his cleaning.

The *sesshin* ended and the several participants proceeded to Reiun-in Temple for the customary service at the grave site of Japan's most revered philosopher, Kitarō Nishida. When the inevitable group photo was taken, Toyoshima-san, in accord with his custom, was not to be found. I have in my possession only one picture in which he is present; he's crouched, face ducking the camera.

But heading home from the temple compound, I noticed him ahead of me as I started toward the Myōshinji gate. Quiet as I knew him to be, he must have been intent on hammering the point of the morning's conversation until it fragmented my veins. For he reversed direction, walked up to me, and said: "Hsueh-yen mentions that for three years he looked one meter in front of him when sitting, two meters ahead when standing. I understand the first phrase to mean, 'Don't see others.' The second I take to mean, 'Don't seek others out.'" Then, perhaps concerned I may not have understood, he said—in English: "Don't see other people!" It was evident that he was trying with the full force of his sincerity to persuade me that if I would follow this advice, I would see the result, whereas if I persisted in subverting an effort he obviously respected, decades of driving myself would probably prove futile. "Just for one year," he concluded. "For one year."

I watched as he ambled off in silence toward the gate. I was moved. I was honored. I was afraid. I knew I would not do as he said.

———◆———

The Saturday before my slated return to the United States, an informal farewell was held at the Reiun-in. I was not sure whether Toyoshima-san knew I was leaving. I telephoned, asking him to come to Kyoto, not so much for the gathering, which I'd have done without, but because a Japanese translation of the biography of the great Tibetan ascetic Milarepa had just been published and I wished to make a gift of this as a goodbye. When the get-together had ended and the weekly Saturday evening meditation was about to commence, I pulled him out of the meditation hall and he, Urs App, and I absconded, making our way downtown. Thus far I had seen the book in only one shop. We arrived there and ran into a sizable picket line. When I expressed my disappointment aloud, one of the strikers cheerily bade me not to worry; the strike would be concluded at seven o'clock. Such are the joys of being a foreigner in Japan. We killed two hours, came back in time for the punctual disappearance of labor, and made our purchase. Urs and I both added inscriptions on the inside cover.

Urs was likewise beginning a slow preparation to return to Switzerland, from where he was to catch up with me in the States. When the time came for Toyoshima-san to take the train back to Osaka, this man, whom an astonished witness of his *sesshin* effort had called "one of the toughest human beings on the planet," partly asked, partly told Urs in a voice traced with a whisper of plaintive hope: "You'll come back to Japan"; he repeated to me in identical tone: "You'll come back to Japan."

He started to bow, but I extended my hand; in his firm grip I felt him already recede into his loneliness. Our hands parted. He bowed and turned to go. Smiling and waving repeatedly, he descended the stairs, stepping past the reach of my vision to where he would pay his fare and pass through the turnstile to the abyss.

———————◆———————

It took more than seven years to fulfill my promise and make my way back to Kyoto. The FAS Society,[29] the lay Zen group that had centered around the great Zen master Shin'ichi Hisamatsu before his retirement, to which I owed so much, had weakened tremendously. Only in *sesshin* did it occasionally flare into life. Even those could appear moribund, a fate reflected in the unwelcome turn that at the first *sesshin* after my arrival, it somehow became my task to give a series of lectures. I spoke to the only thing I could: the way humans are blocked on the Zen quest—blocked by the way we evade it with an ambivalent will, blocked by the way it evades us even where the will is unsplintered.

Toyoshima-san, I was informed, had been transferred from primary to middle school, and the resultant increment in responsibilities had made his participation in *sesshin* sporadic. It was not unexpected, therefore, that he did not appear. Mid-morning of the second day, however, sitting with my back to the entrance of the meditation hall, I heard to my left someone enter and bow, and a few paces later caught sight of the bowlegged gait, towel hanging from the back pocket.

Toyoshima-san was extremely well versed in Zen literature, but he was of a decidedly anti-academic bent. He read from existential, never mere intellectual, motivation. The *sesshin* talks seemed to hold little interest for him, and though he never divulged himself where someone would be hurt, I suspect that he saw them largely as an intrusion into a task far more fundamental. I do know that he located in these talks one advantage—the speakers were generally long-winded, and he used this as an impetus to sit without respite through the long afternoon.

In the aftermath of these lectures, I invariably asked his opinion. He responded on every occasion in one Japanese word: "Wakaranai"—"I don't understand." So I was surprised and not unpleased when the day following the first of my attempts, which I knew as well as he had no bearing on anything, I found him stretched on a blanket propped on an arm, sunning himself on the veranda, offering as his first words to me in seven years: "I understood yesterday's talk." That was our conversation. Four days later, as the *sesshin* was moving to its close, he told me: "I really understood your talk."

"How's your meditation?" I asked.

"I still haven't resolved the problem. I've just given up. From enduring, I've moved to just giving up."

A shudder should have come over me then, but I simply nodded. My boyishness seemed for an instant to consume itself. A decade had vanished since I'd first beheld him dangling from the cliff's edge. I had come back to find him, impossibly, still at the brink, and I now knew, and knew that he had always known, that it was possible to be trapped there for a lifetime.

———————◆———————

I was in Osaka for the New Year. On the thirty-first I thought I'd give Toyoshima-san a call. We agreed to meet later that afternoon at Umeda Station.

The coffee shops were mobbed, the last explosion before the virtual shutting down of the city for much of the weeklong holiday. We found a table in one of the underground establishments that populate the major intersections of the subway arteries.

The December *sesshin* was only nine days past. I had noticed that Toyoshima-san no longer experienced any of the convulsive spasms that had marked his meditation in previous years.

"Are you still in pain when you sit?" I asked.

"As long as I live."

"At what point does the pain set in?"

He laughed. "From the beginning!"

"I myself am plagued by a weak ankle. Too much pressure from the full lotus. Do you think it could be strengthened through exercise?"

"Probably. But whether there's pain or not is irrelevant."

I inquired if he sat at home. "A little," he said. I had to smile at what he must have meant by "a little." He still arrived at school early each morning for upkeep on a small patch of land that he'd farm later in the day with his students. Class and clubs went until five o'clock, paperwork until seven. I come home, eat, meditate, and go to sleep. Meditation's good for the health—except during *sesshin*. It helps me fall asleep. Meditation," he said in a voice filled with self-critical irony, "is my hobby."

"Everything I do is a waste," he continued. "But there are two kinds of waste: waste for the sake of waste; and waste for the sake of oneself, of seeking for oneself. For me, this last means meditation."

He sketched out a diagram on a sheet of paper. "You can think of meditation in terms of better and best," he said, writing both words in the English he could barely speak. "By *best* I mean the realization in meditation that there is nothing whatsoever. But this state of nothingness in which the 'I' is extinguished does not resolve the problem. In my view, it is preferable not to enter this state. *Better* is better.

"With me, in a weeklong *sesshin*, this realization of there being nothing whatsoever happens two or three times. But, as I said, it resolves nothing. Nor is it a matter of extending this state. It's not a matter of extension. Even if you can preserve it while standing, it's not awakening.

"The best meditation is what Zen means by *mokushō*—'silent illumination.' Mistaking this for enlightenment, monks would sit around like corpses, as Hakuin and others have criticized, or try to maintain it while walking. Beyond this best is awakening. But you don't reach this by going beyond best. Rather, the whole matrix of the meditating 'I,' with its distinctions of better meditation and best meditation, must be broken through. It's my understanding that Hisamatsu broke through this matrix first. He awakened first. Only later did he master the technique to achieve what he calls 'particular *samadhi*' or 'nothingness *samadhi*.'"

I glanced at the diagram crowded by now with the Chinese characters that Toyoshima-san had scrawled in the appropriate places as he talked.

"Meditation will not resolve the problem," he continued. "Yet I must sit. Which is different from sitting for the purpose of bringing about a resolution. I've completely given up. Everything other than meditation is a waste, a diversion. But meditation, the waste for the sake of myself, is also a waste."

"Then why bother to sit?"

"Meditation was the one way out. But it too is a waste. And yet I can't stop sitting. This is not yet *giza*, a sitting that congeals the great doubt block just prior to awakening, but it moves in that direction. In the failure of meditation—the best meditation—the paths of escape, the chinks, disappear. Meditation at its best fails, and this brings into greater clarity that there's no way out. Meditation should be the one means of escape, and when you can take it no further and it still leaves the problem unsolved, you are thrown back into daily life with the problem pressing in ever more intensively."

"Then you're saying that you sit so that the futility of meditation drives you back into the problem of everyday existence all the more?"

"I sit because I have to sit. My sitting is passive, a giving up. Sitting is meaningless. Still, I must do *sesshin*. But I can't break through. So I am thrust back into an increasingly unendurable daily existence that in turn drives me into another *sesshin*."

We were asked to pay up, as the staff was preparing to close early for the holiday. The iron grate had been pulled down in front of most of the shop windows, and there was difficulty finding another venue. We stayed underground, at length locating a place of similar stripe to what we had just vacated, and ordered some tea.

"How long did it take you to conclude that the realization of 'nothingness *samadhi*' is not awakening?"

"Not long. It doesn't continue. It is something that occurs in time. Awakening breaks through time. If you talk of it in terms of a kind of technique, when you reach the limit of pain, you can no longer move, can no longer escape, and the 'I' is extinguished. But all states of meditation are irrelevant to awakening. The same holds true for breathing techniques. They're irrelevant. I no longer search for states in my meditation. For me, the method of meditation is nothing conscious or intentional. The problem just presents itself and you can't get away from it."

"So there's nothing to do then but to give up?"

"Yes. But you can't really give up either. When giving up also will not do, what do you do?"

Most of the discussion after that I do not recall. At some point I noticed that we were all that remained of the clientele and that this shop, too, would soon be shutting down. The days of celebration of the New Year in Japan have always left me with a touch of desolation. I thought of my mother and my father, not knowing I was never to see him again. I asked Toyoshima-san if his parents knew of the suffering he'd borne for so many years. They knew nothing, though they lived under the same roof. "I'm exhausted," he said. "Especially from the job. It's an agony for me that the beautiful children I used to teach grow into the middle school students I now try to contend with. *Sesshin*'s a vacation. Day-to-day existence is a lot harder than *sesshin*.

"My breathing is strained. I'm a block of anxiety. You try to divert yourself, but precisely in the recognition of the meaninglessness of diversion, the meaninglessness of my life becomes incontrovertibly clear. Still I press on, following my interpretation of Hsueh-yen. I don't see others. Or rather, without seeing others I see them. And I don't seek others out."

He raised his hand just below his chin in the familiar gesture indicating that he was drowning in the bottomless pit that had encompassed him without respite for twenty years. Then, as if the hand were overcoming a potent resisting force, it suddenly tugged upward, stopping just above the eyes. "Compared to what I was going through before, things now are a lot rougher."

It was New Year's Eve with all its implications. I watched, as we walked, the current of the world. Somewhere in the roar of moving trains, we shook hands and parted—I to a woman who was waiting, he to where one returns when there is nowhere to go.

From this noble being, still battling for himself as if he were fighting in the jungles of Vietnam, I have learned that a man can inspire the whole world and still be worthless to himself. With whatever truth that is in me, I hope that he makes it. And that this essay has not failed him if he does not.

The Divine Comedy of a Tragic Buddha

PART ONE: WAR AND PEACE

KITAHARA—in Bermuda shorts with socks that reached his knees and sunglasses reminiscent of pilot's goggles vintage World War I —pedaled an undersized bicycle erratically toward the Kamakura Station entrance where Urs App and I were waiting. He was fifty-six, a Zen practitioner of more than thirty years and sanctioned as a Zen master. He had no disciples.

Kickstand booted into place, Urs bowed, Kitahara bowed. I shook his hand, a gesture he accepted as if it were from outer space. Then, feet spread apart, arms dangling at his sides like a wrestler who has just thrown his opponent to the mat, he jumped a few inches off the ground three times in quick succession, each jump turning his body forty-five degrees, his head darting in staccato movements as he surveyed the storefronts that crammed the perimeter of the station. He ran toward the shops to the right of the ticket machines, hurried back to Urs and myself, and executed a second round of quarter turns punctuated by birdlike pokes of the head. Unable to find what he wanted, he ran once again toward the shops, turned to us without gesture or word, about-faced, and then seemed to fall through an automatic door. We trailed him into a combination coffee shop/ice cream parlor of the sort to be found everywhere in Japan, selling iridescent green soft drinks no Westerner has ever dared swallow.

Urs App, at twenty-eight, was already—of those known to me personally—what I regard him as still: the sole Westerner among my generation marked by greatness. In those days he and I edited a no-budget rag sent out, whether or not they understood English, to members of the FAS Society. We had finally persuaded Kitahara to consent to an interview. This he apparently had forgotten, planning instead a hiking expedition through the Kamakura hills. To this end he produced a map of the terrain from a black shoulder bag and began studying it in silence. The ice cream sodas he ordered for the three of us arrived. He took several mouthfuls, his eyes never leaving the map. Spoon by spoon, vanilla ice cream dripped on it; Kitahara saw only hills and wooded paths. Urs and I exchanged glances. Fifteen wordless minutes passed when Kitahara, bug-eyed, blurted out an astonished, "Haauugghh!" We and his half-filled glass of ice cream were in that instant obliterated, as for another fifteen minutes his moistened forefinger moved from tongue to map, which he returned, inch by inch, to pristine, if soggy, condition. When the last stain was removed, he resumed studying the map in the same rapt silence until, content that he had grasped the contours of the day's undertaking, he looked up, called for the bill, and stormed out of the shop and into the hills for a several-hours journey.

At one *sesshin*, Professor Tokiwa told this story: Rushing to the koan interview with his master, a monk ripped off a large hunk of toe on a nail protruding from a floorboard. The meditation hall chief—the last of the monks to depart the sitting hall and bringing up the rear—barked to the monk, who was halted in shock: "Present your answer to the koan to the master first! Then come back for your toe!"

These meditation hall bosses were, as a rule, tough disciplinarians. Not just the Thief, chief of the meditation hall at the monastery where I trained, who, elusive and flowing as the cloud water whose ideo-

hs form in Japanese the compound for *monk,* would distill himself of these elements into thunder. When he'd relinquished this post, his successors—lacking his elegant power, his insight into the root that made him in every way tremendous—were drill sergeants, seduced by the hierarchical authoritarianism they latched onto in the absence of anything real of Zen to draw upon.

So in July 1977, when in addition to the monastery *sesshin* I began to attend the weeklong intensive sittings of Hisamatsu's group and had to contend with an unknown meditation hall boss, I was apprehensive. This one—a burly middle-aged bear with a resemblance to the actor Robert Mitchum—maintained a rigid meditation through the morning. By the fifth sitting period, my eyes closed from pain, I finally heard the rustling of kimono sleeves from the vicinity of the chief's cushions, a sure indication that the bell would be struck to mark hell's end. My heart started to pound in anticipation. Custom had it that no one would break from his sitting posture until the chief had risen, overlapping palms pressed to his chest as he crossed the hall and vanished through the exit. I slit open my eyes, mentally willing him to hurry. To my joy, he rang the chime and hit the wood blocks to end the sitting. His hands slipped beneath his *hakama* skirt and released his crossed legs. He stood, bowed formally with palms pressed together, and disappeared through the wrong door.

No one moved. Perhaps I merely imagined the silent, collective groan from the other sitters in the room. Wild thoughts of relief from the pain in my shoulders, back, ankles, and knees died on the vine. I frantically tried to endure. A few minutes passed. Suddenly, muttering apologies, the chief came racing back into the meditation hall, retraced his steps, crashed his rear onto his cushions, refolded himself into the full lotus, immediately unfolded himself out of the full lotus, rose, performed once more the requisite bow before leaving his cushions, and exited through the proper door.

This was my introduction to Ryūtarō Kitahara, enlightened blunderer. The following morning we awoke at five for the predawn sittings

on the veranda overlooking the garden. At seven we moved our cushions into the meditation hall for the worst chanting in the history of
religion, tone-deafness an apparent prerequisite for group member-
ship. This concluded, Kitahara prostrated his upper torso to the floor,
straightened once more until seated on his shins in the *seiza* position,
and sang out: "Ohayoo gozaimasu. Good morning. Buenos días.
Guten Morgen. Bonjour. Zao an. Buongiorno. Dobroe utro. Born dia"
and a mispronounced cascade of morning greetings in several other
languages. Then he added, in an attempt at English: "And we salute
. . . Dr. Daisetz Suzuki . . . Dr. Sunshin Kitarō Nishida . . . Dr. Hōseki
Shin'ichi Hisamatsu . . . and all the Buddhas . . . and bodhisattvas . . .
throughout the . . . WHOLE . . . UNIVERSE!!!" This he punctuated
with a countenance something along the lines of a cartoon character
who has been conked on the head by a falling boulder.

I wrote of him, under the name Nishihara, in my novel *The Atheists
Monastery*: "The general impression was of a man who at some point
in his life had stumbled upon a moment of supreme silliness, but whose
inner apprehension of this silliness, even after the moment had passed,
remained forever after stuck in the groove." Only on the last day of
the *sesshin* did I learn that during World War II—in an act the heart
inherited from his famous poet father made *impossible* for the younger
Kitahara to forgive—he had, together with the rest of his unit, carried
out orders to thrust bayonets into a group of helpless Chinese captives.

———————————◆———————————

Everyone called him "Kitahara-sensei." But he was not a sensei—a
teacher—at all. As far as anyone knew he had never held a job of any
kind, though he always claimed to be busy, in part due to endlessly
editing his father's collected works for publication. DeMartino, when
I once broached Kitahara's busyness while back in the States, laughed:
"*One* day we'll find out what it is he does."[30]

ɔt in dispute was that in his Kita-Kamakura home, Kitahara

spent—or had spent—much of his time in meditation. He suffered from insomnia, the consequence of a constant and ferocious ringing in the ears—the right ear being especially damaged—resulting from auditory nerve injury caused by punishing blows from his superior officers while he was a new recruit on the Chinese front. He had once told Hisamatsu that by concentrating on the noise in his ears, he could more readily go into *samadhi*. Hisamatsu said: "Stop it. You'll go mad!"

There was talk of a rock in a garden where he sat his nights, a kimono sash tied about his legs so that he wouldn't break position. There was talk that he kept a transistor radio plugged in his ear to suppress the awareness of the shrill ringing in his ears. But that only explains the radio, not the foreign language programs that were his preferred listening. These, I discovered later, were a response to some deep promise made to the Chinese war corpses that he would reject nationality and identify with all humankind. Judging from the English lessons I heard on the radio, the programs never went very far before restarting from the beginning for new listeners. The result, ecstatically proclaimed in English one *sesshin* as Kitahara leapt up from his meditation cushion: "I . . . study . . . seven languages and . . . I cannot . . . speak . . . ANY OF THEM!" He dreamily attempted Esperanto as an eighth.

Toyoshima-san, the meditation Prometheus, said of him: "He is without corners." When I told DeMartino that Kitahara gave me hope that someone as clumsy as I am could awaken, he answered: "He's not clumsy. He's absorbed." Is it Gary Snyder who writes that animals and insects spend most of their time in *samadhi*? In repose, Kitahara was a praying mantis on a leaf. Cigarette burning in the bizarre cigarette holder held in his half-raised hand as he relaxed after meals during each *sesshin,* his eyes peered into the back of his head. During the daily chanting of the Heart Sutra, he would take a wrong turn and lead the group into a repetitive verbal maze, unable to bring the sutra to an end. Lost in meditation, he would forget to ring the bell, driving the stiff-legged Westerners to despair. We loved him for it. Left hand unaware of what his right hand doeth, he bungled his way through the Kingdom. This was his authority, in lieu of the monastic beatings and shouts he associated with the militarism he despised. Once, having lost count of the meditation periods, he left the hall and went to the toilet, an indication that there was still, after nearly two hours of sitting, to be no walking meditation, only a momentary break. A British woman chased after, pleading as he emerged: "Sensei, you've *got* to let us walk!" "Hauugghhh!" he shouted, stymied at his obliviousness. Then, with his teddy bear look that nullified any possibility of reproach, he confessed: "I too am on the cross."

———————◆———————

Kitahara barreled through the Kamakura hills in silence, covered in mud. It seemed impossible; the day was cloudless, and while the trails were still damp from a previous rain, only the bottoms of my shoes were encrusted. The same held for Urs; his clothes were spotless apart from his shoes, but Kitahara's kneesocks, shorts and shirt were filthy. Mess and mistakes seemed magnetized to him, but the magnet was joy. This, to me, was his great secret—life's great secret: to screw up ecstatically.

For two hours we'd seen no one. When we finally did—approaching from the opposite direction—it was, surprisingly, a Westerner, a young woman: Swiss, like Urs. After a brief chat, Kitahara, in German, asked her to join us. She said she had a train to catch late that afternoon. Kitahara promised he'd get her to the station in time, and the four of us hiked on. Another hour in, we rested on a flat part of the trail. I asked Kitahara—as the son of the most revered Japanese poet of his generation yet as someone who had published little of his own—if he thought it was better to focus exclusively on the struggle for enlightenment and to forgo making art until one awakened. "Hmmm," he said.

Around 3 p.m. we began to descend into a residential area. This was Kita-Kamakura, where Kitahara lived. He stopped before one of the houses, nodded his head toward the gate, and proclaimed in English: "My *enemy!*" This was the home of Daisaku Ikeda, head of the Buddhist and politically conservative Soka Gakkai, whose unsuspecting hippie American members in late-1960s Philadelphia had combed the downtown streets for recruits to their gatherings, during which congregants chanted for the fulfillment of desires. The word *enemy* was uttered so preposterously that Kitahara hardly seemed serious. Yet I recalled pieces of a story I'd heard, which my friend Mrs. Maeda later confirmed: A musical production staged by a troupe affiliated with Ikeda's organization had scandalized Kitahara's father and his works. Suits and countersuits were threatened—and later dropped.

———————◆———————

Seated on the floor next to me—at the low table where Mrs. Kitahara was serving the inevitable cakes and tea—was a sculpted bust of Kitahara's dead father. One of his eyes, at the exact level of my own, stared into mine. Mrs. Kitahara was beautiful at thirty-four. They had married when Kitahara was almost fifty. She took her place at the table and joined the conversation. It didn't get very far. Within minutes Kitahara bolted to his feet and sped from the room, trailing mud along the immaculate carpet. He returned in short order with one of his father's notebooks. No sooner had he begun to share its contents than a line of poetry he was reading triggered a further connection and he again darted out to the library. (When we'd entered the house, we'd sped past the vastest personal collection of books I've ever seen, rack upon rack of tall shelves along the entire length of an endless room.) Kitahara reappeared with a slim copybook in hand. It was one of hundreds of notebooks he'd filled over a forty-year period; almost all of them contained some reference to Hisamatsu. Barely had he shown us a page of this when he jumped up and ran off once more, back five minutes later with his father's translations of *Mother Goose*. He had guided us through this with impassioned explanation for a minute or two when he realized the time. He flew to his feet—our Swiss companion had to catch her train. We hurried out. I glanced over my shoulder at the chaos of mud and books. Mrs. Kitahara had a job on her hands.

———————•———————

Forty minutes later Urs and I were drinking chilled tea in the Kitaharas' kitchen. Their little daughter Rumi dashed in. Kitahara swooped her into his arms and set her on her back along the kitchen table: "When whatever you do will not do, what do you do?" he challenged her with his master Hisamatsu's fundamental koan, tickling her all the while.

"Eat ice cream!" she blurted through her laughter.

"When eating ice cream will not do, what do you do?"

"Drink soda!"

"When drinking soda won't do, what do you do?"

"Lots and lots of chocolate!"[31]

No sign we were overstaying our welcome. Less sign there would be an interview, though it was getting dark. Urs finally reminded Kitahara why we had come. "You must be hungry," was the reply. Up he stood. We made our final goodbyes to Mrs. Kitahara and off we went.

The restaurant specialized in eel. While we waited for the meal, the waiter brought beer. I've never been a drinker, but Urs was trying out abstinence, and for courtesy I let Kitahara fill my glass. He knocked off a couple of glasses and put a cigarette between his lips. Rummaging his shoulder bag for a lighter, he extracted one unwanted item after another, but since he dropped each rejected object back into the bag, he pulled out the same things repeatedly and the hunt went on and on. Around the five-minute mark—face full of suspense—he unclenched his fist and broke into a grin; the lighter was in his hand. He lit the cigarette and, as he exhaled, dropped the lighter back into the bag. Two drags later he snuffed the cigarette in the ashtray. When he finished his next beer, he wanted another smoke. He ransacked the bag as before; several minutes later it was in his palm. Kitahara lit the cigarette and, absorbed in the inhalation, dropped the lighter into the bag. He tried to pour beer in our glasses, but mine was still full and Urs again declined. Kitahara shrugged. Emptying the bottle into his glass, he said: "I studied aesthetics at Tokyo University. But with the outbreak of the war, I knew that I could die at any time and that if I didn't achieve some kind of realization, my being born in this world would have been completely in vain. To have a chance to be born only to die so soon!"

"So your interest in religion stemmed from that time?" Urs inquired, having started the tape recorder he had waiting by his knee.

"Yes. My father died. My father was a poet. But with his death, I felt that art did not penetrate the ultimate dimension. Watching my father die, I suffered terribly. He was a very great man. His death disintegrated completely my interest in aesthetics, and my preoccupation with religion took hold. It was at that time that I experienced a Christian conversion, in which I was saved from the depth of my despair by Jesus Christ. This occurred when I was about twenty years old. And then I became interested in theology and philosophy, because I wanted to get to the ground of that experience. This brought me to the study of Kitarō Nishida's philosophy at Kyoto University.[32] It was not Buddhism or Christianity that I wanted to study; rather I wanted to investigate the source that is common to both. I don't understand Nishida's philosophy well, but its difficulty charmed me. It's very difficult, and these difficult and at the same time charming points are connected to Zen."

"Was it from that time that you became interested in Zen?" Urs asked.

"Well, when I went to China to serve in the military, I carried a Bible because my interest was in Christianity. But I also brought with me a book by Nishida."

"How did your going to China relate with the Christian ideal of loving one's neighbor?"

"Really, I hated the idea of going to war. But I felt that I had to enter the very troops I detested as an apostle of Jesus Christ. God's light is shining everywhere, so it's just to that kind of place that one must go. It was with that feeling that I entered the army. I promised myself that even if I went to war, I would never kill a man. It didn't work out that way. I did not realize that's what it would come to. It was precisely in the army that I wanted to live the way of the cross. I wasn't baptized and am neither Catholic nor Protestant."

"Was there any change in your faith at a certain point?"

"You know, war is a truly miserable thing. We were ordered to violently bayonet a group of Chinese captives—I was thus forced to confront this kind of situation in which my faith was severely tried. As a Christian, in such a situation one should have been willing to be crucified rather than harm another man. But it was a real *Grenzsituation* [limit situation]. I wasn't able to tell them to stop that cruel deed. In a circumstance where one is in jeopardy of losing one's own life, one betrays one's faith. Peter betrayed Jesus three times before the cock crowed—that's how I felt.

"I was persecuted by an officer who found me with a Bible. He said to me: 'You believe in the God of America and England! You don't believe in the Japanese gods!' I said: 'God doesn't belong to any country on this earth. The love of God pervades the whole universe.' The officer got terribly angry, tore the Bible from me, and stomped on it vehemently. A sergeant later came up to me saying: 'Belief is free,' and he returned the Bible to me. I had a small English Bible that I read on the toilet. And sometimes when we had a break, everyone would be resting with their heads propped against their rucksacks and I'd look up into the star-covered universe and wonder what, after all, human history is. Even China with its long history of over three thousand years was full of wars and all kinds of events, and standing in the midst of this history I asked myself: What is the universe as a whole, which is transcendent to history? Once, when we passed a church that had been destroyed in an attack and I saw the words 'God is love and sacrificed His own son' painted on the ruins in Chinese characters, I fell into deep thought. There were German Catholic missionaries in some regions of China who refused to flee in spite of the war, and they may have been persecuted and later killed in communist China. People such as these are truly great. Christians have this missionary spirit wherever they go. That's something that one rarely finds in Buddhism, at least up to now.

"In Chinese towns, the Chinese intelligentsia regarded us with icy contempt, with hatred. I could understand how they felt. On one occasion there was scrawled across a fortress wall in large characters: 'Resist Japan and save our country.' I could really understand that the people on the other side felt this way.

"Thirty years later, a Chinese, Dr. Chang [Chung-Yuan], who is the English translator of *The Transmission of the Lamp,* sat next to me during a *sesshin.* Tears were rolling down my face because I was sitting in meditation next to a Chinese. The true dharma—the essence of Buddhism—transcends the boundaries of states and nations. It's been about eight hundred years since Zen Buddhism was introduced to Japan in the Kamakura era, when Chinese priests fled from the persecution of Kublai Khan, and it is likely that it will spread throughout Europe and America, transcending all national boundaries . . . "

———————◆———————

The execution of the Chinese captives when Kitahara was barely twenty-two, just three months after he'd been sent to the battlefront, he described, in one of his essays, with a single sentence: "I collided with a shocking experience that was later to become the driving force of my quest to awaken the Way of FAS." Demobilized, he returned to Kyoto and resumed the study of philosophy and religion that had been interrupted by his conscription. Something about Shin'ichi Hisamatsu, then lecturing on Buddhism at Kyoto University, impelled Kitahara to divulge, front and back of the final examination sheet, his war experiences. He grew apprehensive that he was detaining the professor, all the other students having one by one left the classroom. But when at length he approached the podium and submitted what he'd written, Hisamatsu responded—to Kitahara's astonishment—with a deep, reverential bow. The effect was magical. "Having been subjected in the army to nothing but irrational beatings and shouts, I was suddenly enthralled to discover that there was also in this world such a Buddha-like existence."

There was thus forged an irrevocable link between the Zen master, who devoted his life to the elucidation of what he called the "ultimate crisis" of the human being and its solution, and Kitahara—dreamy and sad-eyed in photographs from the late 1940s—for whom this crisis included "experiences on the battlefield that even Dr. Hisamatsu had not known."

His "discipleship"—Hisamatsu refused to be regarded as a Zen master—began at a time when Kitahara's inner world, self-described through a phrase he borrowed from the *Record of Lin-chi,* was "utter darkness." It culminated with Hisamatsu's words, in their last meeting before his death: "Knowing you has made life worth living." Of the intervening thirty-three years, Kitahara occasionally published a glimpse:

> The night before [Hisamatsu's] Zen talk I escorted him, in the snow, back to his dwelling at Hoseki-an. Entering, I was served powdered green tea. But when I had finished about half, Dr. Hisamatsu suddenly scolded: "Drink it without using your mouth." Cornered, I dashed the tea in my face. He said, "No good!" with a scowl, and then, extending his hand charged: "Pass that teacup without using your hands! . . . Take this plate without using your hands!" I was utterly at a loss, but Dr. Hisamatsu pressed me: "Sitting will not do; what do you do? . . . You can do anything—stand up!"

Standing, I was told: "Standing will not do, what do you do?" Then, when I'd assumed a crouching position: "Remaining motionless will not do; what do you do? . . . As you are, leave!" When I'd descended from the veranda, I was bombarded with: "Return without walking!"

He often punned D. T. Suzuki's English translation of *dhyana* as "cross-legged sitting" to mean crucified sitting; it was a critical element of his view of legs pulled into the full lotus, a posture he'd been told would lead to *samadhi* twice as quickly as the half lotus and that Hisamatsu himself had urged him to employ. The intensity with which he had superimposed the cross formed while sitting on the cross his past made of his present, suggested—despite his gentleness, despite the comedy—that he was made of steel. I first sensed this during a *sesshin* meal when, as part of the serving crew, I poured scalding tea on his hand as he held out his bowl. The hand did not waver. Later he wrote that it had once been his custom to bind his ankles into the full lotus position with a towel or a dog collar during his hours of solitary sitting. He had trained for three decades under one Zen master and concurrently for twenty-plus years with a second and several years with a third. He wrote: "I have sat meditation in this place and that: with a friend in a graveyard, in three training monasteries, in various temples, at the Hannya-dojo, in the mountains, up a tree, on a rock, in the small shrine at Shunkō-in Temple [on the grounds where Hisamatsu's house was located], and elsewhere."

But meditation proved to be an ever-diminishing aperture. He insisted to Hisamatsu: "Sitting is all I have!" Hisamatsu parried: "Sitting won't do!"

———————◆———————

Kitahara's rare essay "Makujikikō" ("Straight Ahead!")[33] gives a sense of his intensity in the years after the war:

That night [July 4, 1949, during the *sesshin*], in my interview Dr. Hisamatsu said: "You can't go on as you are. Somehow you've got to break through. Not anything, yet everything. What is the sitting that is not the sitting in the full lotus position, but the sitting whether walking, standing, sitting or lying? Where is the sitting when you are walking? In all bodily positions, whatever you do will not do. So what do you do? Absolute negation. Death. But this, at the same time, is absolute affirmation. That's true sitting. So far, I've given this problem only to you. You're the first. Do whatever it takes but I want you to realize absolute Self. There would be no greater happiness for me than for you to throw your entire being this sesshin into grappling with this problem. If you can solve it, you, too, will be able to save others. If sitting in the ordinary sense won't do, what do you do?"

I bolted to my feet and charged towards to Dr. Hisamatsu. He straightened his posture in preparation for the assault and said: "Stuck, aren't you? But to be unstuck is true sitting."

. . . On Sunday afternoon, December 2, 1951, after I had been sitting in the small shrine in front of Hōseki-an for an hour and a half, I went up to see Dr. Hisamatsu: He told me: "Don't pay any attention to whether or not your body has ceased to exist. Instead, proceed by concentrating exclusively on the koan. Even if you are the only one to solve this koan of 'cornered, there is a breakthrough,' I can close my eyes in peace."

. . . Running through the falling snow [during the December 1951 *sesshin*] I returned to Reiun-in Temple and together with Naha hurried back to the small shrine in front of Hōseki-an to spend the night. We resolved to sit through the night but unable to endure the extreme cold we both fell asleep. At dawn we awoke and sat continuously.

... Exerted myself [at the same 1951 *sesshin*] even during the rest periods, seated in the full lotus position approximately 14 hours a day, about 100 hours in total, but nothing came of it.

... In the interview room at the 1954 spring *sesshin,* a small desk was situated between Dr. Hisamatsu and any Zen student who wished to engage him. During one interview I lifted the desk and flung it against the tatami; one of its legs smashed, scattering the pieces. The vividness of Dr. Hisamatsu's Zen functioning brought me to an immediate standstill; he said not a word of reproach about my breaking the desk but later—the desk was master Mumon Yamada's favorite—secretly sent it out to be repaired.

... On April 9th, 1957, in the interview room on the sixth day of the *sesshin,* when I counterattacked Dr. Hisamatsu and—despite repeated failures—once more tried to "crumble Vaisali City and topple Vimalakirti," he said: "It won't do. It won't do. Stop shouting. Be more calm. Grapple with the koan in every daily activity. You've made considerable progress. But it still won't do."[34]

The Kyoto tea master Shizue Yanagida, in the video that Urs App and his wife, Monica Esposito, made for her eighty-sixth birthday, had this to say of the Kitahara she knew when they both lived on the grounds of Ryōanji Temple in the early 1950s: "He painted on his ceiling: 'Die, absolutely!' That room of his was incredible."

———————◆———————

From Kitahara's 1978 interview with Urs and me:

It was after my return from the war that my interest in Buddhism began to deepen. Yet even then I viewed the world with

Christian eyes and thought of Dr. Hisamatsu's standpoint as one of hubris. I couldn't understand it at first. I couldn't understand when Buddhism speaks of the absolute Self as opposed to emphasizing the absolute Other as they do in Christianity. The statement that the true Buddha is ourselves was a complete enigma to me; I felt resistance to words like these and harbored an ill feeling. But gradually, as I got to know Dr. Hisamatsu, I came to realize directly that he is really an enlightened man, a man who has died completely, has really died and been reborn. In Christianity as well, we truly die on the cross, die as the old Adam and are reborn in Christ. "It is not I but Christ who lives." From such a place I gradually found a point of entry into Dr. Hisamatsu's standpoint. In the beginning I was utterly incapable of comprehending the utterance: "Kill the Buddha, kill the patriarchs, kill God!" From Dr. Hisamatsu's standpoint, God or something like that which is conceived in the head is negated. But I think the standpoint of Christ himself is fundamentally not in contradiction with the awakening of Dr. Hisamatsu. For after all, Jesus Christ was, is, and will be always a Formless Self, an awakened one.

"You really think so?" asked Urs.

"I do."

"Then you entered into Zen practice without abandoning your Christian faith?"

"Actually, rather than being forced into a confrontation between the two, I suddenly found myself absorbed in the problem: What is the awareness of Dr. Hisamatsu?"

"And it was at this time that you began to practice Zen meditation?"

"I began my practice of meditation at the Gakudō-dōjō [the original name of the FAS Society] and started doing *sesshin*. That was in 1947, thirty-one years ago. During the war I was forced into a spiritual struggle of an intensity similar to what one encounters in the struggle with the Mu koan in Zen."

"Did you practice under Dr. Hisamatsu for many years?"

"Yes, but . . . you know . . . I still cannot grasp Dr. Hisamatsu's ultimate point."

"Did you also undergo traditional koan practice?"

"Yes, I trained also in the traditional way [under the lay Zen master Kōryu Osaka] at Hannya-dojo, starting from twenty-four years ago."

"Why was it that you undertook traditional koan practice?"

"Yaaaugh!!! Because I couldn't penetrate Dr. Hisamatsu's fundamental koan: 'Whatever you do will not do. Right now, what do you do?' So I went to the master of Hannya-dojo and put it to him: 'Whatever you do will not do. Right now, what do you do?' The master blurted out: 'O yoi yoi!' I quickly retorted: 'If that won't do, what do you do?' He said: 'I can see that you're really at an impasse. How about training in the traditional Zen way?' So I came to feel that I wanted to know the traditional method as well and underwent koan practice starting with the Mu koan. But even as I proceeded koan by koan, I always bound each particular koan to Dr. Hisamatsu's fundamental koan: 'Whatever you do will not do. What do you do?'"

"What kind of connection do you see between the 'solving' of particular koan, koan by koan in the traditional way, and the solution to the fundamental koan as set forth by Dr. Hisamatsu? For example, I assume you already passed several koan . . ."

"Actually, I passed all the koan used in traditional Zen, about three hundred in all."

"Isn't this like climbing a ladder rung by rung [with the possibility that one never reaches the top rung]?"

"Well, it has that element, but it's a mistake to see it solely in those terms. It must also be seen that each koan is fundamentally related to the ground. In this way one must set about koan practice. From

Dr. Hisamatsu's standpoint, however, this approach is merely an end-less adding of sides to a polygon; however many sides you add, it never culminates in a perfect circle."

"If that is the case, what is the value of this step-by-step approach?"

"Dr. Hisamatsu's standpoint holds true for his awakening, but this is something we do not yet understand. What Dr. Hisamatsu is criticizing is the mistaking of a particular *samadhi*—such as may result from intensive struggle with the Mu koan—for genuine awakening. For Dr. Hisamatsu, particular *samadhi* is quite inadequate. . . . But even the repetition of Mu, if taken to the final point in a thoroughgoing way, is quite sufficient. There are numerous cases in the past of people who have attained awareness by proceeding in this fashion. . . . In any case, I wanted to know Zen in terms of both the traditional way and Dr. Hisamatsu's way."

"And you have been practicing along both lines for many years?"

"It's been thirty years, but still I am unable to stand on equal footing with Dr. Hisamatsu, as was Lin-chi when he said to Ta-yü: 'There's nothing much to Huang-po's Zen'—it's a height to which I cannot attain. I cannot help but think there is an even deeper satori that still remains outside my grasp. In the final analysis, when seen from Dr. Hisamatsu's standpoint, one ought probably to say that the Zen masters of today's traditional Zen have not yet penetrated deeply enough. . . . Nevertheless, I have to reiterate that a criticism of traditional Zen coming from the mouth of someone who doesn't know anything about it is likely to be an erroneous one. Basically, my view on traditional koan practice can be summed up by the Zen saying 'When a cow drinks water it turns it into milk. When a snake drinks water it turns it into poison.'"

———◆———

Each time Kitahara wanted to smoke, he rifled his bag for his lighter. Invariably he prolonged the search by dropping every item that was not the lighter back into the bag. Around ten cigarettes into the interview, when after several minutes Kitahara could yet again not find his lighter, Urs asked the waiter to bring matches. "Sensei," he called to Kitahara, engrossed in his search. Kitahara looked up, received the matches in utter amazement that Urs had hit upon such a brilliant idea, lit the cigarette, and, as he exhaled, dropped the matches into the bag.

PART TWO: PRICE OF A TICKET—ONE FULL LOTUS

During the discussion that invariably followed the Saturday evening meditation of the FAS group, I one night expressed that the Zen quest demanded a courage I could not find. Yamamoto-san, a Kyoto University graduate student in agriculture, advised to eat brown rice.

A year later, after I thanked him for the meal he had prepared for me in his apartment—plenty of brown rice included—Yamamoto-san chastised me for the inappropriateness of my gratitude: "A Buddhist never does anything for thanks."

The amazing Miss Hoshi, who breezed through the *sesshin* with a light heart and through the world with a will to help others, had nicknamed Yamamoto-san "by the book." And between the fall and winter *sesshin,* he *did* seem to have added a book to his collection—a book on techniques for deepening concentration. For he'd now adopted a new practice: During the five-minute interlude between sitting periods, he would break the silence of the meditation hall with a repeated owl-like exhalation, "Huuuuuuuuuuuuu! . . . Huuuuuuuuuuuuu!"

I had begun sitting two meditation periods in succession. The minutes between sittings, when moving was permitted but I did not, were grueling to endure. Here's what deep meditation did for me: After four days of Yamamoto-san's hooting during these breaks, I wanted to kill him. But since that necessitated moving, I opted for shutting my eyes and toughing it out until the onset of the next sitting period silenced him. Toughing it out didn't go very well. I glanced over at Kitahara-san to see if he was ready to begin the next meditation. He was still as a mannequin. Suddenly he sang out, "Whooooooooooooo ... is saying ... Huuuuuuuuuuuuu?" Eyes looking through the back of his head as always when he spoke in English, he cracked the two wood blocks together and the sitting resumed.

———————◆———————

Resting on the wide veranda that separated the meditation hall from the garden, I watched Kitahara lift himself into the air and belly flop on the hard wood floor. This, it turns out, was yoga, for as soon as his chest smacked the ground, his arms flung back, he grabbed hold of his raised ankles, and he was locked in the bow pose. Though he was far from fat, Kitahara could have lost a few pounds, and his agility was impressive. He was on his feet with striking speed. Immediately his limbs fell out from under him and he crashed to the floor on his spine, legs thrown over his head into the plow position. This posture he held for but a few seconds—hardly enough for a stretch, I thought. Then, as if by antigravitational force, he was on his feet again, smashed his butt against the veranda, and was in the twist asana.

Looking up at his audience of one, he told me: "Zen training is bad for the health. Yoga is good for it."[35]

———————◆———————

During the walking meditation, along the veranda that fronted the garden, when we thudded too loudly along the creaking floorboards, Kitahara would give one of his rare commands: "Soundless!" This was not just a reprimand demanding that we make less noise, it was a koan, in the words of his master Hisamatsu: "to break ... the bottom of the world of sound"; the "paradox of sound negating sound"; "sound ... [as] the expression of the soundless"; the "Great Silence [that] is nothing but True Self, Formless Self."

As I soon learned, Kitahara, in consequence of the terrible ringing in his ears, was an odd sleeper. He sometimes wore earplugs, and once when I came back from night sitting in the garden, the light of the descending moon refracted through the paper-paneled door showed him sleeping with two tiny black objects placed over his lids. Another night, walking past his futon, I heard the sound of a transistor radio plugged in his ear. Because—or in spite—of all this, he overslept the 5 a.m. wake-up call several times.

Since it was Kitahara's job as hall chief to wake the rest of us, his inability to rouse from his slumber—at times because he didn't hear the alarm, at times because he forgot to set it—gave us extra sleep. This caused an ambivalent reaction. I wanted to sit, above all in the last days of the *sesshin,* when time was running out. But I was also relieved by the delay, especially in the December cold, and since no one else budged from his futon, I assume the relief was consensus.

Once, though, on the next-to-last day of the *sesshin,* Kitahara slept so long that, given the July warmth and the fact that little sleep is needed as concentration deepens, I decided to rise. Soon everyone other than Kitahara followed suit. Doors slid loudly along their rails; folded futons were dumped in a huge pile; we dressed, rinsed faces and mouths, and chatted. Kitahara slept through it all. Even the carrying off of the futon from the tatami mats next to him had no effect. Finally everyone had transported cushions out to the garden veranda to commence the predawn sitting. Kitahara slept on alone. I stood over him, fascinated. My friend Tanemura-san, cushion under his arm, joined me. I pointed to Kitahara's still body and whispered, almost inaudibly: "Soundless!" Kitahara bolted to his feet and bellowed: "Awake!"

———◆———

Kitahara was overjoyed that Zen was moving west. When Urs App published a list of Zen centers around the world, Kitahara poured over the dry columns of names of Zen groups in Europe and South America with a child's pleasure. He delighted in the handful of Westerners who joined each *sesshin,* translating much of what he said in Japanese into his wonderfully rotten English. He charmed us with the deluded optimism of the announcement he invariably made before the long-winded talks (usually by academics) that occurred three afternoons per *sesshin*—two hours with no bell, a torture to Western legs: "After one period of sitting, we will deeply enjoy the afternoon lecture of Professor X."

At the outset of each block of sitting periods, Kitahara would preface our opportunity to be whacked by announcing the name of the person patrolling the meditation hall. Kitahara liked to assign this task to Iki-san, with the announcement, in English: "Mr. Iki will carry the patrol stick for us."

It's poor style to digress, but Mr. Iki warrants a quick digression. I haven't thought of him for years. I should have, for this reason:

Iki-san, twenty-four, was studying psychotherapy in the graduate school of Kyoto University. He was very diligent, clean-cut to the extreme. One afternoon after lunch, I found him alone, his back propped against a wall overlooking a secluded inner garden of the temple. We had never really conversed, and as I was looking for an excuse to stay clear of the meditation hall, despite promising myself that I would sit through all the breaks, I decided this was a good time for a chat. Simply as a diversion, without much interest in the answer, I asked Iki-san how he had become interested in Zen. His reply, in stunningly well-pronounced English: "When I was sixteen, my mother died suddenly, and I was seized by the terror of death." He burst into a torrent of tears and wailing that brought the conversation to an end.

———————◆———————

At the end of the final sitting period of our first *sesshin* together, Kitahara announced, in Japanese and then English: "I . . . have received . . . news . . . of the death . . . of my father's . . . great disciple. I withdraw . . . at . . . ONCE!" Seated on my cushions, I burst into tears.

As I was packing my rucksack to go home, Mrs. Maeda asked me to accompany her and Miss Hoshi to Hisamatsu's former dwelling, in a temple in the same Myōshinji Monastery compound, just north of where the *sesshin* had been held. "You're a sensitive one," Maeda-san said. My puzzlement at her remark must have shown on my face, for she added: "Obviously, you weren't crying over the death of someone you never even heard of!"

She'd seen, correctly, that the cause of my tears was Kitahara—the beauty of his dignity as he announced his departure. So I didn't expect, when we'd ascended the steps and entered Hisamatsu's rooms, to find Kitahara dusting away, unable to leave Kyoto until he'd cleaned the tiny temple house where his teacher had lived. He rummaged through everything with excitement. "Look, Hisamatsu's mother!" he said, pointing to small framed photo. He jumped about examining one item after the other, finally handing me a wooden container for calligraphy brushes and pens. He gave Hoshi-san one of the brushes, kept a pen for himself—items Hisamatsu had apparently once used. The snapshot, which was then taken by Mrs. Maeda, my mother discarded in a fit of post-stroke dementia years later. But I try to summon Kitahara's tragicomic expression as he held his pen aloft when I need to remember that Zen is a matter of life and death, and silly.

———◆———

Zen training prior to a breakthrough is a striking about with a fly swatter in a universe without flies. Nan-yüeh had criticized his meditating disciple Ma-tzu: "If the oxcart does not move, do you whip the cart or do you whip the ox?" This is the problem of method in Zen. You try to corner yourself through sitting—or when not sitting—but the self that is cornered is merely the object of the self's awareness. The self as subject, elusive to these exertions, looks on at its efforts from a remote distance.

Effort won't do, so what do you do? More effort. The result was a lot of unwanted pain that threw me over the cliff—probably the wrong cliff. I felt myself in jeopardy if I continued at this intensity, in greater jeopardy if I did not. Divided on whether to escalate further or to retreat from the full lotus back into the half lotus, I sought out Professor Tokiwa-san. He heard me out with characteristic care and said: "Let's ask Kitahara-san before I say something that will get us both into trouble."

Kitahara, as usual when he was not meditating, was to be found in the small *shoin* where the *sesshin* participants drank tea and, in the winter months, warmed themselves. He was seated in his kimono, inhaling a cigarette through the strange cigarette holder that always called to mind the hookah-smoking caterpillar in the Disney film of *Alice in Wonderland*. I asked: "Will the intensity caused by the pain of the full lotus posture help precipitate the great doubt block [held in Zen to be the precondition for awakening]? Is it meaningful to try to deadlock myself through this type of practice?"

Kitahara never once glanced in my direction. Arm at a right angle holding the cigarette in its holder, eyes gazing within, he said without hesitation, "Nothing has any meaning, including pain."

Camus wrote in *The Myth of Sisyphus*: "Life . . . will be lived all the better if it has no meaning." I've read biographies of Camus. For him, this was simply not true. Yet Kitahara's assertion of meaninglessness was entirely positive. *How*?

————◆————

On the fifth day of the December *sesshin*, warming ourselves in the sun on the veranda after lunch, Urs App—this was his first *sesshin*—expressed to me his doubt that the pains in his legs and back had anything to do with the problem he was grappling with, which at that period he described as nihilism. It was the only time I have ever seen him unsure.

That afternoon was one of the three slots per *sesshin* where one could bow before another participant and, if he or she agreed, go off to a designated room in the temple for an exchange. Urs bowed before Kitahara. I subsequently learned that he confessed to Kitahara that all this counting of breath seemed pointless. Kitahara said: "I always found that attending to one's breath got in the way. I just tried to cut to the source." That night, when I was coming back from peeing to rejoin the walking meditation, Urs was waiting for me at the entrance to the veranda. "Something incredible has happened," he said. "I'll tell you later tonight." When the sitting was over and we chanted to close the evening, Urs's voice, with its beautiful lilt, seemed to come not from his body but from the air.

The following night—the last—when the sitting concluded, instead of proceeding into the chanting that closed out each evening, Kitahara snatched up the patrol stick. He tramped over to Hisamatsu's large calligraphy of the Chinese character for mountain, formed so that it suggests someone sitting. There was an accompanying inscription: "Unmoving, like a mountain." Speaking German, Kitahara waved the patrol stick at the calligraphy like a wild TV weatherman and lectured ten minutes exclusively to Urs.

Setting out our bedding to prepare for sleep, I asked: "How's Kitahara's German?"

Urs laughed. "As bad as his English."

———————◆———————

When I first sit on my cushions, the problem of existence asserts itself. Steadily it expands outward into every cell. Like pancake batter dropped into a heated pan, it spreads but won't fully congeal. A wave surging toward its breaking point but not arriving. A substance forming into a shimmering gelatin, where what is needed is that it solidify into stone.

So I pushed harder. One three-month season of *sesshin* sitting, my head lashed violently against the back of my neck for hours on end.

I could see Kitahara eyeing me from his cushions, but I could not stop my head from jerking. "Awake!" he shouted finally. But my eyes were wide open; I guess he soon realized I was not sleeping and that the spasms were beyond my control. At the period's end he jotted into the notebook he kept by his cushion to record—in shorthand—his observations during every *sesshin*.

That night, when the sitting was over, my entire body convulsed as I sat with legs extended on the tatami. When I opened my eyes, Kitahara was crouching next to me.

"Are you all right?"

"Yes." Actually, I wasn't sure.

"I understand that feeling of trying to push to the bottom. But you don't have to force it [muri shinakute ii]."

"Do you mean it's okay not to force it?" I asked. "Or that it's *better* not to force it [muri shinai hō ga ii]?"

"Better not to force it. The Buddha drank milk."

I'd been hurling myself over the ledge. Yet the ledge receded infinitely. So I hurled with greater force, despite my ambivalence, and the advice to hold back coming from a man whose past was streaked with asceticism confused me.

"You're sure you're safe?" he asked.

I nodded.

"Well, if you're safe, then it's all right." He seemed worried. That worried me.

———◆———

Toyoshima-san described to me how in an early *sesshin,* when the pain at the base of his thigh had reached an extremity, he suddenly disappeared. Wanting to know what to make of this, he broke his custom not to seek out others and went to Kitahara, who dismissed his experience with a warm: "Probably there's some acupuncture point down there that causes the body to vanish."

———◆———

Sesshin lunch, which usually lasts twenty to twenty-five minutes, is tolerable for about fifteen, after which—seated on my shins and without cushions—my anklebones, squashed under my butt, start digging into the hard wood floor. Today there are two reasons that even the Japanese, usually untroubled by this position, are starting to squirm: (1) Howard Curtis, six foot four, all-county basketball, serious mountain hiker, meticulous in both English and his fabulous Japanese, is sitting with legs loosely crossed rather than on his shins. With his Gary Cooper steady-in-a-crisis calm, chopsticks in hand, he is plucking the remaining rice in his bowl one grain at a time, not a care in the world, while I, his good friend—so I thought—am dying. One by one I notice that the rest of the participants, long finished eating, are growing restless along the two rows of benches except for: (2) Erica Horn, a glamorous Brit almost as tall as Howard, recently arrived from India, who is chewing each morsel of her meal in ecstasy. They seem to be battling it out over who can eat more slowly. At the half hour mark, even the most stoic postures have sagged, torsos lifted off heels to reduce the pressure on the feet and knees. The two chew on, extracting flavor from each savored grain, sip of soup, or tea. By minute thirty-five, no telepathic skills are required to know that in the mealtime silence, thoughts are criminal.

"Take all the time you need," Kitahara merrily announces, breaking the silence. "All of us are diligently working on our koan."

Twenty embarrassed spines whip into upright position.

———————◆———————

Oyabu-san and little Suzuki are on the veranda agreeing how regrettable it is that I never met one of the sitters no longer able to attend the *sesshin*. Kitahara was standing alone several paces off.

"When did he die?" I asked.

Immediately, Kitahara's feet cut from under him and his back smashed against the ground. I assumed this was more yoga—the corpse pose—but when Kitahara started to writhe with his eyes clenched shut, I feared that this time he really had injured himself. Then I noticed the tears rolling down his face were of silent laughter; I had confused *nakunaru* (to die) with *inakunaru* (to no longer be around [in Kyoto]).

————————◆————————

It's a terrifying mirror to run into decades-long meditators who are jerks. They are living warnings. Professor J was one of them.

He was in his early seventies when I met him at a *sesshin*. He moved elegantly, sat meditation beautifully, spoke English well. He had trained as a lay practitioner at a Zen monastery for years.

At the conclusion of Masao Abe's talk on the second day of the *sesshin*, Professor J launched into a diatribe. Abe paid him no mind. Professor J was not to be deterred, but his new gripe with Abe's rather academic talk ended with a complete non sequitur: "For this group to prohibit use of the patrol stick except at the voluntary request of the sitter, when I can sense that a hit from me may change that person fundamentally, is a profound error." It occurred to me from then on that something was amiss.

Professor J took a liking to me though and invited me to an elaborate dinner at his home. It was clear that he was on the make for a disciple. I eluded capture. He never forgave me for it.

One night during the group discussion after the Saturday meditation, I made a brief comment. When I stepped out of the Reiun-in Temple gate, Professor J was waiting. "Your point was asinine!"

"I'm sure it was." But something occurred to me, and I thought I should confirm it. "By the way, what *was* my point?"

"Tell me again!"

So I ambled off. He shouted out after me: "You Westerners come to Japan to study Zen, find it too difficult, then cry and moan about everything."

Masao Abe said to me at his home: "One night, years ago, I got a telephone call from Zenkei Shibayama, the great Zen master. He asked:

'Who is this Zen master J, a member of your FAS group giving talks on Zen in America?' 'There's no Zen master J,' I told him. 'There's a J-san, a physics professor. He's recently been in the US lecturing about Zen at some university in Illinois.' Shibayama said: 'Well, it seems your Zen master J has been denouncing me as a fraud.' I reported what Shibayama had said to D. T. Suzuki, who was never angered by anything. Suzuki exploded. He said: 'I begged Zenkei Shibayama for years to visit the United States. I told him repeatedly that many Americans had become interested in Zen but that they now needed to experience a true Zen presence. Shibayama always refused. Finally I wore him down—and something like this happens.'"

Abe said to me: "Professor J has been trouble for decades. Some of the senior members have wanted to kick him out, but it is my view that FAS must stand on the standpoint of all humankind and embrace everyone. J is an interesting case. He's had more formal training at a Zen monastery than most lay practitioners. Perhaps he's had a kind of Zen experience. He thinks he has. The result is vast egotism."

A few *sesshins* later, two high piles of a booklet newly published by Professor J—his version of the Busshinji Incident—were stacked by the entrance to the meditation hall. For some years FAS had convened its summer *sesshin* at Busshinji, a temple in the western prefecture of Okayama. At one of these, an argument had erupted between Professor J and the temple priest. The priest struck Professor J, who, by his own account, absorbed the blows with profound calm. Professor J gloried in the incident. The publication of the booklet some years after the event showed, perhaps justifiably, that he was determined not to let the episode go.

The consensus among the elderly members of the group was that the priest's behavior had been unconscionable but that Professor J was not without blame. The group never again returned to Busshinji.

The publication of Professor J's booklet—which we were obliged to pass each time we went into or out of the meditation hall—dominated much of the Japanese chatter the entire week of the retreat. But as always during a *sesshin,* I was too overwrought to concentrate on a language not my own if the words were not directly spoken to me.

On the last afternoon of the *sesshin,* before striking the bell to begin the last sitting, Kitahara cried out in a sad, forceful voice—in English: "Violence has nothing to do with us. We are F . . . A . . . S Zennists. We are not FAScists."

———————◆———————

En route to the temple outhouse during the walking meditation, I stepped on X-san's heavily bandaged foot. She exploded at my stupidity. Back on my cushions, only an hour left in the *sesshin,* guilt merged into koan combined with time running out drove me to frenzy. The bell ending the final sitting rang. Another failed retreat. I exhaled—partly in regret, partly in relief—and before the breath had ended, I was floating in a transparent bubble severed from the room. And having a grand old time—until I heard Kitahara call over from his cushions that I had neglected to strike the *han,* the wooden board suspended from two ropes out on the garden veranda, ritually hammered with a wooden mallet in a preordained rhythmic pattern to announce the time to the world. And what a way of telling the time! The struck board bears these words:

> Life and death is a momentous matter.
> Death strikes swiftly.
> Don't waste an instant.
> Time waits for no one.

Bad Angel says: "If you move, your ecstasy will disappear. Just sit here; he'll call on somebody else."

Somewhat Good Angel says: "Your sitting pals can't move their agonized legs until you get your ass off the cushions and strike the *han.*"

Bad Angel: "Sit still, fool! This is spectacular."

In sum: Enraptured in the exquisite result of a training designed to break egotism, I ecstatically plot to worm my way out of my job. Quick Justification 1: The entire *sesshin* I have botched striking the *han*. Kitahara knows this. In fact, during my most recent pathetic effort, he sprinted out of the meditation hall before the cacophony could persist any further, grabbed me by the wrist as I struck the board with the wood mallet, and futilely tried to guide me into the proper technique. It would be happier for all if he gave the task to someone who does it with finesse, or for Kitahara, as often occurs, to do it himself. Quick Justification 2: It's taken nine years to achieve this freedom. The others will understand. Quick Justification 3: Justifications 1 and 2 aren't going to succeed—he's clearly waiting for Antinoff-san—but you can at least stall for time and milk it as long as you can.

Joyous seconds later, Kitahara, the gentle hulking bear, charged my way, grabbed me under the armpits, and lifted me to my feet. He nudged me out onto the veranda, where I whacked the mallet against the wooden block incompetently as ever, largely because of the shooting pains in my forearm from the shock of the mallet against the board. Bad Angel: "Cracking a mallet against a trivial slab of wood is a duty hardly worth expulsion from heaven." Somewhat Good Angel: "That's the point of the whole thing, stupid. Forgotten the bodhisattva vow you've been chanting all week?—to save others before yourself?"

When I finished, I replaced the mallet in the hanging rope loop where it was stored, hurried back into the meditation hall, and crossed my legs atop my cushions. Ecstasy had vanished, of course.

———————◆———————

Returning from the garden veranda after the night sitting, I found someone sleeping in the futon I had prepared. It was 2 a.m. and I did not want to wake the others by sliding open the door to the room where the unused futons were stored. So it was with relief that I spotted empty bedding, complete with cover and pillow, one row from the paper-paneled shoji that separated the meditation hall from the veranda. As I undressed, I noticed on the futon between the shoji and where I stood a black mask covering the eyes of the sleeping figure. Kitahara! Once under the covers, I soon had a guess as to why someone had stolen my spot. Kitahara's body, by the force of some subconscious torment, unexpectedly crashed against the shoji. When it happened a second, then a third time, knowing I would not sleep, I sat up and watched. After several minutes, his body, without his knowledge or intention, lifted once more and hurled itself against the rice-paper panels. The door shook but the panels did not tear. It happened twice more. There followed a long calm. I leaned my head against my pillow. Kitahara, sound asleep, began singing. It was a child's song, the melody tender and consoling and so, so beautiful. I lay awake till morning working through the math of this uncommon denominator: As in Kitahara's eyes, so in his sleep—quarrels even his enlightenment could not extinguish.

———————————●———————————

From the August 1978 interview in Kamakura:

Me: It's long been said in Zen that there are three essential factors: great faith, great determination, and great doubt and that when even one of these is lacking, awakening is impossible. Could you elaborate on this?

Kitahara: What is it that's unclear?

Me: Well, as someone who is engaged in Zen practice, I'm very much aware of the possibility of failure through insufficient effort. When I hear these three phrases I am frightened. I feel that I lack the requisite inner strength. In terms of actual practice, not merely theoretically, what must great faith, great determination, and great doubt entail?

Kitahara: Great determination is the will to penetrate to the ultimate point even should one's legs break. Whatever harm may result, however sleepy and distracted one becomes, however much pain one must undergo, one never allows the slackening of the will until one's goal is reached. This is what is meant by great determination. I think you already know this. Great faith and great determination are present in Christianity as well. And various doubts arise should one undertake to penetrate the root of great faith. It's not a faith without doubt but rather a faith that is maintained in the midst of one's doubt and agitation. Nevertheless, generally in the great religions, doubt is not emphasized. This emphasis on doubt is peculiar to Zen Buddhism—is in fact its most important characteristic. In philosophy also—for instance, in Descartes—one tries to reach a point of certainty through doubting and doubting until further doubt is impossible. There is a similarity between this and the great doubt of Zen. But the great doubt of Zen differs from such a philosophical, methodical doubting. In Zen one doubts with one's whole body and mind; the totality of the person's being is drawn together into one mass of doubt. It's not doubt in the ordinary sense of the term where one goes: "It's not this and it's not that" but rather—for example, in the case of the Mu koan—a thoroughgoing concentration; such a state of concentration is called doubt, great doubt.

Urs: A state of concentration?

Kitahara: Actually the word *state* is probably inapplicable. But there is an aspect of great doubt for which the phrase "state of concentration" can be used. Total concentration of body and mind—this is great doubt and great faith, and the taking of one's pursuit to the final consequence is great determination. And even though they are designated separately, they are after all one.

Me: So that by concentration you're not referring merely to a technique?

Kitahara: It's not merely a technique. Whatever technique is involved, before one reaches the goal, one cannot but encounter various doubts along the way. The unwavering in the midst of all those doubts is great determination, great doubt. Finally, everything culminates in a lump of doubt. At that point, some chance occasion may give rise to the opening up of a new viewpoint. When one says *doubt,* the reference is not to doubting some object. Even if one doubts various things in an objective manner, this doubting should finally culminate in the great doubt. The doubt of Zen tries to penetrate to the ground of the world, the universe, the self. It calls into question everything; everything is included in this doubt.

Urs: What is the relationship between doubt and *samadhi*?

Kitahara: Doubt itself is a kind of *samadhi.* Of course, what I'm referring to may be considered by Dr. Hisamatsu still as merely particular *samadhi.*

Urs: But isn't it correct that great doubt is not a particular *samadhi*?

Kitahara: Hmmm . . . but great doubt is not yet Great Awakening, perfect awareness, and thus differs from universal awareness in Dr. Hisamatsu's sense.

Me: Dr. Hisamatsu says that great doubt constitutes, in terms of the emotions, absolute anguish; in terms of the intellect, absolute contradiction; in terms of the will, absolute dilemma. What is necessary, practically speaking, in order to arrive at this point?

Kitahara: The essential thing is that all the problems of one's existence be thrown into one's fundamental human dilemma, that all problems are thrown into one pot, so to speak, and faced as a totality. By struggling on in this way, this all-encompassing problem finally crystallizes as the great doubt. In traditional Rinzai Zen, for example, one must throw all the problems and contradictions of one's life into the Mu koan. Even in *shikantaza* [where one sits without koan], when one is fully determined and tries to break through, one inevitably runs up against the various contradictions of everyday life. The attempt to solve these contradictions always involves agony. It's never merely a matter of technique. Even the practicing of *zazen* brings with it, through the mere fact of pain, a kind of dilemma.

In the past, I thought there was no other way for me than *zazen,* and

I tried to break through. When the pain increased to its limit, I broke into fits of convulsions. The practice of *zazen,* even without koan, brings one up against an enormous wall. In koan practice as well, one brings oneself to this kind of limit situation. When you are deprived of all recourse, thrown into a limit situation in which you are driven to the last extremity, what do you do? This being deprived of all recourse can be found in the koan method as well. It can be seen in the koan in which a man is hanging by his teeth to a branch that extends over a precipice and is asked: "What is the essence of Buddhism?" Another koan demands: "Without using your mouth, speak quick!" Through these injunctions, one is driven into a dilemma and one must extricate oneself from it. In the koan of old there were many limit situations. If you are put into a gas chamber in Auschwitz, what do you do? Ultimately, there will probably be no other means of exit than as smoke up the chimney; I don't know. In such a situation, what do you do? Such inquiries are numerous in Zen. When death is absolutely certain, how can one escape. Where do you go when you die?

Urs: Isn't this dilemma the source of all koan?

Kitahara: Yes, and at the same time it's also given as a particular koan. Whether one is awakened or unawakened, when it's time to die, death is a reality for everybody. From the standpoint of Zen, whether one dies in great agitation or in tranquility, this reality cannot be denied. Even if you die suddenly in a traffic accident, you have to face it. The Zen master Hakuin, when he was young, was thrown into a state of serious doubt when he encountered the story of the Chinese Zen master Yen-t'ou, who when being murdered by robbers shrieked "Gyaaaa!" in a horrible voice that is said to have traveled many miles. Hakuin couldn't believe that a great, enlightened Zen master could die so ignominiously, and his faith was severely shaken. But later, when Hakuin himself awakened through the Mu koan, he exclaimed: "Just now he lives!" There is also the cruel story of the cat who, when severed in two by the Zen master Nan-ch'üan, died shrieking "Gyaaaa!"

The point is: This "gyaaaa"—death itself—is the absolute reality. This is what one has to see in a koan. In the Pure Land sect, they believe that at the moment of death, they will be saved by Amida Buddha. That may be all right, but from the Zen standpoint it will probably have to be viewed as an illusion. For Zen, one cannot be saved merely by such a belief. In Zen, whatever the circumstances and manner of one's death, that dying must be beyond life and death. Traditional Zen has certainly reached to this extent. In the case of the koan of "the sound of one hand," or in the Mu koan, there are various ways of inquiring, such as: "What is Mu before you are born?" or "What is Mu after you have died and become ash?" Even if one just penetrates the Mu koan solely by uttering "Mu, mu," this "before being born" and "after dying" is always present in the Mu itself. Dr. Hisamatsu would say: "When even the Mu *samadhi* won't do, what do you do?" One must awaken to the ultimate ground. In traditional Zen, there are many problems accompanying the koan—secondary problems. But for Dr. Hisamatsu, a method must be established that can dispense with all this.

When I went to the Hannya-dojo and asked Master Osaka: "This instant, unable to do anything whatsoever, what do you do?" he said something and I retorted: "When you can't say that, what do you do?" Finally the master roared and attacked me like a dragon. Because I was young at the time, I pinned him and at that moment the words of Rinzai, "Everywhere else the dead are cremated, but here I bury them alive at once," uttered from my mouth. The master said: "Okay, okay," and I let him go. When I glanced at him, I saw that his kimono had been torn during our great battle.

Before I went to the Hannya-dojo, confronted with the problem: "Whatever you do will not do. Right now, what do you do?" I shouted, pushed over the desk, and attacked Dr. Hisamatsu. Then he said: "Take hold of me without using your hands!" I was at a loss what to do, and he said: "No good!" In Zen there is a well-known koan where the master demands: "Stand me up without using your hands!" If you can do away with the discrimination between self and other, this is not a difficult problem to solve. When working with the Mu koan as well, if one really becomes nothingness, one can readily respond to all the subsequent problems as they arise. The method employed by traditional Zen, while said to be irrational, has its extremely rational aspect. The problems themselves appear to be contradictory and an object of bewilderment, but this is only apparently the case. If one opens up a viewpoint beyond the contradiction, the contradiction itself disappears.

In some sense, the traditional koan method is concerned with what a thing *is*—for example, this soup bowl, its roundness and hardness, its essential form, and its form when being used. With each koan one tries to see it from a different angle. But even without koan, through the diligent practice of *zazen* alone, all things come to be seen as if they were sitting. Just by doing *zazen* it can become quite clear that, for example, these things on the table are sitting as formless form, having both body and action.

Ordinarily, the working with the Mu koan or the koan of the "sound of one hand" should bring with it what may perhaps be called a glimpse of absolute oneness. Without such an understanding, even should one proceed through the various koan, they will remain incomprehensible. There are so many things [pointing to things in the room], one . . . two . . . three . . . four . . . five . . . six, and yet they are all one. When one sits, with koan or without, this comes to be seen very clearly. Absolute oneness manifests as the many, and the many again return to oneness.

The Zen master Hakuin in his "Song of Zazen" says: "Your coming and going takes place nowhere but where you are." Whether coming or going, everything is an "event" in formless, absolute oneness. Today we have walked from Kamakura to Kita-Kamakura, and this is also formless absolute oneness. Absolute oneness itself is eternal stillness. Pascal said: "The eternal silence of these infinite spaces terrifies me." But in Zen, perpetual silence is joyous, joyous in a sense beyond sorrow and joy. The silence of Vimalakirti expresses the great joy of the dimension in which neither joy nor sorrow arise. We have been walking around all day, yet within all that movement, that absolute silence is always present. Always. This absolute silence is the *un-grund* [unground], even in activities such as drinking. Absolute oneness, formlessness, is not something that is present only during *zazen*. It is in all activity. When I say *is,* this is not the *is* which stands in opposition to *is not*. Rather, it is the *is* which transcends the dimension in which the discrimination between *is* and *is not* takes place.

———◆———

When the interview was over, Kitahara, wanting a cigarette, hunted the bag for his lighter. His hand latched onto something—the map of the Kamakura hills. He pulled a black ink pen from his pocket and for a quarter of an hour marked out the path that we had traveled. "Antinoff-san, for you," he said, handing the map to me. "To remember our journey today."

I thanked him, took note of his markings, and said: "Sensei, the one part of our hike that is not indicated is your house. Could you mark it on the map?"

The suggestion pleased him tremendously. He took back the map, examined it with great care, designated the exact spot of his house, closed the cap on the pen, and dropped the map into his bag.

Part Three: Formless Meditation (1991)

A woman achieved what even cancer proved too feeble to do: tear wide the metaphysical bullet hole that all my adult life had dwelt in my chest, broadening it past my shoulders, feet, and head so that it swallowed me whole. Every cell in my body felt crushed in an ever-tightening vise. For the first time in twenty-two years, I could not meditate. One difficult night, hour after hour I repeated on my back the closing line of the

Heart Sutra. Twice I fell asleep, but I soon woke to find the sutra line reciting itself; I clung to it for dear life.

In the morning I called Mrs. Maeda in Kyoto and asked her to inquire if I could speak with Kitahara. I had not had contact with him for twelve years: seven in America when I'd gone back for my doctorate; the last five back in Japan. Age had retired him from the weeklong meditation *sesshin,* and he had always been a private man. I said: "Tell him I don't want to intrude but I'm in despair." Mrs. Maeda rung back to say that I was to phone Kitahara that evening. He had once told me that to call him at night was "dangerous."

As soon as he heard my voice, he interrupted: "Despair, Antinoff-san? The cherry blossoms are fabulous! Come to Kamakura. We'll have a look." His voice was so kind that I burst into tears.

I was to meet him at the entrance to Kita-Kamakura Station that Sunday. He was not there. After a half hour I concluded that I'd misunderstood and that he'd actually said Kamakura Station, our rendezvous point when Urs App and I had come to interview him years before. I took a taxi the one stop. He wasn't there. I took another taxi back to Kita-Kamakura and waited at the original spot. An hour and a half after the appointed time, I happened to glance past the ticket wicket back into the station and saw a lone man sitting on a bench on the far side of the tracks. I doubted it was Kitahara; this fellow was much older, thinner, almost frail. One excellent feature of the Japanese railway system is that for a few yen you can purchase a ticket that allows you onto the platform for the purpose of greeting visitors and seeing them off. I bought one and crossed the tracks. The man was contentedly eating a toothpick-sized chocolate-covered wheat stick, a product called Pocky, especially loved by children. When I was a few feet away, as uncertain of my identity after a dozen years as I was of his, he said, in English: "Mr. Antinoff? . . . Did you have an accident?"

"Kitahara-sensei, I'm so, so sorry. I've been waiting in front of the station. Isn't that where you said to meet?"

"It *was*. But then I said I'd wait for you on the platform." He pulled the red cardboard Pocky box from his sports jacket pocket. He peered into it, then sheepishly showed me the empty box and shrugged.

We crossed the tracks and exited the ticket wicket. Once outside the station, he asked: "Shall we talk about despair or have something to eat?" Before I could answer, he said: "Let's talk about despair later." He prodded me into a cab.

Minutes later we were seated at opposite ends of a table. A waiter set down the mandatory cups of tea. For the past weeks, I had been spitting up stomach acid. I couldn't stop coughing. Some customers at the other tables turned their heads. Kitahara hurriedly called for a glass of water. Finally it quelled the cough. The waiter returned with beer, then was back again to place on our table two trays, each containing square lacquered bowls of eel and rice, soup, and a small plate of pickled radish slices.

"I *too* am in despair," said Kitahara in English after a mouthful of eel. "I am in despair about my wife," he said in Japanese. "She criticizes me for not being Dr. Hisamatsu. We'll talk about despair later." He popped more eel into his mouth.

For many minutes he ate in silence, washing the eel down with beer. Finally he said: "My wife . . . is in despair. My wife married *me*. She's resentful. At university she studied French literature. Now she's a housewife."

This seemed an opening to tell him of my personal situation. To my surprise it seemed useless to do so. I was fully aware that what afflicted me bore no ultimate relation to losing someone's love and preceded any particular event of my life. I did explain that a woman who had proposed marriage had ended our relationship without letting me know. Kitahara drank and ate, offering no comment or advice. He became very interested in his soup. Slurping the last bit, he waived his chopsticks over the table, saying, "These bowls, these glasses, these cups—all are emptiness! Without time and space." His face, his voice were ecstatic. I realized then that his way of speaking *to* the human problem was to speak exclusively *from* its solution. He was inviting me to the Zen rendition of the Last Supper. Pointing to the items on the table, he beamed at me as he indicated them one by one. It wasn't just that he was turning each into a koan, as if to say: "These are eternal, these are absolute emptiness—don't you see?" He was telling me, without words: "I am incapable of speaking to your suffering in any other way than to show you that these bowls and cups are the obliteration of suffering." But all Kitahara actually said was, as he rose from the table: "Let's talk about despair later."

We ascended single file into the same wooded hills where Urs and I had hiked with him thirteen years before. An hour in, it started to rain. Kitahara glanced up at the sky darkening above the treetops, turned around to me, and said in Japanese: "I too am in despair. My son loves rock and roll. When I ask him to turn the stereo down, he ignores me. My wife takes his side. My wife says: 'You stand on the standpoint of all humankind and aren't even nice to the person next to you.' She means my son. I guess we all have a selfish point." He walked on a few paces, turning again to add: "Marriage is [he used Kitarō Nishida's phrase] absolutely contradictory self-identity. By never marrying, Dr. Hisamatsu experienced in his private life only self-identity. Antinoff-san, if you do marry, it's best to marry someone with a religious mind and heart. Antinoff-san, whether you marry or do not marry, you must break through the distinction between hoper and despairer. We'll talk about despair later."

The trees reduced the rain to a drizzle as we walked on in silence. A cawing bird flew out of a tree. Kitahara thrust a finger into a suit jacket pocket and immediately a notebook was dangling from a cord at his hip. The same finger went behind his lapel and a pen was hanging from a cord around his neck. The appearance of both items had taken in total less than two seconds. He halted, jotted into the notebook, and both pad and pencil disappeared. I remembered mentioning to

DeMartino when I was back in America that Kitahara had assured me that he almost never wrote poetry. DeMartino said: "He'd never tell you that he did."

Another half hour passed, still without a word. Kitahara paused at a fork in the path; I took the occasion to grab a small carton of apple juice from my bag. A miniature straw wrapped in plastic was taped to the side of the carton. I stuffed the straw into the carton and handed it to him. Kitahara gulped down the juice in evident pleasure, pulled out the straw, and returned the half-filled carton. As I finished it off he said: "It would have been even better if we'd had one carton each. And Antinoff-san, one more thing." He pointed his thumb to the forked road. "We're lost."

He contemplated the two paths, then stormed off on one of them. Scurrying to keep up, I began to question:

"Is a breathing technique in meditation essential?"

He answered, "Dr. Hisamatsu, asked what breathing technique he used in meditation, said: 'I have no breath.'"

"Do you still meditate?" I asked.

"No. I do formless *zazen*. I sit in the full lotus while watching TV."

"Do you think *sanzen* [an interview with a Zen master] is necessary?"

Kitahara said: "Do *sanzen* with yourself." He halted and turned: "Dr. Hisamatsu told me to stop doing *sanzen* with Kōryū Osaka. As a Zen master, Osaka was a *maegashira* [the lowest of five ranks in the top division of sumo wrestling]. When I began koan interviews with Master Osaka, it was as an equal. Dr. Hisamatsu did *sanzen* until 1935. He might not have finished to the end; there was no need for it. Everyone was impressed with the speed of his progress."

"I can no longer form the koan mentally while sitting. It has ceased to be an object of my awareness."

"You don't need a koan when sitting. The koan is the one who sits."

"When sitting I can't even mentally say my name. I am simply aware of my despair. I focus on that."

"To be focused on despair is a form of sickness." Kitahara pointed to houses visible below us as we traversed a bend in the path. Only when we began our descent did he add: "True meditation is to *break through* despair. This can be achieved anywhere, and without a teacher. During the war, some did *zazen* in Siberia. We'll talk about despair later."

As we passed the first houses and hiked out toward the main drag, Kitahara said: "Meditation does feel wonderful, doesn't it!"

We reached Tōkeiji—the divorce temple—where for centuries women fled abusive husbands, who were barred by law from entering the nunnery grounds; a three-year stay could legally end a marriage. Kitahara wanted to show me Matsugaoka Library, where D. T. Suzuki had lived and written in his last years. It is not open to the public. Kitahara was untroubled by this; we passed through a gate and climbed the hill. He called out. No one answered, and we couldn't get in. When we circled back into the Tōkeiji Temple grounds, Kitahara spread his arms wide, inhaled deeply, and said: "What *isn't* Zen art?"

Did that include the rows of gravestones he now hurried toward? Kitahara stopped before one of the graves, pressed his palms together, bowed, and said: "Thank you, Iwanami-san, for publishing my father's works." He zigzagged along the cemetery paths and stopped before another headstone. Engraved in the stone was the name Kitarō Nishida. Kitahara began chanting the Heart Sutra. It's the only sutra I ever learned in Japanese, largely forgotten now, and I joined in. Then he announced that we'd recite the "Vow of Humankind,"[36] the short prayer for a peaceful, awakened world composed by Dr. Hisamatsu after Japan's disastrous war in the hope of helping Zen awakening achieve what it had failed to achieve in its long history: an activist, *healthy*, political-historical expression. But Kitahara chanted it in Chinese. He recited it again in French. He recited it a third time in Russian. Then in English, then in German, finally in Japanese. The study of foreign language broadcasts was not, apparently, simply to block out the ringing in his ears.

We moved on to the grave of Daisetz Suzuki. Again we chanted the Heart Sutra. At its close, he again announced that we would recite the "Vow of Humankind." I prepared for a repeat of all six languages when he added: "Japanese only, to save time." He finished and marched out through the temple gate.

I followed him off the main road, past neighborhood houses, to a bus stop. We waited and waited for a bus that did not come. It eventually occurred to Kitahara to examine the schedule posted on a street pole, after which he announced: "Wrong stop." We walked to the "right" one. The bus did not come. After a further forty minutes, Kitahara opted to call a cab. We crossed the street to a telephone booth. Kitahara, disclosing our whereabouts to the cab company, spotted a taxi in the distance, hung up the phone, and started to run. The taxi halted; the bus appeared. Kitahara reversed direction, and as we raced back to the bus stop, the bus pulled off. The taxi also was gone. Kitahara smiled at me like a naughty child. Rapidly running his index finger several times up and down his lips, he summed up our waiting for a ride for an hour and a quarter: "Blib-blib-blib-blib-blib-blib-blib-blib!"

He once more studied the bus schedule, apparently rejected the length of the wait, and ran off in search of another cab. A human giving machine, churning out giving—however cockeyed its employment. He was trying to help me with every bit of his strength. I feared he'd be sleeping off my visit for the next two days. Age had crept into his face. A man whose compassion could kill him. I don't even remember getting into the cab, which toured exquisitely lit streets of cherry blossoms—fabulous as promised—in the Kamakura twilight. I do recall sitting in yet another restaurant, where Kitahara confided how sad it made him that the FAS group after Hisamatsu's death had become weak. I recall another cab to a train station. That two tickets were purchased and that we were on the train platform—to where I had no idea. That the train rolled in. That while waiting for him to board first, he nudged me gently through the open door. That as I turned around, the door closed; he'd returned me to myself. Kitahara was tap-dancing on the platform with the kindest, kindest smile. And as the train pulled off for Tokyo, I knew this was his discussion of despair.

PART FOUR

This postcard from Kitahara, January 1, 1992:

> A HAPPY NEW YEAR! Last year, both at Myōshinji Monastery's Reiun-in Temple and Shōkokuji Monastery's Rinko-in Temple, I served as meditation hall chief, sitting *sesshin* together with my elder daughter, Rumi, who is a student at Kyoto University.
>
> FORMLESS SELF itself is the true teacher. "Throughout the Great Tang Empire there are no Zen teachers." (Blue Cliff Record)[37]

Kitahara in public was not an event to be missed. If he had come out of *sesshin* retirement, it could only be because his daughter was in Kyoto (where the FAS group was centered), because he wanted her to experience the *sesshin,* and because the best way of encouraging her to do so was to participate himself. I supposed—rightly, it turned out— that when she graduated, he would stop, and for good. But I could not get to Kyoto for nearly a year.

To find that Rumi Kitahara—who I'd first and last seen being tickled to the accompaniment of Hisamatsu's fundamental koan as a small child—had grown into movie star beauty. Her stillness in meditation was astonishing; during the entire week of sitting, neither her back nor a finger stirred. At Kyoto University she studied French literature—her parents' alma mater and her mother's major. I was told there had been a skirmish over her course of study: Kitahara hoped she'd study philosophy; Mrs. Kitahara had won.

Rumi was accompanied by a handsome young fellow—her boy-friend, apparently—who seemed to regard the *sesshin* as a date. He wore an exquisite knee-length overcoat, combed his hair impeccably, and later asked if I had an electric razor that he could borrow, explaining with concern: "I've got a heavy beard." He, too, attended Kyoto University—a philosophy major who like many Japanese university students rarely went to class. His reasoning was novel though: "What's the point of showing up at the lecture if you haven't first understood the books?"

"What are you reading in French literature?" I asked Rumi during a break.

"Marquis de Sade," she said, all innocence. "I investigate evil. I want to understand the evil human being." These words from a woman *that* pristine, *that* beautiful put on my tongue a question or two. But Kitahara was her father, and I said instead:

"You are completely still during meditation."

"I'm so cold at night I can barely sleep."

I was amazed. "How long have you been meditating?"

"I never meditate—apart from these *sesshin*. My father would like me to. I rebel."

"Your father is a very funny man."

"*Very* funny. And a little strange."

———◆———

When I'd entered the Rinko-in Temple before the start of the *sesshin*, Kitahara was a kind, elderly man in suspenders, sitting with his feet dangling over the veranda, not unlike the pensioners I would meet in the public bath. Changed into *hakama* skirt and kimono, he transformed into charging rhino crossbred with frolicking bear. His love of Zen and of those who pursued it poured from him and fueled him. Zen poetry from the Tang and Sung Dynasties, memorized in Japanese and English translation; utterances from the ancient masters; poems of his father sung terribly—all burst from him at whim as he circled the meditation hall with the patrol stick, all lumbering power and youth; as he readied to strike the blocks to commence a sitting period; as he struck the blocks again at the period's end. On the second day, when we finished the walking meditation and had resumed our cushions, he said: "*Zazen* is not a *samadhi* that begins at a particular time in a particular place and then ends; it is the source of time and space; it is timelessness . . . spacelessness. Any sitting posture is okay. True meditation has no form."

———————◆———————

In the predawn December cold, dressing for the third day's sitting, Kitahara was standing over his small carrying case. He reached under his loosened kimono with both hands and pulled off his underpants, placing them in a transparent plastic bag that was neatly marked in black ink: "Tuesday, December 22." Then he lifted from his case a second plastic bag labeled "Wednesday, December 23." The bag with the used drawers was placed beneath the bag marked "Monday December 21." He then slid on the December 23 underwear.

I mentioned this to Mrs. Maeda. "His wife," she laughed.

"Good thing," a voice said from behind me. "Otherwise he'd go into *samadhi* and put on the underpants he just removed."

———————◆———————

I hadn't slept more than an hour each of the first three days. Age forty-three, no longer seeing the point of lying awake shivering as I always did during cold *sesshin*, I decided to stay the remaining nights at a cheap inn a half hour's walk from the temple. Next morning I streaked across Kyoto in the freezing darkness, passed through the Rinko-in Temple gate, which Oyabu-san—always reliable—had unlocked as promised, and pulled my sitting cushions out onto the veranda for the 5 a.m. outdoor meditation. At 9 p.m., without a hint of tiredness, I strolled back to the hotel, pleased with my new plan of attack.

The next morning was so cold that it hurt to breathe. I half-ran to the temple. The gate was locked. I'd made rapid time, so it was probably not five. At six, it was definitely not five. At 6:10, footsteps scurried along the path leading from temple to temple gate. The bolt was unlocked and the gate pulled open. "Kitahara-sensei overslept," Oyabu-san said. "Very sorry." He bowed.

———◆———

Participation in the *sesshin* had declined to the point that meals were no longer eaten communally at the temple; we foraged for them alone. The one place I could find open at 7 a.m. was a McDonald's—I hadn't been to one in decades—though six-foot-four Howard Curtis extolled the company for installing the Western-style toilet that he proclaimed, after three years of squat toilets in Japan, to be "the greatest invention in the history of man."

Days two and three, not wanting to meditate while trying to digest hamburgers or sausage, I breakfasted on McDonald's pancakes without syrup. On the fourth day, Tanemura-san, reading a newspaper while he sat in a booth, glimpsed me eating and fled the restaurant. Not wanting to deprive him of his favored place, the fourth day I hunted for a coffee shop that opened early. Turning a corner, I saw coming toward me both Kitaharas, Rumi smiling with her arm through her dad's. He suggested that I join them at a place they'd frequented the previous days.

During the meal, Kitahara filched a potato slice from Rumi's plate and popped it in his mouth. "Li drinks the wine, Chang gets drunk," I quoted the Zen adage. Kitahara lit up, stole another bit of potato, and exclaimed: "Kitahara eats, Rumi gets full." He cracked up as he stole several more bits of her breakfast.

"Your daughter is so still when she meditates," I said.

"Better . . . than . . . her father." He turned to her. "I was falling asleep leading this morning's walking meditation. Want to see how I stayed awake?" He crinkled his face muscles into preposterous positions and bulged his eyes. "During my student days I used to fall asleep during Dr. Hisamatsu's lectures."

He rose and went off to pee. Rumi said to me in English: "My father is good. Very, very good. For this reason I study the evil man."

———————◆———————

Rumi Kitahara sat two cushions from mine on the opposite side of the meditation hall from where her father sat with his eyes closed. He could not see, consequently, when several times during the week she silently pressed palms together in request to be whacked with the patrol stick. On each occasion, however, the split second before the first of the four blows, Kitahara's eyes shot open. When the last blow was struck and he was sure that she had come to no harm, his eyes immediately closed.

Her Zen education cost him. When the week's struggles had ended, I overheard eighty-one-year-old Professor Kitayama ask: "Will you be attending the next *sesshin*?"

"I don't know," said Kitahara. "I'll be sick for a week from this one."

———————◆———————

On the penultimate night, the last to leave the meditation hall, I walked past Kitahara's sitting cushions. Despite the December cold, they were soaked. A living example of the Zen dictum: "Unless at one time perspiration has streamed down your back, you cannot see the boat sailing before the wind. Unless once you have been thoroughly drenched in perspiration, you cannot expect to see the revelation of a palace of pearls on a blade of grass."

Or illness?

The last bitter-cold morning, Kitahara—always silent while sitting—twenty minutes into the meditation said: "Feel your hand resting on your lap. Where in the touch does the hand end, the lap begin? Touch the floor with your palm. Where is the separation? Absolute oneness."

Before the final period he said: "On December 3, 1915, Hōseki Shin'ichi Hisamatsu broke through in a manner not seen for hundreds of years. He has said: 'If you cast off body and mind, then . . .'" Kitahara paused. He seemed to have lost his train of thought. Then said: "Find out for yourself what follows."

Retrieving my rucksack to go home, I happened upon Mrs. Maeda trying to give Kitahara an envelope containing money for leading the *sesshin*. Kitahara, refusing it, said: "Dr. Hisamatsu [now dead] would be angry."

Kitahara did show at the next *sesshin*. It was held in the meditation hall on the top floor of the Institute for Zen Studies on the grounds of Hanazono University. When the final morning's sitting had ended, I dangled my legs over the edge of the sitting platform until I could walk; by the time I slipped into my sandals, the meditation hall was empty. I descended the hall by the back stairs, past the small storage area where we kept out gear. As I stepped outside, Kitahara—this had never happened before—was waiting for me.

"Antinoff-san!" he excitedly pointed to the ground. "Your *relatives*!" Thousands of red ants were zipping about on the hard dirt that lined the grassless university baseball field. "During the war I used to watch the ants in China," said Kitahara, switching to Japanese. "Ants make no distinction between China and Japan. Only humans do." He watched their movements spellbound. After a time he turned to me and said: "I died in the war." My face must have shown incomprehension, for he offered a revision: "I should have died in the war." Another pause. "I came back. I took care of my mother." Pride in his voice as he added: "She lived into her nineties." He pondered the ants a half minute more and said: "As I plunged my bayonet into a Chinese captive, I chanted: 'Namu Amida Butsu.' Utter hypocrisy!"

I had read the story of the elderly fisherman and his wife who, terrified that killing fish morning till night to earn a living meant eternal damnation, asked Hōnen, the founder of Pure Land Buddhism, if hell could be avoided. Hōnen promised that if they chanted "Namu Amida Butsu"—the saving chant in Pure Land Buddhism—despite taking so much life, they would enter paradise. Kitahara clearly had that tale, or one like it, in mind as he killed. And wasn't buying it.

The first full day, after the predawn sittings, Kitahara ran through his litany of "good mornings" in fifteen languages. He'd added Dutch, for a reason I'll soon explain, but my favorite bit: "And we salute . . . Dr. Daisetz Suzuki . . . Dr. Sunshin Kitarō Nishida . . . Dr. Hōseki Shin'ichi Hisamatsu . . . and all the Buddhas and bodhisattvas throughout the . . . WHOLE . . . UNIVERSE!!!"—had been omitted. When the morning chanting, tone-deaf as ever, mercifully ended, I went up to Kitahara. "What happened to Dr. Suzuki, Dr. Nishida, Dr. Hisamatsu, and all the Buddhas and bodhisattvas throughout the whole universe?"

He looked at me quizzically.

"You always salute them after your 'good morning' greetings."

"I've never done anything of the kind."

"Every sesshin for years."

"You're mistaken."

The next morning, still no mention of them. When the chanting ended, we cleaned the meditation hall. I was on my knees dipping a rag into a water pail when I looked up and saw Kitahara standing over me. "Where are Dr. Suzuki, Dr. Nishida, and Dr. Hisamatsu now?" he demanded. Before I could respond, he slapped me on the back with the flat of his hand and said: "Dr. Suzuki," slapped again and said: "Dr. Nishida," slapped a third time and said: "Dr. Hisamatsu"—a greeting from each (overly careful not to injure) from beyond life and death.

The following morning, after the predawn meditation and the list of "good mornings," Kitahara continued: "And we salute . . . Dr. Daisetz Suzuki . . . Dr. Sunshin Kitarō Nishida . . . Dr. Hōseki Shin'ichi Hisamatsu . . . and all the Buddhas and bodhisattvas throughout the . . . WHOLE . . . UNIVERSE!!!" He was beaming, looking straight at me.

The following day, just before striking the wood blocks to begin the morning sittings, Kitahara said: "National teacher Bukkō's words to Hōjō Tokimune,[38] 'Maku mōzō!,' are often taken to mean: 'Have no deluded thoughts!' What Bukkō really means is: 'There *are* no deluded thoughts.'"

Another symptom of the weakening of the FAS group was that the annual weeklong July *sesshin* had been reduced to a four-day combination meditation retreat and academic seminar. The opening day convened not in the meditation hall but in a small conference room on the Hanazono University campus. We went around the room for self-introductions. From the ever-silent superhuman meditator Toyoshima-san: "My name is Toyoshima. I'm from Osaka. I'm a schoolteacher. I am unable to be here for the whole *sesshin,* can only be here for a little of it; I came to exert myself to the utmost for that little bit." From Kitahara, his daughter Rumi seated next to him, glasses on his forehead, a drooping tuft of hair obscuring the bridge of his nose: "My name is FAS—actually it's Ryūtarō Kitahara. My heart is half-Chinese, half-Japanese. My home is the universe. After Japan's violence in the war, Dr. Hisamatsu felt we must stand on the standpoint of all human-kind. Dr. Suzuki said: 'Life is death; death is life.' Today I understand this well. According to the data Urs App-san has published listing all the Zen centers in the world, there's hardly a country on earth where there isn't one. Zen, which in the form of Zen Buddhism has been transmitted from India to China and from China to Japan, from now on will spread through this whole world as a powerful force. But it must do so on the standpoint of all humankind."

At the end of the afternoon—all talk, no sitting—Kitahara was requested to give introductory instruction on meditation for those who wished it. A few of the professors suggested that the starting time of the evening meditation be pushed back from 6 to 7 p.m. on account of the heat and asked that the instruction be postponed until then. Kitahara objected: "If you cut down the sitting time any further, it won't even be a *sesshin*. We'll go to the meditation hall now." When I arrived in the hall, Toyoshima-san—one of the greatest meditators in Japan and the last man on earth to need instruction for beginners—was sitting on his cushions. After a brief discussion of posture and breathing, Kitahara rang the bell for a sitting period to commence. At its conclusion, he added this postscript to his instruction: "Try various ways of medi-tating, but when you are forced to confront what to do when every method of meditation has failed—that is when you must throw your-self into Zen meditation." We sat another period and broke for supper.

As I was exiting the meditation hall, Toyoshima-san came up to me and quoted: "Forced to confront what to do when every method of meditation has failed—that is when you must throw yourself into Zen meditation." He broke into a grin and said in his terrible English: "Best instruction."

———————◆———————

When I resumed sitting with FAS in the 1990s, an aged man—eighty easily—would at times appear. He wore a goatee, monk's robes, and high black combat boots. This was M-san, back after an absence of many years, an ardent right-winger during the war.

He attended parts of this summer *sesshin* as well. A young professor new to me was giving a talk in the conference room. Since the day was so hot and the seminar room air-conditioned, he invited us—typical of the modesty of so many Japanese—to pay no attention as he spoke and to go to sleep. Both Kitaharas did just this, heads nodding side by side as they napped. Kitahara had conked out while taking notes; his hand gripped a pencil pressed into the table.

During the discussions, M-san made a remark revealing markedly left-wing views. Kitahara woke abruptly; even his subconscious was taking notes. When the afternoon concluded, I walked up to where he was sitting and asked: "Wasn't M-san a far-right nationalist during the war?"

"M-san is very practical."

"No duality between left wing and right?"

Kitahara shook his head with displeasure. "That's not what nonduality means."

———◆———

For a brief period, FAS was affiliated with the running of a *sesshin* in Amsterdam. To my amazement, Kitahara had never been invited to attend. I asked Mrs. Maeda why, since she had once said to me: "I would like as many Westerners as possible to meet Kitahara-sensei." She was as puzzled as I was.

"Westerners need to see a meditation hall boss who is comical," I said. She doubted her influence but agreed to look into the matter. Whether her efforts were relevant to the result I am not sure, but a year later Kitahara was bound for his second trip to Europe and his first in thirty years.

When I next took the train into Kyoto, a few months after the event,

I asked Mrs. Maeda how Kitahara's Holland experience had turned out.

"Half failure, regrettably."

"Did he lead the *sesshin*?"

"No."

"Why the hell not?"

"He wasn't asked." I couldn't believe it. She shrugged, then added: "He was bowing before these European sitters with tears pouring down his face, apologizing for the Second World War. Not all of them understood."

———◆———

A Buddhist adage reminds that it is more difficult to be born human than for a blind turtle to fall into a log floating in the ocean. Rarer still to hear of the Buddha dharma. Rarer still, I would add, to encounter a spiritual friend who *is* that dharma.

Such beautiful gifts, so insanely wasted.

On the day I learned, in a letter from Mrs. Maeda, that Kitahara had died, I rummaged through the folder containing all the notes I had taken during our encounters, the few photos—mostly group snapshots after *sesshin*—in which he and I appeared, the three postcards I'd received from him, the program booklet I had bought when he'd mailed me a ticket to a Tokyo concert of musical settings of his father's poems, the transcript of the interview he had given to Urs App and me, and Japanese photocopies of five of his small output of essays. Toward the bottom of the folder was the letter he had sent in response to my own letter of thanks following my 1991 visit to him in Kamakura. I had written of my fear that I would die without resolving the problem I had struggled with for so many years. Traditionally, in Japanese letters, the addressee is mentioned only at the conclusion. I have not corrected his English:

I have read your earnest letter. I'm sorry for your lost love. What has been joined may come apart. Those who meet are bound to part. Let the leavers go their way.

But I guess it would had better for you. Because an ill marriage will be spring of ill fortune. A bad wife is one hundred years of bad fortune.

I think with Nishida-sensei that the world is an adequate (sufficient) expression (realization) of absolute oneness with all its miserable reality. What a contradiction! And truth!

I understand your uneasiness (inquiétude, Angst). But Zen master Bankei awoke to "Unborn" formless Self at this very moment of life and death crisis.

No pains no gains. If you wake to "Unborn" Self, you can not pass away for ever.

Now I say unto you: 放下着 ("Give it up. Cast it away.") If you cannot do so, then carry it away.[39]

> 放捨諸縁 Severing all secular relations
> 休息万事 Rest everything what you concerned with.[40]

This is the essence of Zazen.

True Zazen has no form. That is your formless Self just right now.

衆流截断 The marvelous activity of severing deluded thoughts.[41]

From this very formless activity, right now, as Rinzai said, "You can go, when you want to go; you can sit, when you want to sit. You are free."

You can go around the Pacific Ocean from Japan to America and return from U.S.A. to Japan. This action also occurs from the absolute activity of your genuine Formless Self.

Mr. Antinoff it isn't so that you cannot break through absolute Antinomie. In your everyday you are breaking through this "Antinomie" Already. When you see, You see, When you hear, You hear.

FAS Sesshin in this Summer will be from July 21st at the Institute for Zen Studies. Won't you and Ours(?) App join us?

Bon courage!

Sincerely yours, Kitahara Ryutaro

To Mr. Anti-antinomie Antinoff

(You are not an ant, but—the true Man without Title!)[42]

Better Hakuin's Tremble Than to Want to Be a Zen Master

S WEEPING THE STONE path that bisected the garden, En-san, who loved Beethoven, bowed before me, snatched the broom from my hand, and said: "Quickly. Change into your robes. Bunko-san will wait for you at the monastery gate in ten minutes." Bunko did not look at me when I arrived. I trailed him in silence for several minutes until we boarded a tram—then a small train—to a region beyond Kyoto I've never since seen. The monk said nothing of our destination. We walked from the station to a tiny, detached house adjacent to an ugly highway. Bunko called politely from the door. An elderly woman appeared—all goodness, bowing endlessly—and sat us at a floor table, where she served us watermelon and tea. The two Japanese chatted. Bunko rose and stepped up to what I now understood was the family altar. He began to chant. I stood next to him with palms formally pressed in the Buddhist way, unable to understand a word he sang.

Two photographic portraits of men in military uniform were on the mantelpiece. Both, it seemed clear, had been killed in the war ending twenty-seven years before. The elder was the woman's husband, the other her son. Chances were not small that one or both had been killed by an American.

Making our goodbyes, the woman followed us to the street corner, thanking me, thanking me, thanking me.

Bunko for me was a fawn given human speech and a human's need for enlightenment. He loved Zen more than any monk I have known. Each day of his life he read Zen texts. In later years, by his sitting cushions, he kept a book containing the reputed words and acts of one Zen master or another, which he read three to five minutes before each period of meditation. Zen, he said, was his "everything."

Apart from the Thief and Dr. Ebuchi (the latter pronounced Bunko a future Zen master), the monks in the monastery found his dedication weird. He hid in the bell tower, sitting extra meditation to avoid standing out. He pored through yellowing journals about Meiji- and Taishō-era masters in the storage area behind my tiny room. His speech was unhurried and subdued, but if a fawn to the world, he was a tiger within himself. The arduous weeklong *sesshin* he described as "my life's purpose."

Bunko came to Zen after failing the entrance exam to the elite Kyoto University and losing all hope in his worldly prospects. A strange motivation to produce such breakneck determination. He started reading about Zen and meditating in his room, then for several years as a lay practitioner attended Sessui Harada's *sesshin* at Hosshinji Monastery near the Japan Sea. At least once, exhilarated after days of meditation, he walked the seventy kilometers back to Kyoto. "At Hosshinji," said Bunko, "I first experienced the joy of the Zen path." An elder monk who trained there, Setsugen Morishige, befriended him and told him that by focusing the *katakana* syllable *mu* in his lower abdomen while sitting—at one stage wrapping a *mu*-inscribed stomach band around his gut—he had lost all bodily awareness, was stripped of the koan and every other thought, and was completely unable to exert himself in meditation. In consequence, at his master's advice, he cut down brush and, whenever possible, threw himself into his round-the-clock activities with a madman's fury; only thus was he capable of active assault on the koan. Bunko subsequently wrote him, asking for advice on how to advance his own koan struggle. Setsugen complied but added that letters were a waste of time that could be spent meditating and that he should not write again.

Bunko was thirty when I met him, three years after he'd become a monk. Mine was his second monastery (excluding Hosshinji). I never asked why he left the first. The fifth afternoon after my arrival, he slid open the paper-paneled shoji and climbed into my room. "Are you homesick?" he asked. The kindest of the monks, the one who made his concern my daily well-being.

———————◆———————

The ferocity of his meditation he kept invisible. He silently bellowed "Muuuuuu" into his belly with aggressive force; I know this because a groan, while he exhaled unintentionally, slipped from his mouth from time to time in the meditation hall. During *yaza,* the outdoor night sitting that ended each evening of meditation, he was the last monk to depart for sleep. I—desperate to leave but unable to unbend my stiff legs or stand—witnessed him end the day's struggle with a final grunt before rolling off his cushion and sprawling onto the veranda. When I mentioned that I was reading Hakuin's account of his Zen sickness, caused by the overexertion that led to his first great break-through at age twenty-four, Bunko said: "It would be a pleasure to meet someone nowadays who meditated hard enough to get sick." He told me of Hakuin's great disciple Torei, several times dangerously ill and whom his fellow monks had to force to stop sitting. He admired the monk and ex-samurai Suzuki Shōsan, who scrawled the Chinese character for death on his chest multiple times each morning with his index finger and with bulging eyes and clenched fists meditated sitting and standing in imitation of the fierce-faced statues of the bodhisattva Vajrapani that guard the entrances of certain Buddhist temples. "It's not an approach for everyone," Bunko said, "but it's worth knowing that it exists." I asked him if his brother monks shared his devotion to meditation. He said: "During *sesshin* most of them think about their girlfriends, about food, about their next visit home, about getting out of the monastery for good. Everything but their koan." Yet from an opposite motivation he said: "I never try to come up with the answer to a koan on the sitting cushions. Meditation is *my* time. I concoct answers for the master on the toilet."

———————◆———————

One night, when meditation was canceled, we took a tram to the eastern edge of Kyoto and hiked twenty minutes up a steep incline that led to his parents' tiny home. His kind, kind mother fed us nonstop. "She's a country girl," he said. "She'll never let you quit eating." His father, a sailor and to my eye much older than his mom, was home for a brief stay. When I next set foot in their house five years later, Bunko was on a rare visit home from his third monastery. His father had suffered a severe stroke and could no longer talk.

This was a time when the words "Buddhist compassion" rolled off my tongue easily and I'd not yet realized that the phrase consists of barbed wire. I asked Bunko about his relationship with his father since his affliction. He said, in English: "I look at him . . . He looks at me." I thought this insufficient—until my mother's stroke years later. In silence he massaged his father's shoulders, arms, and hands.

Bunko left his mother to become a monk. His father left her for the sea; illness brought him home, where he left her even more. I was invited to spend the night. Bunko set out our futons and turned off all but the overhead nightlight. Sitting on a folded-over cushion prior to his pre-sleep meditation, he said: "After Huang-Po attained enlightenment, he returned to his home district for the first time in over twenty years to see how his mother was faring. He did not know she had cried over him day after day until it made her blind. She would visit the inn by the ferry terminal where itinerant monks could get a free night's lodging and—because her son had a deformed foot—washed the guests' feet so that she'd recognize him should he arrive. Without her knowing it, he *did* arrive. After she washed her son's good foot, so strict was his renunciation that he retracted the bad one and offered the healthy foot a second time. His mother, learning later that her boy had been at the inn and was departing by boat, hurried after him, fell off a bridge, and drowned. Huang-po, hearing this news, said: 'We monks are taught that if a child renounces home to pursue the Way, the spirits of his relatives will be saved for nine generations. If my mother has not attained salvation, the Buddhas are liars.'"

Bunko's third monastery, Seitaiji in Yamanashi prefecture, was one of a kind. The monks to a man did not train there to become temple priests but from existential motivation. The well-known Zen master and ruling spirit of the place, Sōgen Ōmori—his ultranationalist stances prior to and during the war notwithstanding—energetically welcomed Westerners.

I attended my first Seitaiji *sesshin* at Bunko's suggestion. Months earlier, during a Seitaiji break, he had returned to Kyoto and visited his former monastery. Hearing that I'd resumed training there but was living on my own, he had tracked down my lodgings. Not finding me, he headed for his mother's home. By chance, returning from the Heian shrine, I spotted him. I was very happy.

I asked why he had sought out another monastery. He said he needed to train under a better master. I asked what he found lacking in his previous (my current) master. He made a sour face and stuck out his tongue.

He invited me to visit Seitaiji for the April *sesshin*. Only upon arriving did I learn that Bunko was now at the top of the monastic command. It was currently his six-month rotation as chief monastery administrator, and he'd have to forgo the meditation hall. To compensate, in every room where his duties were performed—by the floor desks, by the telephone—he'd set out cushions for whenever the chance to meditate came his way.

He was reading at a knee-high floor table when the monk who escorted me to him announced my arrival. I asked what he was studying. "Ma Tsu Tao-I [an eighth-century Chinese master]. Let's read some." He indicated that I should sit at his side of the table. But while flipping pages in search of a passage he thought I'd like, Bunko abruptly closed the book and began describing instead the skirmishes between the eccentric Meiji-era monk Hara Tanzan and the rule-obsessed Eikido. One tale: When their master Fugai had completed his sermon, Tanzan shouted out: "We monks have come from far away to study the Buddha dharma, and here you are talking crap." Eikido, furious at the insult to their teacher, demanded that Tanzan apologize. Tanzan stood, flipped up the back of his robe, and patted his rear end at the master. Eikido now insisted that Tanzan be expelled from the monastery.

"Let's keep him around," said Fugai. "He's an interesting fellow. In the future something good may come of him."

"Did it?" I asked.

"Later Tanzan worked the Tokyo streets for a time as a fortune-teller, reading palms with a magnifying glass. Eventually he became a professor of Buddhism at Tokyo University. He was known to wear his monk's surplice over his business suit. When it was time to die, Tanzan sent invitations for his friends to come and watch. Lying on his side, he thanked them in politest Japanese for taking time from their busy schedules to attend. 'There go my feet,' he said. 'There go my legs . . . There goes my chest . . . my throat. Sayonara!'"[43]

———————◆———————

Walking me to the meditation hall, Bunko ordered my hands out of my pockets as soon as I tried to protect them from the still cool April air. The *sesshin* was beginning, and he was letting me know that while it lasted, we would not be friends. The full day of sitting had hardly commenced when a huge brute of a man in kimono and *hakama* skirt shouted me out of the meditation hall for talking during a break. This was Kobayashi-sensei, like his Zen master an expert in the martial art of kendo and allegedly so delicate in his movements that, despite his hulking size, mice would appear in the practice hall as he maneuvered his sword. He was said to have competed with not only bamboo weapons but steel blades. In the meditation hall, he crouched so deeply as he struck the monks with the patrol stick that he terrified me as he neared. While sitting, I contorted my face into a fake ferocious grimace out of fear that he would strike me for sleeping. His face was blotched and violent; he looked as if he'd happily yank a man's neck off his torso and then polish his fingernails with the blood. "I'm a block of meditation" ("Zazen no katamari"), he'd once bellowed, bursting into master Ōmori's interview chamber. "Unwring it," Ōmori had negated him, gesturing as if untwisting a towel.

"Very nice guy," Bunko assured me.

On the third day, another man in kimono rather than monk's robes—beautified by an austere dignity—circled the meditation hall with the patrol stick slung over his shoulder and said: "There are those who, sitting at the risk of their lives, have broken through on the third day." Later that afternoon, standing next to him at the urinal, I said: "It's not easy to reach that kind of determination."

"Many die en route," he said.

I liked him immensely. After the *sesshin,* I told Bunko that the fellow had impressed me. He said: "He quit being a monk and shouldn't be wielding the patrol stick."

Fifth afternoon, as the monks traversed the monastery crop fields during walking meditation, Emma, an attractive Brit obliged to meditate apart from the monks because she was a woman, was digging up the turf with a hand spade. The monks stormed the dirt path behind her, faces concentrated, one hand atop the other and pressed flat against their chests. Emma paid them no attention. *Every* monk, as they neared her, turned his head.

Minutes later I dropped onto my cushions. A gunshot rang between my ears, and my head vanished. I sat merrily through the afternoon. But as always the *sesshin* ended too slowly and too soon. I took a bath and went to sleep. Soon I was awakened by a Japanese layman with a scrunched face who'd been—or was still (I was never quite sure)—a boxer.

"Everyone's gone," he said.

"Gone where?"

Mishearing his next sentence as "Let's go outside" ("Soto ni deyō") instead of "Let's leave the monastery" ("Sōdō o deyō"), I threw on my cheap kimono, slipped into my borrowed pair of hard rubber sandals, and left the meditation hall. To my surprise, he walked through the monastery gate. I was completely underdressed for the chilly night and could not walk well in unfamiliar sandals. I started to shiver. He traipsed on, me trailing behind, sorry that the monks had left him behind and not wanting to further hurt his feelings. Car brakes screeched, a door flew open, and we climbed into the backseat. Driving was one of the monks. I was relieved not to be cold. The car pulled into a large parking area. I followed the others out of the car. Seconds later I entered the most palatial sushi restaurant I have ever seen. Already seated at a long floor table was the Seitaiji head priest (not master Ōmori, who lived in Tokyo and came to Seitaiji only for the last four days of the *sesshin*, but the priest in charge of the temple). Next to him was a tiny Japanese in his sixties, completely drunk. "He's an important politician," the chauffeur-monk informed me. The temple priest responded to everything the politician said with a forced laugh.

The politician brought a large bottle of alcohol to the lip of my glass. I covered the glass with my hand.

"Drink!" shouted the politician.

I declined.

"Drink!

"No thank you."

"You drink, Foreigner-san! . . . Foreigner-san must drink!" Patrons in the surrounding table were watching.

"Let him fill your glass. You don't have to touch it," the chauffeur-monk leaned into my ear. This simple solution had never occurred to me. The politician poured the liquor into my glass and I was instantly forgotten.

As I ate, the head priest said to the boxer: "If you answer one koan, truly penetrate it, one is enough."

"How do you truly penetrate?" said the boxer.

"Now, *my* master—*he* was severe."

The politician stood on the tatami and boomed at the top of his lungs: "I have six women and satisfy every one of them. Six. I satisfy them all." The head priest turned to him and laughed: "Heh, heh, heh."

What on earth was he doing with this creep? When the priest paid the politician's bill, that was a *koan* I *did* know how to answer.

———————◆———————

The next morning, the assistant to the meditation hall chief, still drunk and sound asleep in the full lotus, smashed his forehead against the hard wooden edge of his meditation platform with such force that his upper torso bounced him back into upright position. When he started to snore, his boss kicked him out of the meditation hall. When I made my goodbye to return to Kyoto via Tokyo, Bunko said in English: "Getting drunk after all that meditation makes no sense. Still, am I not same? Big effort during *sesshin*. Big promises after. Then, *sesshin* over—I eat too much, sleep too much."

Haga-san, a layman with movie star looks—physics major and

lover of classical music who later became a monk—rode the train with me, though I barely knew him, all the way to Tokyo simply because I expressed interest in the bookshops in Jimbo-cho. We spent hours together and he never said a word of his own initiative, yet each time I asked a question, he answered enthusiastically before again falling silent. Side by side on a sidewalk bench, we meditated as the throng moved among the outdoor bookstalls. Opening my eyes, I said: "It's easy to concentrate in a crowd after *sesshin*." He replied: "Whether you've been in *sesshin* or not is irrelevant." I never saw him again. Urs App did, months later, at the November *sesshin* I could not attend because of the *sesshin* at my own monastery. The last night, Urs reported, Master Ōmori announced that only those who'd broken through during the week would be permitted to see him in his interview chamber. At this announcement, Haga-san alone jumped down from the sitting platform and left the meditation hall. In the bathhouse after the *sesshin*, when Haga-san got out of the tub, the monks splashed the bathwater onto their naked bodies and cried: "Haga-san's enlightened wisdom is in the water!" They splashed one another. "Hurry, grab some! Before they drain the tub."

Urs also recounted this bit of one of Master Ōmori's *sesshin* lectures: "What's the point of meditation if you don't die the Great Death? You might as well spend the week lying on your side reading a porno magazine."

———◆———

I partly supported myself during my second stay in Kyoto by bicycling to the famous Gion district, where I taught English at a coffee shop frequented by *maiko*—young geisha in training. Faces and necks painted white and in gorgeous kimonos, they chatted and giggled over their coffee, never at a table but always huddled at the extreme corner of the counter. The power with which they excluded the outside world by denying it their gaze was riveting. I'd once briefly penetrated their world though. Ikeda-san, a woman lodging in Saburi-san's small temple, where I also stayed, had a friend who wanted English lessons. The day of the first lesson, to my astonishment, Ikeda-san brought me to a miniscule Gion bar (known in Japan as a *snack*) owned by a homely, nervous geisha incapable of learning the most basic sentence. She had in her charge a nine-year-old girl to whom she was not related. This little protégé, who when she came of age was to be the geisha's disciple and was unofficially already being groomed as such, was treated, from all I could discern, not with affection but as a future cash cow. The child liked the lessons, and she liked me. When I asked if she had interest in going to the cinema with me, she was overjoyed. The next week I arrived to a canceled lesson and was told by the geisha that she had become too busy to continue studying. The girl cried and cried, and I did not meet them again.

Eight years later, taking the afternoon off from my doctoral thesis for a stroll through Gion, I saw the old geisha, nervous movements unmistakably hers, on Shijo Street. Walking beside her, beautiful and poised in a luxurious kimono, face powdered white, each step perfect in white socks and traditional wood clogs, was the girl. The old woman chatted at her. Not once did the girl's face turn to the left or right. I so much wanted to cross the street to apologize for never having taken her to the movie. She would never have accepted my eyes.

The coffee shop where I taught, a few blocks from the old geisha's bar, was named Java. The owner had been stationed in Indonesia during the Pacific War. I gave lessons to his wife, a woman of great humility who loved to smoke cigarettes and paint. (Her husband permitted only the former of these loves.) I also taught her linguistically gifted married daughter, Rika-san. I brought Bunko, in Kyoto in January while his monastery was out of session, to meet them. Glancing around the place, he said: "Maybe they need a dishwasher. I should make some money for mom."

"You'll be good for business," I said. "You're very charming."

"*I* think so," he said, pure innocence in English.

So for the next month of lessons, Bunko was behind the counter in apron, baggy Western slacks, and cheap white sneakers minus the laces. Top monk at Seitaiji, he calmly, silently rinsed the cups and plates as if he were not there. That he'd switched from highest to lowest would never have occurred to him.

One English lesson finished, one to go, we chatted at a corner table during his brief break: "Each person has his unique way of meditating," he said. "Over time, this becomes visible in one's idiosyncrasies." I finished teaching Rika-san just as Bunko was getting off work. At the Yasaka shrine, we parted. I leaned against my bicycle, watching him head north along Higashioji Street for home. As he walked, he glided his left arm in slow motion back and forth through the air. His solitude was what my solitude failed to be.

Two days earlier, Professor Nishitani had said at his Wednesday seminar in the office of the *Eastern Buddhist*: "When I did *sesshin* at Shōkokuji, I would sweep the leaves as if I alone existed in the universe. It wasn't enlightenment. But it was the beginning of something."

———◆———

On the television screen in Bunko's mother's home, a Tendai Buddhist monk, staff in hand, strode the several hours before dawn up the inclines and down the valley paths of Mount Hiei. This he repeated for a thousand days within a seven-year span. After the seven hundred–day mark, permitted neither food nor water nor sleep while chanting nonstop in seclusion for nine days, he performed a daily ritual requiring him to walk up the aisle to the temple altar. It took hours on the last day, as he could barely move. A kamikaze pilot reprieved by the sudden end of the war, he had become a monk in the wake of his new wife's suicide.

"So severe," sighed Bunko's mother.

"*Zazen* is better," said Bunko.

"Why better?"

"*Zazen* goes much deeper, and without the extreme asceticism. Any training dependent on physical strength weakens with age. *Zazen,* as you age, gets stronger."

"Even if I *try* to take it easy during a *sesshin,* it spills into asceticism," I interrupted.

"I have no pain in meditation 99 percent of the time," Bunko replied.

Upstairs an hour later, as we pulled futons from their cupboard and spread them on the tatami, I asked: "Do you work on a koan while falling asleep?"

"No. Only during the waking hours. When it's time to sleep, I drop the koan and let the body curl into a soft ball."

"Can't one meditate through the day in the same way, letting go all effort and simply giving oneself up to the power of the meditation?"

"Absolutely not."

"It's necessary to put power in your lower abdomen?"

"I put tension into my body anywhere and everywhere."

"If I do that, my body can't bear the strain."

He gave this some thought. "My approach may not be good for everyone. I'm unable to stop."

"What do you mean by everywhere?"

"I contract the sphincter, for example. It's a good aid to concentration. But it's not something one can do all the time—for example, when the stomach is empty. There *are* softer methods. After his breakthrough, Master Ōmori was told by his master to abandon the koan and for three years just to silently repeat the last line of the Heart Sutra. When I trained as a layman at Hosshinji, Sessui Harada had us work furiously on the koan for the first six days of the *sesshin,* then on the seventh day cease koan struggle and devote ourselves to pure sitting. There's Chūdapanthaka, who the Buddha found crying after having been expelled from the community of monks by his own brother—a big deal among the early disciples—for being so stupid that he couldn't remember his own name.⁴⁴ The Buddha said: 'Stay and sweep around my quarters while reciting the mantra "Removing dust and impurities."' Chūdapanthaka attained enlightenment in this way. There was also a fishmonger with no time to sit, who for hours in front of his shop bent his legs with each exhalation and straightened with each inhalation." Bunko showed me how this is done. "But *my* meditation is aggressive."

I glimpsed what "aggressive" could entail when Bunko stayed with Urs App and me in Philadelphia the following year. When I descended the stairs to the living room where we meditated, I found Bunko on his sitting cushions, fists clenched, eyes bulging, mouth stretched open to its limits, teeth bared.

———◆———

Stopped in front of the *honzan,* the ceremonial building in the center of the monastic compound that separated the subtemple where I lived from the meditation hall, were two bearded young Western men in their twenties, one black-haired, one blond. They looked puzzled. I asked if they needed help.

"In which of these buildings lives Shin'ichi Hisamatsu, the Zen master?"

"Hisamatsu is not a monastery Zen master," I said. "He's not a monk. He lives in Gifu prefecture with his nephew."

"You're wrong," said one. "He's master of this monastery. The book says so."

They produced a German translation of one of Hisamatsu's works and pointed out the back inside flap of the book jacket. I don't read German, but it was evident that they had confused an advertisement for a different book published by the same company, written by the now deceased former master of the monastery—my master's master—with the Hisamatsu book they were carrying.

"We've come all the way from Germany to meet Zen master Hisamatsu."

"Did you make prior arrangements?"

"No."

"I don't believe it's possible to see Hisamatsu without an introduction. He's almost ninety and retired. He left Kyoto so that relatives could take care of him after his housekeeper died." A discussion between the two in German followed. They weren't pleased.

"I do have a suggestion," I said, "though it's far from what you planned. Two days from now will begin a meditation *sesshin* run by a monk for non-monks in Chiba, in eastern Japan. The master of this monk, Mumon Yamada, will attend. He's probably the greatest Japanese Zen monastery master alive. Whether you could meet him or not, I cannot say; I never have. I'll take you to the *sesshin,* if you like, and if you'd also like, when it's finished, I'll take you to Seitaiji Monastery, which is likewise open to Westerners."

It took us six hours to get there. The venue was modern, referred to by my friend Priscilla, a disciple of Mumon Yamada's, as a "hotera," a term derived from the words *hotel* and *otera,* Japanese for "temple." It was far less severe than a monastery *sesshin,* but every *sesshin* tears the heart. Mumon Yamada, under whom Bunko had wanted to train but was forbidden to do so by his sponsor priest, arrived on the second or third day. I had glimpsed him once before. Walking toward the north gate of Myōshinji after the Saturday night meditation of the FAS Society, Renny Merritt had said in my ear: "Mumon-san!" I turned just in time to see an old man, white goat tuft hanging from his chin, pass us like a whisper in the darkness. On this day, by contrast, he bubbled with happiness in the bright afternoon, bowing endlessly to the *sesshin* participants who lined the path to the building in greeting. He was beautiful. Whenever he appeared in the meditation hall, he somehow infinitely retracted from the room. On the last day, he told of the tuberculosis that had almost killed him as a young man—DeMartino said that he had but one-eighth of one lung—and of the meditation that had cured him. He ended with: "May you all live to a hundred."

He departed the meditation hall. Noritake-san, the priest in charge, asked the participants for comments, as the place was still in its experimental phase. I forget what I said when my turn came, but Priscilla approached as I was packing my things and said that Noritake had announced that I had redeemed myself by my remarks (two days earlier he had shouted at me for napping in the afternoon) and that he might be able to arrange an interview with Mumon Yamada.

"Fabulous, if he can pull it off," I said.

She set off back to Noritake-san. Immediately I was accosted by the Germans.

"We're very disappointed," one said. "You said we'd glimpse a great Zen master. He's not at all like a Zen master."

"What's a Zen master like?"

"He should have a long robe and a flowing beard. I hope the next place will be better."

I said I might have a chance to meet the master and would wait until I heard.

"We want to go *now*."

This I explained to Priscilla, and since it was still uncertain whether the meeting with her master would take place, it was agreed that the Germans and I would head off. We arrived at Seitaiji in the evening and were led to our rooms. (There was no charge.) I unpacked and went to see how the Germans were doing. A pair of well-worn sneakers was strewn on the tatami.

"I wouldn't keep those there," I said. "The monks won't like it."

"You're so attached to the rules! We prefer European Zen, without all these rules."

Next morning, after the predawn chanting, the Germans made their debut in the meditation hall. One German squatted on his shins with pillows between his rear and thighs as he had at the *sesshin* in Chiba. The head monk said: "Here, we meditate with legs crossed." The German, who had a bad knee, reluctantly complied.

Sweeping the grounds after breakfast, I spotted the Germans coming toward me, luggage packed. "I like it here," said the German with good knees. "My friend insists that we leave."

I took them over to Bunko, sweeping another part of the temple grounds, so they could make their goodbyes. The German with the bad knee said: "In Europe we respect the individual. Rules suppress individuality."

Bunko spoke very gently: "We who train here do so having discovered it's easier to struggle together than alone." He bowed. The Germans departed.

———————◆———————

When I returned for my third trip to Japan, Bunko was the sole priest at a country temple. In his forties, he had entered his fourth training monastery. This former head monk, who'd already received a teaching certification from Sōgen Ōmori, was starting once again at the bottom. But his aging knee could no longer bear the strain of the ritualized bowing while he lugged—arms extended at the shoulders—the heavy containers of cooked rice when he served meals to his fellow monks (among other physical tasks). He had no recourse but to abandon the monastery and wait for his sponsor priest to find him a temple.

I learned the address, purchased a train ticket to Mishima, and found the place. His mother was with him. During a visit, her leg had given way as she walked a temple corridor. She never rose again; the break was so bad for someone her age that the doctors could do nothing. Cooking, feeding, bathing, and bedpan Bunko undertook entirely alone. He barely left the temple for longer than it took to bicycle to and from the market. He had virtually no companions apart from his mom. Later, living at his temple, I had the chance to observe him daily for several months at close quarters. He flowed through these tasks without grievance, a coming to life of the title of the seventh volume of Hisamatsu's *Collected Works*: *Taking Things as They Come*.

We talked about meditation, of course. He said he now achieved Oneness (*hitotsu ni naru*) at almost every sitting and that when he didn't, he knew why. "About meditation technique I have no doubts."

"Do you still inject tension into the body?"

"Hardly any."

"Still contract the sphincter?"

He laughed. "There *was* a period when I did that, wasn't there?"

A few nights after I came to live with him, he said: "I sit in Oneness. But I am unable to dissolve it, break it, bend it, shatter it." Not long after, he pulled a book from his beloved collection of Zen writings, stacked on a small shelf near his meditation pillows, and showed me an exchange wherein a master,[45] asked by a monk about enlightenment, replies: "The greatest sickness." These words affected him powerfully, and he mentioned the story several times.

Suzuki Shōzan wrote as an old man that a single day of his current meditation was worth more than an entire year of it in his younger days. Bunko now meditated three periods a day: morning, afternoon, evening—far less than in previous years but to much greater effect. "In my forties," he said, "I felt melancholic and lonely. I thought: All this meditation, nine years in training monasteries, what had it produced? Then everything began to change." One afternoon when we finished meditating, he said: "The Buddhist texts call it emptiness. But it is really joy."

He wanted to do *sesshin* but couldn't leave his mom. I suggested that *sesshin* required only two people and that we do it there. Word of the event spread through his monk friend An-san; several priests and a nun from other temples came for all or part. One of them brought an electrifying bit of gossip: monk X, who had secluded himself in meditation for two years, was to sit with us for the final three of the seven days. He did not show on day five. He did not show on day six. But at 7 p.m., during a quick break between periods, a hulking monk with a fierce bearing entered the chanting hall where we meditated, his intense face relaxing for quick smiles to the admiring brother monks who greeted him with bows. "X-san!" murmured a monk to the left of my cushions, referring to him, according to custom, by the name of his temple. The wooden blocks were struck, and the remaining three sitting periods of evening six came and vanished.

On my way to my room and sleep at the far end of the chanting hall, I heard someone say: "X-san will be meditating through the night." It seemed an unnecessary announcement—only X-san himself could have originated it—but it's an awesome feat to sit without sleep, then meditate a final full day, and I was duly impressed. So impressed that I felt guilty when forced to pass X-san's sitting cushions in the dark when I woke to pee. No monk X. Probably he was meditating out on the temple veranda in night sitting. Early the next morning came the report that directly after breakfast, X-san would depart. My good friend Lee Roser, in from Tokyo, was sweeping the chanting hall before the morning sitting commenced. He told me he had woken in the dead of night and needed some air. Walking down to the rice paddies and again upon his return, he passed a huge monk sitting in his car, chatting away on a cell phone.

———◆———

Nearly two decades before, I'd presented Bunko with a tale of seclusion of a very different sort: the biography of the great Tibetan ascetic Milarepa, who sat naked in Himalayan caves, fed on nettles until he turned green, and cut the garment his sister had given him to cover his nakedness into gloves, socks, and a cover for his penis. The book folded out like an accordion, and Bunko was absorbed in it for days. One day, looking up from the text, he said: "So sad you can't find anyone like Milarepa in Japan anymore."

Now these many years later, I took a shot at exposing him to the greatest Hindu of the twentieth century. For a week his Zen books remained in the small shelf by his sitting cushions as he read Ramana Maharshi, whose name he could never get his mouth around. Bunko's conclusion: "He's the real thing. What I'd like to know is: To what extent is he the real thing?"

He then told a story of monks who (with one exception) were *not* the real thing: The twelfth-century master Ta-hui was so fed up with his disciples' imitations of the mighty ninth-century master Lin-chi's famous Zen shout that he banned it from the monastery. Ming Ta-ch'an—his huge, big-bellied, iconoclast disciple—barged into Ta-hui's interview chamber, roared out a shout, and withdrew. His master then sent out a written proclamation saying that violators of the ban on the Zen shout would be fined. Ming Ta-ch'an entered the interview chamber, threw down a thousand *sen* that he'd concealed in his sleeve, reeled off several shouts in succession, and withdrew. Furious, Ta-hui distributed a new proclamation: Anyone who gave a Zen shout would have to treat the entire assembly of monks—numbered at one to two thousand—to a meal. Ming Ta-ch'an went to the chief monastery administrator, told him that Ta-hui needed five *ryō* in cash, walked into the interview chamber with the coins stuffed between his robe and his chest, tossed them to Ta-hui, and let out a shout. The master asked: "How'd you come by so much money?" Ming Ta-ch'an told him. Ta-hui burst out laughing.

———————◆———————

Bunko often said: "You've got such a big smile that it's hard to believe you're not healthy."

"I *am* healthy. My body is like a hypersensitive circuit board. Switches flip and something goes out of order; switches flip back and I'm fine."

At the first autumn chill, I vomited up some peanut butter. The toilet was far, and to avoid puking in the chanting hall that separated it from my room I carried around the plastic basin I used when bathing.

After five days of this, Bunko said: "Now I understand the type of body you have," and he proceeded to tell me of two monks. One had to measure every meal to the ounce; if he made a mistake, he'd be ill. He felt best in meditation. The second, from another sect of Buddhism, had no legs and pushed himself about on a wheeled cart.

———————◆———————

Bunko was distrustful of intellectuals. Zen academic writing he dismissed. Even among Zen classics, the books that mattered to him most were *Whips for Breaking through the Zen Barrier,* with its detailed autobiographical recounting of Ming Dynasty monks' tribulations and breakthroughs, and the great existential Zen writings such as Hakuin's, whose emphasis on the quest to awaken was more vital to Bunko's life than the revered *Record of Lin-chi* and similar celebrated works, which focused more on expressing enlightenment than on how to attain it.

The first Zen story Bunko ever told me was how Hakuin, despondent at the fraudulence of Zen after reading of the great master Yen-t'ao's screaming reaction to his murder, elected to allow his future direction to be determined, with eyes closed, by whatever text he plucked from a pile at a book airing. Hakuin selected *Whips for Breaking Through the Zen Barrier,* opened to a random page, and read how the monk Tzu-ming, when drowsy in meditation, would jab an awl into his thigh. The passage returned Hakuin to Zen with redoubled force.

Entering the chanting hall one afternoon, en route to my sitting cushions, I passed Bunko atop his cushion, open book in his hand, grinning. I heard "Steve-san" at my back and turned. "These letters of Yuan-wu, read in tandem with those of [his disciple] Ta-hui, give advice for advancing on the Zen path that is truly wonderful."

———————◆———————

Just after dawn each day, Bunko entered the chanting hall, monk's robe pulled over his work clothes, and sang—at times half-asleep—the obligatory morning chant. With no other priests at his little temple, he could have slept a bit longer or chanted another day. He never did, which is intriguing in the light of his confession one evening. "I hate sutra chanting."

———————◆———————

When Bunko came to his country temple, he married, an arranged marriage for sure. His new wife, bred in the city, had no idea what the life of a priest's wife in a small, rural temple would mean. She couldn't endure it and departed. He referred to this only once: "I failed at marriage." Pondering this, he added: "I don't believe any married couple is completely happy."

Somerset Maugham writes in *The Razor's Edge*: "Larry lacks just that touch of ruthlessness that even the saint must have to win his halo."[46] Bunko was too innocent to be married.

I said: "Did you ever again have contact with Emma-san [the Brit who turned the meditators' heads] once she left Seitaiji?"

"No. Emma-san was really good."

"Also very pretty."

"Pretty? I never thought of her in that way. She was special: the way she patted the excrement into the crop soil, carefully, without hesitation."

———————◆———————

So here's how, unintentionally—with no interest in doing so prior to the fact but plenty of interest thereafter—I resolved for myself a problem in aesthetics:

Twice when I talked with Bunko about my meditation, he began rowing an imaginary boat and asked: "Are you moving?"

I was not. For him, this ended the discussion.

In my first weeks living with Bunko, before temple duties and the needs of his mother forced him to cut back to his normal sitting time, I had convinced him to sit nine periods: three each—morning, afternoon, and night. In the evening he turned on the overhead lights in the chanting hall where we sat, something he never did when alone. Though in meditation my eyes involuntarily close, the increased lighting affected me, and I started to float in Pure Beauty, as if the details of every painting in an art museum had been extracted; the canvases, frames, walls, and archways had all been extracted; and all that remained was the greatness of the paintings and their content-less beauty. Beauty so beautiful that no one who experienced it (I was and am convinced) could fail to perceive it as beauty. In that sense it was objective beauty—beyond the relativity of subjective judgment but accessible only through a hard-to-achieve subjective experience. Two nights later, Bunko cut the overhead lights to save electricity. The floating ceased. Step cousins of that beauty still pay visits.

———————◆———————

To Bunko's "I believe it is right because Buddha says it," I said: "I believe what Buddha says because it is right." He lit up at that and told several people. The exchange seemed to suggest to him an essential difference between East and West that intrigued him. Critical thought was something absent to his nature, a dimension of mind he wasn't sure what to make of. Once preparing a meal, he said: "Zen is to become one with nature."

"Nature destroys ten thousand people in thirty seconds in an earthquake" (a line I stole from DeMartino), I reminded

"Zen is to become one with *good* nature," said Bunko. The untenability of this position never occurred to him, and he was too sweet a guy to argue against. He wouldn't have argued back anyway.

We almost did squabble once. He wanted me to pull weeds from the temple grounds, which was truly his right, since I was his guest. I was determined, when I wasn't meditating, to write as much as I could.

"Artists make art only for themselves," he said. It's a partial truth at best, yet since Zen demands the negation of the ego, insofar as my religious need trumped my artistic need, he was within his rights to criticize me with this too.

But as a general proposition, not as a justified criticism of me, I thought I oughtn't let it slide. "Would it have been better for Michelangelo not to have created?" I asked.

Bunko looked pained for a second. But he didn't respond. That he said nothing because he felt I'd made a valid point is doubtful.

———◆———

Bunko's mother lay eternally on a futon in his room; he chatted with her often through the course of the day. At night, so far as I could tell, he slept beside her. Her speech and manner had been as relaxed as her son's, and I'd known her only healthy and vivid. Now she was eighty and all bones, under a single blanket so thin, despite the late autumn cold, that in her circumstances I would have caught pneumonia. From my room at the opposite end of the temple, I would hear her laugh and laugh. When I remarked on this, Bunko agreed: "She really laughs hard, and a lot. Once in a while she realizes her situation and cries."

"Your mom told me she plans to return to Kyoto when her leg heals."

"I let her think she'll get better. The house in Kyoto has been sold." We were sitting at the floor table where he entertained his infrequent guests. "Sometimes I hope she'll die. Then I think of how *she* experiences her situation and vow to help her every way I can." A few days later, at the same low table, he said: "Do you know the story of the scorpion and the frog? The scorpion wants to cross the river but cannot and so asks the frog to ferry it across. The frog refuses: 'I can't do that. You'll sting me and I'll die.' The scorpion says: 'I will not sting you.

That would be unkind after such generous service.' The frog is suspicious but is at last won over. As they reach the other side of the river, the scorpion stings the frog, who complains as it is dying: 'You said you wouldn't sting me.' The last words the frog hears are: 'Of course I stung you. I'm a scorpion.'

"If I am the scorpion," said Bunko, "I'm going to strain with all my might not to use the stinger. If I am the frog, I am going to strain with all my might to silently absorb the sting."

———◆———

This was at the time of the Bosnian War, after the breakup of Yugoslavia. He'd read in the newspapers that Serbian fighters were raping Bosnian Muslim women to impregnate them as a form of genocidal ethnic cleansing. I had gotten used to monks making ill-informed political pronouncements. In a Zen talk, the master at the monastery where I first met Bunko had this to offer on the Vietnam War: "Both sides are acting like children," a comment so distressing to professor disciples of his who taught at Kyoto University that they asked him to steer clear of politics. Bunko's monk friend An-san, a bright and kindhearted fellow, blamed the cruelty of the Japanese soldiers to fellow Asians during the Pacific War entirely on the Industrial Revolution, which made advanced weaponry possible. The undeniably great Professor Nishitani, in a skirmish with DeMartino, challenged: "So what's wrong with Hitler?"

"He killed six million Jews," DeMartino countered.

"Besides that, what was wrong with him?"

But Bunko, naive in many ways and admittedly politically conservative, told me in his kitchen, as tenderly as I've heard anyone say anything: "If I could talk with the kids of these raped Bosnian women, I'd ask: 'What is your original face before the birth of your father and mother?'"

———◆———

Six-foot-two Lee Roser gave Bunko a pair of wool moccasins to keep his feet warm on the freezing temple floors. Bunko's judgment of Lee ever after: "Big body. Big heart." Bunko matched both kindness and unkindness with kindness. So he surprised me with his comment a few days later, when he had finished telling me of the affection a monk he knew held for poet-monk Ryōkan, the infinitely kind idiot-sage of eighteenth- and nineteenth-century Japan, famous for removing his sole kimono and presenting it to a thief, giving a daily sunbath to his lice before returning them to their home in his chest hair, burning down his hut with a candle in an attempt to make a hole in his thatched roof so that a bamboo stalk could grow, sticking a leg out of a mosquito net that a guest insisted upon so the mosquitoes wouldn't go hungry.

"I don't care about Ryōkan—*or* compassion," said Bunko.

"Aren't all enlightened people compassionate?" He knew as well as I that Zen claims that compassion (along with wisdom) is an inherent feature of enlightenment.

He shrugged. "Some are. Some aren't."

———◆———

Bunko said to me over the years, "I don't understand your disquiet." I understand it *this* way: Marcel Carret's account of his years as physician to the Algerian Sufi Ahmad al-'Alawi records an unforgettable exchange, directly after the doctor narrates that he had remarked to the shaikh: "Since everyone is troubled by the enigma of his existence and his future, we each seek some explanation that will satisfy us and set our minds at rest."

Dr. Carret: "Everyone follows the course which suits him best. If he finds what he is looking for, then for him this course is the right one. They are all equal."

Shaikh al-'Alawi: "No, they are not all equal . . . They are all equal if you only consider the question of being set at rest. But there are different degrees. Some people are set at rest by very little; others find their satisfaction in religion; some require more; it is not only peace of mind that they must have, but the Great Peace."[47]

When I was twenty, I fell over the cliff. I tried to break my fall. The fall has kept falling: past romance, past what DeMartino called "vacuous having fun," past trying to write sentences on a page, past the gorgeous stillness of meditation. There is a disquiet that the most adept meditation of the ego quells but does not root out. It drove Prince Gautama from the royal life to meditate naked with thorns growing through his thighs. He later rejected this, of course. He could *not* reject that being set at rest short of the Great Peace had become impossible.

———————————◆———————————

At his floor table, seated opposite me, Bunko drew with a pen on a blank sheet of paper one side of a mountain from base to summit. "Meditation takes you to *here*," he said, tapping the tip of his pen at the apex. "But that's not Zen. Zen," he said, drawing the line from summit to base to form the far side of the mountain, "is the movement from here to here."

Later that afternoon, between the afternoon and evening sitting, I spotted Bunko, broom in hands, charging along the flat slabs of stone that formed the path by the side of his temple. With each mighty sweep of the broom across a flagstone, he grunted out his koan from his lower abdomen: "Muuu't . . . Muuu't . . . Muuu't . . . Muuu't . . . Muuu't . . ."

His battle for an antidote to "the greatest sickness" of the summit of meditation, by moving Oneness in the world?

———————————◆———————————

Bunko said to me: "I think I can die calmly. I think I can die in meditation or am close to being able to do so." Then, reflecting on this pronouncement, he said: "Probably if I got cancer, I'd fall into a huge panic."

One afternoon, before we commenced sitting, he complained: "Does your meditation ever cause big pressure in the top of your head?" His face was uncharacteristically flushed. He tapped his bald pate a few times, then shrugged and dropped his butt onto his cushions.

———————◆———————

"When Hakuin was thirty-four," Bunko tells me, "and attracting notice as a Zen master, he was invited to the famous Myōshinji Monastery for a grand ceremony. Obliged to recite a Buddhist verse before the decked-out assembly of monks, his voice and legs trembled. Some bigwig priests in attendance mocked: 'Hardly worth your reputation, are you?'—his anxiety proof to them that he was not truly awakened. Hakuin countered: 'Don't think I tremble on your account. I tremble because I stand in the monastery where Kanzan Egen [its fourteenth-century founder] once stood.'"

This story of a great monk—part of whose greatness was to quake at the memory of a greater one—may seem quaint to a culture where too many scurry for certification in one Eastern technique or another to make a buck or an identity. The documentation from Sōgen Ōmori, entitling Bunko to officially function as a teacher, he'd dismissed and stuck away in a drawer. He had no inclination to be a Zen master and was dubious of those in a hurry to set themselves forward as one. He was much more the elder brother monk who helped whoever asked. Bunko sometimes meditated with the local children, though they could concentrate only for five minutes. He meditated with some adults in his village; they lasted not a whole lot more. When he heard that an international Zen center had started up outside Kyoto, he made a sizable donation; staying there to assist for a time, he was made to feel unwelcome by the man in charge. Yet Westerners pursuing Zen always fascinated him. When he read the Japanese translation of my essay on

Promethean meditator Toyoshima-san, he liked only the opening two pages that described my tribulations in the monastery. Toyoshima-san's superhuman strivings made no impression: "There are lots of sincere Japanese."

The quaking-hand episode illustrates Bunko's entropic Buddhist cosmology (which I never did accept). "Not even an enlightened Zen master of today reaches the level of the Buddha, nor even the level of Hakuin. He was the greatest of the Tokugawa masters, but he's not at the level of Sung Dynasty masters like Ta-hui or Yuan-wu, who weren't as great as the Tang Dynasty masters like Lin-chi. The further removed from the Buddha, the weaker the realization, however strong."

So it wasn't cockiness the evening he said: "In current-day Japan, I'm number one. That's *current-day* Japan, mind you." He clearly rejected his Zen as not good enough. "I need to run into a master Hakuin. Someone capable of crushing me. He'd scare me to death. But I need it."

The day before I left his temple (and a week later Japan), he said: "I'm not ready yet." He shook his head at himself. Then, switching to English and beckoning the world with his hand, he added: "After five years, I say: 'Everybody! Come!'"

The Fire in the Lotus

WALKING THROUGH THE GROUNDS of the monastic compound where I lived—in a three-mat room five minutes from his home—Professor Abe let out one of the occasional pieces of autobiography he would divulge when he thought it might help me advance. "In my late thirties and early forties, I was pressed to the wall. It was a situation of near collapse, and it impelled me during the *sesshin* to resume meditation immediately after the midday meal and to sit without break, forgoing supper, until the sittings concluded at nine. Later I had some problems with my knees." With this last sentence, we both laughed, but there was an infinity of difference in our laughter: his nonchalant in its relaxed recollection of a hardship borne and long since cast off; mine nervous, apprehensive at the abysmal difficulty before me.

This was one of those fascinating glimpses of the Masao Abe of a previous incarnation, when age had not yet blended with compassion to give him the tinge of the grandfatherly. It was rather the Abe-san of the tales of his friend and my teacher Richard DeMartino, who told of Lamplighter, the American who'd appeared in the circle surrounding Suzuki in the 1950s "thinking he had something."

"So you're the great Abe," he challenged as he stood opposite the newly arrived Japanese outside the Lion's Den at Columbia University. Abe ripped the pipe from his mouth and tossed it back in his face.

It is said that the lotus born in water can be destroyed by fire but that the lotus bloomed in fire cannot be burned. Abe bloomed in fire. He told how when listening to a talk on Pure Land Buddhism, the words "Amida Buddha is not far from here" pressed him to the ground and had him clawing at the tatami in anguished recognition that it was he who would not permit Amida to enter. He recalled how in the after-years of a conversion that he felt had empowered him to embrace the whole world, the nihilism that at the depths of his religious experience had been dissolved through Amida's grace broke forth anew in a second, now God-resistant strain; how in the midst of a last-ditch effort during a winter *sesshin* to achieve the "no-mind" through which he sought to undercut this obliteration of his salvation, he had run from the meditation hall and—tearing the kimono from his shoulders—doused himself repeatedly with the freezing water of the temple well, only to hear the words: "Everything is a lie; everything is a lie" pour from his mouth despite himself and draw even the sacred *nembutsu*[48] into their nihilating caress. Above all, there was Hisamatsu, the great lay Zen master and his teacher, the one being in the world who had remained, of course without intent, elusive to Abe's all-encompassing faith and who in existence as well as word had rejected Abe's realization as insufficient, reprimanding simply, "No noise in the meditation hall," when Abe, though formally in the meditation posture, was so absorbed in the *nembutsu* that he unwittingly blurted "Namu Amida Butsu" aloud.

Hisamatsu himself had been reared in a Pure Land milieu, only to see his faith give way to the demands of a human reason that at length likewise proved powerless against the crisis of being human. The resulting double impotency, of human existence and of God, stood at the root of his insistence on a "religious atheism," religious in that it broke through the "I," atheistic in that this breakthrough had to be obtained in the absence of any divine agency. "Whether walking, standing, sitting, or lying, whatever you do will not do. So what do you do? Absolute negation. Death. But this at the same time is absolute affirmation." These few seconds of talk once thrust before Ryūtarō

Kitahara were the core of Hisamatsu's existence as well as his religious teaching. Kitahara's writings chronicle an episode in Abe's attempt during the postwar years to contend with both:

> Following Hisamatsu's lecture [during a *sesshin* at Reiun-in Temple in 1951], when the chanting of the sutras had also been completed and the group in its entirety was sitting together, Abe-san, seated in one of the spots on the row to the left of the front gate and diagonally opposite Hisamatsu, suddenly shouted: "Sensei! If sitting will not do, what do you do?" I was astounded. This was the very koan I had been struggling with day and night for the past seven days, in fact, for the last three years. Hisamatsu engaged him in an aggressive exchange:
>
> "That's your problem."
>
> "I am asking you," said Abe.
>
> "You're the one with the problem."
>
> "Deceiver! I am asking you. If sitting will not do, what do you do?"
>
> "In your doing it, I do it."
>
> Without warning, Abe burst from his seat onto the area of wooden floor in the center of the room, and was about to pounce on Hisamatsu. I was sitting next to Sensei, and caught up in the bystander's curiosity as to how the situation would unfold, was a second slow in reacting. But when I realized what was happening I grabbed Abe from behind, pinning his arms, like the man who seized hold of Asano Takumi no kami as he slashed Kira Kōzuke no suke.[49] The oldest among us, Tokuhō Nishitani, sitting in the furthest corner, dashed towards Hisamatsu as soon as he saw him in danger, trampling the fallen Abe just like the statue of Vaisravana stomping out evil spirits in the Sangatsu Hall of the Tōdaiji Temple.

Reiun-in was now unexpectedly transformed to a scene of sheer chaos.

Abe, trying to writhe free, at the same time maintained his grip on Hisamatsu and could not be made to relinquish his hold. Finally Hisamatsu shook an arm free, and pressing his hand against Abe's forehead, watched him intently. Abe shouted at him: "Is this the true Self?" "This is the true Self," Hisamatsu replied solemnly. Abe bowed and said, "Thank you very much," then darted off somewhere.

That evening, as we were drinking tea in the *shoin,* Abe reappeared, staring fixedly at Hisamatsu—who had his back to the *tokonoma*—with a strange look. Suddenly with his open palm he slapped Hisamatsu's balding skull. Sekiun Koretsune, sitting next to Hisamatsu, said: "Is that all?" Hisamatsu replied, "More, more." Abe then struck him with all his power, but Sensei was just smiling calmly.

Later, when I came across the Zen phrase: "An angry fist cannot strike a smiling face," I thought "So that's it!" and remembered that strange scene.[50]

Close to three decades later, in the same room, this same Koretsune, now more than seventy, criticized Abe, as we drank tea during a *sesshin* break, for the inappropriateness of his action. Abe simply laughed. "You don't understand. I had no choice. I was completely cornered."

———————◆———————

The Professor Abe I first met in 1972 seemed *kalpas* removed from these struggles. Two monks brought me to his home the day of my entry into the monastery. He explained to me in English the daily monastic routine. There was about him an intimation of ripened virtue, very much the gentleman, who in response to inquiry as to how he was doing would respond, as he appeared at the gate in his kimono:

"Always very busy; always very free." One remark from that first occasion especially intrigued me: "Enlightenment is the goal of your master's life." This was a man, I thought, who would not yield even to a Zen master, an impression subsequently strengthened when Abe confirmed an account I'd heard from DeMartino: The repercussion of a *sanzen* interview, he'd been banned from the very monastery I had just entered for accusing the previous master of play acting.

My own first tenure at the monastery was a failed one. Life hitherto had been too devoid of suffering, of persistence, to ready me for the physical and psychic shock that was to abruptly ensue. Abe visited frequently to bail me out. I could not bow properly, or even dress myself. I could not fold a kimono were it to cost the world. When I bitched that I was getting entangled in a bunch of secondary stuff, Abe noted simply: "The monastic forms are dead. Only you can give them life."

Later I learned that, for Abe, what "gave life" was not mastery but compassion. "It is the law of the Buddha," he said, "not to destroy life. If so, one cannot eat. The notion that it is justifiable to kill plants but not animals is an illusion of anthropocentricism. But if we do not eat, we destroy ourselves, still violating the Buddhist law. This is the significance of the *gasshō*, the pressing together of the palms, before taking a meal. One destroys life so as not to destroy life, but one does so only at the ultimate heartfelt limit."

What beauty of man, what ferocity of inner struggle must have been needed to create such simple beauty of phrase! And thus the *gasshō*, formed by my hands before each sitting, each bow, each meal—dead, illimitably far from an ultimate heartfelt limit I was not yet human enough to achieve—became, as with every other form of this universe, a wall. One that, it soon became clear, would have to be scaled from an encampment somewhat distanced from those of the monastery. Still, as I regrouped in America, something of Abe seemed to abide. He had instilled my failure with dignity, always referring to me in the presence of others as his friend, even as I succumbed to my downward spiral. He had been able, when the pain of meditation thwarted me in my most critical aspiration, to convey to me its gorgeousness, as if to know it in its depths turned the breath to champagne. He had been uncompromising in his insistence that I must be able to persist in meditation alone. And he set before me a cliff that at once gave partial illumination to the austerity of his own undertaking with a spare piece of advice: "You must kill yourself at every instant."

Three years later, a few days after my return to Japan, I met him in his study. He seemed to be testing my resolve. I had arranged a new strategy, sitting the nightly hours with the monks and moving into the monastery for only the weeklong *sesshin* that occurred several times per year. The monastery master had already acceded to this. Professor Abe, too, seemed satisfied. He described me with the phrase "kendo chōrai o kisuru"—to emerge from a setback with redoubled efforts.

Still, the Zen path has its own inevitable logic, in Professor Abe's one-of-a-kind understanding of inevitability. For him, the word meant "the undeniable necessity," as he called it, the necessity that could no longer be dodged. He warned often that one might never reach this point—it was not inevitable in that sense—yet *had to* come to it if one was to prevail. It could not be forced. Failing to arrive at the undeniable necessity, people suffer on in situations they know are untenable for years. "What will you do at the edge of life and death?" he demanded, patrol stick poised over his shoulder at a *sesshin* of the FAS group, founded around Hisamatsu during the war, in which I had become a participant. But how does one achieve the edge of life and death, without which an answer to this challenge is impossible? DeMartino, in an exposition of the "Right Aspiration" of Gautama's Eightfold Path, had said: "It's not enough to want enlightenment. You've got to need it." The disparity between wanting and needing tore at my heart and legs with dramatic force, and the thought of dying without awakening generated an anguish matched only by the bewilderment that the force of this anguish could not be converted into anything more than sporadic effort. One may volunteer for the Zen quest. But one is conscripted into the Zen wars.

I was then, as I suppose must always be the case, pulled into the vacuum in spite of myself. The abandonment of the half for the full lotus became for me the personal symbol in the struggle against the impulse to shrink back from the edge, resulting in an unintended asceticism that bared me to the grid of my ambivalence. Tears fell onto my clasped hands as I meditated, the realization that the last thing I wanted in this world was to maintain my sitting posture even one more period quarreling with the thought that the last thing I could do was to waver. Abe observed only that the struggle with pain and the doubting of its validity was a problem that every serious practitioner of Zen must confront. He assured me that the question would remain in my mind as long as I had the luxury to raise it.

He would say: "Ordinary education is to add on. Zen education is to take away." And he knew well the paradox that an ever-increasing honing of the power of the will could bear fruit only when this power expended itself to exhaustion. At my explanation in the back of a trolley that the intensification of effort had merely brought greater awareness of my powerlessness, he was incredulous: "*You* still think you have power! Self-negation is the only ultimate power."

Presenting me with an English translation of the *Record of Lin-chi*, he inscribed in Chinese characters a line from the text: "Seeking Buddha and seeking dharma is only making hell karma." He remarked that when he had come upon this sentence, it had brought him to the brink of collapse. Intrigued, I asked what had transpired in the wake of that encounter. Letting me know once and for all that curiosity is barren with what really counts, he said, coolly: "Find out for yourself."

———◆———

Aware, during my initial stint in Kyoto, that I would not persevere at the monastery, Abe met my dejection, and more importantly my fear, which was far less transient, with a *juzu,* or Buddhist rosary, made from dried fruit of the Bodhi Tree in Bodhgaya where Gautama—unable to marshal a further step—was brought to the final impasse. It was a precious gift—a symbol of his faith in my capacity to carry my quest to its consummation in the absence of any warranting sign—too large for the wrist and so worn around my bicep. Eventually it was to slip unnoticed from my arm, to my great regret. But the Bodhi Tree is without form and does not slip off so easily. It is planted where man is planted, the contradiction around which human existence is coiled and from which it recoils.

I now see that all of Abe's offerings were the fruits of this tree, beads on a *juzu* that with each addition shrank the circumference of its circle, choking off the possibility of getaway. Inexhaustible in his unwillingness to stop the discussion until I was satisfied how next to proceed, that he held finally that one was to be deprived of every way of proceeding is not to be doubted. This, regarding what might be called "method" in Zen, was the jewel of his inheritance from Hisamatsu. "When cornered there is a change; where there is a change there is a passing through"—words I would later encounter with frequency in Hisamatsu's writings—I first heard from Abe. But it was not his style to press the matter. It was only in response to my overt indication that fleeing might no longer be an option that he advised: "You must try to corner yourself as much as possible." When I showed I could not, there was not the slightest trace of disappointment or disapproval. To my confession that my whole life had been reduced to the duality of confronting the Zen quest and evading it, he merely remarked: "You need not try to find some third position. You need only to get to the bottom of that opposition."

I understood him to mean that the attempt to achieve a "pure effort" that would eliminate the impulse to evade was vain; what was essential, by contrast, was to be deadlocked in the depths of the inescapable oscillation between the two poles. This deadlock—the final cornering—was the "great doubt block" in Hisamatsu's meaning of the term. In his autobiographical account of the situation immediately prior to his own awakening, he describes it as "black, and with no means of escape left open in the entirety of his existence, not even one the size of a hole in a needle . . . as though one were to climb to the tip of a pole 300 feet tall, and then find oneself unable to advance, to descend again, or to maintain one's position." I still own the napkin on which Abe scrawled the diagram wherein he argued that meditation alone, while approaching it, could never achieve the crown of that pole, that sitting, too, would have to be undercut if the great doubt—in Hisamatsu's sense of absolute contradiction, absolute agony, and absolute dilemma—is to be achieved. Hisamatsu had hammered this in emphatically. "I was at an extremity," Abe recounted to me in his study. "I said to Hisamatsu: 'For many years I have struggled for a place to stand but have not been able to find one.' Hisamatsu replied: 'You must stand where there is no place to stand.'"

This was in consonance with Hisamatsu's strong advocacy of a cherished phrase from *The Gateless Barrier*: "In order to attain the wondrous Awakening, it is necessary for all routes of mind [and body] to be brought to the extremity and extinguished." Yet I who could find no way to bring my paths to an end ran forward but could not get free of the starting blocks, ran away but could not get free of the need to run forward. Abe made me a gift of a calligraphy he had in his turn been given by Hisamatsu—"Extinguish-in-sitting the dusty world"—and a year subsequent, a copy of the painting, attributed to Sesshū, of Hui-k'o presenting to Bodhidharma his severed arm. But these affirmations of my exertions were invariably countered by Abe's insistence that they be brought to a standstill at the cusp of maximum effort and the impossibility of advance. "Gautama deadlocked at the Bodhi Tree is the negation of Buddhist practice," he said, adding, before I could respond: "Gautama at the Bodhi Tree is the fulfillment of Buddhist practice."

I found myself increasingly pulled apart: a tautening of contradictory forces thrusting the mouth open and the eyes dangerously shut as I bicycled from English lessons to the interview with the monastery master; an expanded balloon whose air is anguish in meditation, neck lashing backward in hundreds of paroxysms during a three-month season of *sesshin*. Still I remained what characterizes—contrary to Exodus—man and not God: a tangle of branches that burns and burns but cannot burn out. When I laid this "intensity" before Abe mid-*sesshin* outside the gate of Reiun-in Temple, he dismissed it with indifference: "Psychological, not ontological." This was disturbing, not because he was rejecting any attempt on my part to exhibit a resolution—I had none. Rather, after so much heartache on what I took to be the Zen path, I had been confiscated in my attempt to express even the problem at the first move. Feeling I had no recourse, I challenged his characterization. To this he pressed me gently, just firmly enough between the shoulder and heart for me to fall backward, saying, as he turned to other business: "What are you going to do with that?"

———◆———

Thus does one touch render impossible an entire world, though one touch is sure to redeem it. And when I ask myself why I was worth his bother on so many occasions over so many years, I know it is because he honors what he calls man's "burning problem." That I could not yet burn as the phoenix burns seemed never to be a concern. He regulated his life by the absurd equation of gratitude that I have noted in a few other great beings. As a natural speaker of English living nearby, I could do a little for him by going over his essays; he did everything in his power for me in return. DeMartino's talent was to block you halfway through your question, grasp its intent, and floor you with a single retort. "The mama lion throws its cubs over the cliff and feeds those who can climb back up" were his words, and his style. Abe stood at the opposite remove, willing to talk until two in the morning so that

I left his home clear about the next nuanced step. You could not tire him or make him tire of you. He burned at a low, even flame. I'd go from our editing sessions to my tiny three-tatami room and flop onto my futon; Abe would go to his writing desk with whatever essay I was assisting him with, dropping the revised manuscript in my mailbox before dawn.

The first time Abe visited me in the monastery, days after my arrival in Japan, he said that meditation must be without either bodily or mental tension; instead, a "spiritual" tension was imperative. In the trenches, it is hard to separate this last from the others. Once at a *sesshin*, when the bell rang marking the transition from the seated to the walking meditation, the release from the full lotus set me into uncontainable laughter as we circled the veranda. The next afternoon, as we were both rinsing our hands, Abe was ebullient. "Last night I heard you laughing during the walking. That's the tension . . . Oh. Very good sign!" Later, when I inquired whether it was better, when leg pain made concentration on the koan difficult, to abandon the koan and try to become one with the pain until the sitting period's end, he advised against it: "You may not be able to achieve this Oneness before the bell rings, but if you throw yourself into the koan, it is sure to be intense."

Yet it was without words that Abe gave portent of what spiritual intensity would have to mean. The initial block of the evening sitting periods had terminated, and the bell rang for the walking meditation. Abe fronted the queue, and I, on the cushions next to him, was second in line. As we stepped barefoot along the temple side of the wooden veranda, I noticed a thick line of icy slush along its far edge, parallel to the garden, remnants from a recent snow. It was directly in our course as we turned into the third leg of the lap, but Abe could have easily averted it by establishing the path a foot to the inside. Terribly susceptible to the cold, I urged him in my mind on to the dry wood. Instead, he accelerated, trampling right into the snow, and there was no choice but to follow. Coming back from the urinal, I prepared to resume my place in line. Palms pressed together, I watched him steadily as he stormed round the veranda, for as soon as he was past, I was obliged to bow quickly and slip in behind him. Two seconds from me I caught the full force of his visage. I knew then that he had not simply stomped into that snow; he had blowtorched it.

As an episode, it is inconsequential, but it gave me a glimpse of some decisions Abe had made a long time before. That kind of fierceness cannot be given by another. Nonetheless, in response to a letter I'd written him at Princeton, he made it quite clear that in the end there is no retreat. His response reads in part:

> It is true that Gautama rejected asceticism. But asceticism means undergoing pain for its own sake, or enduring the pain as if that itself were the means of attaining awakening. This is simply a form of morbidity. The unintended pain that may accompany hard meditation practice in the quest for the true Self, on the other hand, was never rejected by Gautama.

Enclosed with the letter was a photocopy of some remarks of Dōgen on the Sung master Ta-hui, one passage from it marked in red. When I'd read it, I knew that I was boxed in, just as I was locked out.

The postmark reads from 1978. Though other discussions ensued, mostly regarding the preparation of Abe's book *Zen and Western Thought,* I consider it our last critical exchange. Perhaps I will make a response, but none is possible now. Too easy to lie to oneself about these things.

———————◆———————

I will not duplicate what I have written previously about the day Abe took me to meet Hisamatsu, who having slain self and universe in what Zen calls the Great Death stood where there is no place to stand. I believe I learned that afternoon what Rilke must have meant when he wrote that beauty deigns to destroy us, for though it was not his design, the encounter with Hisamatsu tore me to shreds, reducing me to a spasmodic wailing of unprecedented intensity and duration. At the time, I saw the meaning of this reaction as the cross formed from the intersection of coming face to face with Hisamatsu's Great Peace and the terrifying dread of the path that loomed before me if that peace were in fact to be attained. But subsequently I came to know that these tears possessed an additional meaning. They brought me to the certitude of what Abe had always maintained: "Compassion is the supreme inner reality." That it was not as its embodiment but as its negation that I found this certainty does not diminish it. Those tears remain the rare "ocular proof" that when Jesus said to lose yourself is to find yourself, when Socrates replied to his accusers that if he was put to death "you will harm yourselves more than me," they spoke truth.

It interests me that Abe's direct comment on my tears was silence. Neither at Hisamatsu's house nor in the taxi back to Gifu Station, where my sobbing endured unabated, nor at any point on the return train to Kyoto did he offer a word. Only in response to a question as we rode the bus toward the neighborhood where we both resided did he finally talk, as if unwilling to intrude on what had transpired for me alone. Then he said only that I had experienced a "great encounter" and, in reply to my confessed fright of being plunged into the abyss: "Today you met a man who leapt into that abyss. Look at the result!"

But though he made no mention of them, I am convinced that he knew those tears even before I had wept them. Abe once told, from a sutra parable, of doves ardently in love with a forest that they discover desperately ablaze. Their sole remedy—soaking their wings in the waters of a nearby lake—is hopeless, the water evaporating in the air en route. The doves repeat the process, again without effect, and repeat it again. A rare droplet douses a flame, no more than this. But love is its own destiny, and the doves are impelled to the perpetual recapitulation of virtually doomed passion. This, without its sentiment, is the vow of the bodhisattva.

Years, too, have evaporated, and Abe with them, since he voiced those words to members of the lay group of the retired, soon-to-die Hisamatsu, encircled on the tatami of the Reiun-in Temple in a lovely evening infused with the stillness of meditation. I am now of the mind that the lake consists of the bodhisattva's tears, hidden in the flames, hidden even from the bodhisattva himself. Hisamatsu, in his explication of Zen art, calls it "austere sublimity" or "lofty dryness," words that explain to me the meaning of tears met with silence. It is this that I first beheld in the passage "As we go to part a tall bamboo stands by the gate; its leaves stir the clear breeze for you in farewell" and sensed the pierced heart of the master, his task completed, who would never again see his greatest disciple. It is this that I was honored to witness in the unshaven countenance of DeMartino the afternoon he made his farewell *mondō* to his deceased friend Bernard Phillips, comrade in the pioneer American quest for Zen, as he sat cross-legged in a small room of students common to them both. It is this that I have loved so well, though from an infinite distance, in Wu-tsu Fa-yen's sole response to his long-struggling disciple Fo-kuo at the moment of his enlightenment, in which can be traced the imprint of Abe's uttermost aspiration: "The great affair of life that has caused the Buddhas and patriarchs to appear among us is not meant for small characters and inferior vessels. I am glad that I have been a help to your delight."

Between Straw Fedora and Wood Clogs

I am not contained between my hat and boots.
—Walt Whitman

WITH THE *sesshin*'s end, I slid open the paper-paneled door. Tokiwa-san stood alone in the three-tatami room, changing from kimono to his street clothes. "I'm so glad nothing happened," he said. "If it had, I would have had to reject it."

His words caused me to double take. I had pushed myself in meditation hard; that "nothing had happened" was the last thing I wanted. Bent over my bags, I looked up at him, his back toward me. "And just now," he continued, seemingly to no one, "as we were chanting the Heart Sutra, I thought: How true, how right!"

It was only that evening, alone at dinner in a coffee shop, that a brief fragment from that sutra entered my mind: "No eye, no ear, no nose, no tongue, no mind, no consciousness."

———◆———

A memory from an early *sesshin*: His patrol round the meditation hall completed, Tokiwa-san, standing in the corner of the hall, patrol stick held erect, speaking in his soothing tone to we who cannot be soothed lest we "die" from our wound: "In their conversation at Harvard in 1957, Dr. Hisamatsu said to Paul Tillich: 'True meditation must be object-less.'" After an extended silence, he added: "Dr. Hisamatsu then told Professor Tillich: 'True meditation must also be subject-less.'"

———— ◆ ————

Returning after lunch to a *sesshin* at Chotoku-in Temple, I spotted, as I turned onto the gravel road leading to the entrance, the form of a young man, twenty-eight to thirty years old, ambling before me in the distance. He slipped into the temple gate. As the *sesshin* was poorly attended, I was curious as to the identity of this new participant. A moment later I, too, passed through the gate and just outside the meditation hall found Tokiwa-san, who'd been in attendance since the first day. I hunted around for the man who had just arrived but could find no one. I went back to the temple foyer. Besides mine, there was only one pair of shoes. Tokiwa-san was sixty-two at the time.

Now, at seventy,[51] with at last some first signs of age, his lightness and the speed of his movement are amazing. He is still fifty from the front and thirty from behind. At a *sesshin* a few months ago, I saw ahead of me in the final walking meditation of the evening a graduate student who, as the line turned, showed a profile reminiscent of Tokiwa-san's, and only after a futile search for him among the others in the darkness did I understand the reason for the resemblance.

The first time I ever set eyes on him, at my first weekly meeting of FAS, he said to me, in English: "My name is Tokiwa. Evergreen." In that play on the Chinese characters of his surname there was already something of his mystery, for I had taken him to be in his thirties when he was fifty-two. But some years later, when I commented on his eternal youth, he explained this mystery away with another one—if one sees beyond the words—of far more interest: "I do not age because I am unable to mature."

———— ◆ ————

Howard Curtis once said of Tokiwa-san: "He's like a utility infielder that plays every day and bats .460."

———————◆———————

Some weeks after being compelled by the departure of all senior members—through age, through death, through busyness, through bruised ego—to take charge of the group that had for decades formed itself around Hisamatsu, Tokiwa-san appraised his tenure with the judgment: "I am a cancer to this organization."

At a *sesshin*, learning from Howard Curtis a new English vocabulary word as they translated Hisamatsu's poem—"The koan / The scarecrow of a monk's soul"—he pronounced himself thereafter a "scarecrow meditation hall chief." The fifth evening of the same *sesshin*, he told me: "During walking meditation, I was thinking: How deeply everyone is absorbed in their meditation. Only I am wandering about with superficial and deluded thoughts." When, having finally freed himself of other obligations, he arrived on day four of another *sesshin*, he responded to my request for some advice, saying: "You have been deep in meditation for several days, and I arrive only now with no concentration. I doubt in such circumstances my comments could be of any use."

At a *sesshin* reflective of the diminished fortunes of the FAS group— only three members present—Tokiwa-san tried to apologize in public for letting Hisamatsu down and broke into tears.

———————◆———————

In an attempt to intensify my effort, I had stopped moving with the period-ending bell, inspired by the meditation Prometheus Toyoshima-san to sit two periods in succession. This achieved nothing, and first night of the next *sesshin*, I decided to see if matters could be brought to an extremity by trying to sit through the night. The next morning I met Tokiwa-san in the lavatory.

"You didn't sleep last night, did you?"

"No," I confirmed.

"I slept like a pig," he said.

With the *sesshin* ended, walking back to Hanazono University from the customary service at Kitarō Nishida's grave in Reiun-in Temple, I ran into Tokiwa-san coming, apparently, from his office.

"I ought not to criticize you, but your method will not bring you what you want," he warned. Then, in response to my silence, he added, "Meditation is the basic posture, to which I always return. I am therefore able to move about freely."

I listened, but I was boxed in. It did not seem possible to change course. Yet the wild spasms that too often accompanied my sitting— and therefore his words—frightened me.

"Zen emphasizes the need to exacerbate the problem," I countered.

"From the standpoint of Buddhism, Zen Buddhism is very young."

To this I again said nothing.

"Meditation is the dharma of tranquility," he continued. "You may be aware there has long been a question as to whether Hakuyūshi, the hermit said to have given Hakuin the method of cure for his illness, actually existed. Some hold that recent investigations confirm that he did. And yet I am inclined to believe that Hakuin, severely ill from the severity of his practice, found it necessary to invent Hakuyūshi. You too, perhaps, will invent him for yourself."

He then offered something I at that time thought unconnected. Now I am not so sure. "When I was a student at Kyoto University, I was obliged to present my understanding of an aspect of Buddhism in a setting at which Dr. Hisamatsu was present. Nine years later he said to me, 'On that occasion you were wrong.' It was then that I realized that Dr. Hisamatsu lives in eternity and exists only for the human problem."

Before the evening meditation, in the middle of a *sesshin,* I ran into Iki-san, a bit tense that he'd been forced by circumstance into the role of meditation hall chief. "What about Tokiwa-sensei?" I asked, as he'd filled that capacity the first four days. Iki-san replied that Tokiwa-san was gone for the day. Two new students who could neither speak nor hear would be entering Hanazono University with the new semester, and he'd enrolled in a sign language course so as to be able to communicate in the event they would be members of his class.

I approached Tokiwa-san with an agonizing concern central to my quest, and to the very *sesshin* in which we were that day embroiled. "Let's ask Kitahara-sensei," he replied, "before I say something that will bring a lot of trouble to us both."

Two days before the summer *sesshin,* to be held in a mountain village north of Kyoto, news came that the cook and his assistant would not be available. An American friend in whose house I lived volunteered to serve as cook. I, inept in the kitchen, agreed to assist him. We did the necessary shopping in Kyoto and, packing the groceries on the back of the American's motorcycle, headed out.

The night we arrived, however, we were suddenly summoned to a meeting of some urgency. Seated around a large dining table were K— the head of the organization in whose premises the *sesshin* was to be held—Tokiwa-san, and a couple in their early forties: the cooking staff, it turned out, who were able to assume their duties after all. Despite our assurances, we were unable to convey to Tokiwa-san that we had not wanted to sacrifice our *sesshin* to the kitchen and were only too glad to be rid of the job. He inferred that our insistence that we'd just as soon meditate was motivated by politeness, and his sense of obligation to our being permitted to cook grew in direct proportion to our dis-avowal of any desire to do so. The meeting, consequently, went on for more than an hour. Finally a compromise was worked out in Japanese among the Japanese. We were to prepare the first morning's breakfast, after which the official staff would take over the task for the duration.

That one meal, consisting of toast and a mixture of oatmeal, wheat germ, and fruit, was the fare I consumed each morning at home. I readily admit it's sad-looking—Urs App once called it disgusting—but I eat for nutrition, not for taste. The next morning, after the predawn meditation, members filed into the dining hall, plunked their shins onto the hard wood floor, and sat before the steaming porridge. They consumed the toast, but with this gone and nowhere else to go except to the remaining food, they began to avail themselves of a technique I had mastered as a child to camouflage hatred of a dish my mother demanded I finish off: squishing the oatmeal in their bowls with their chopsticks in the hope of making it appear a diminishing amount. Though feeling somewhat guilty at being the cause of their suffer-ing, I had to laugh, remembering the times, eating in restaurants in Japan, people I did not even know would approach with the challenge: "Eat this *natto*!"[52] . . . "Eat this squid!" welcoming me, if I passed the test, with a friendly slap on the back that confirmed my manhood, announcing to boot that I was "like a Japanese." But now, the situation reversed, it was evident that these tough Zen practitioners, willing, as they had repeatedly shown, to meditate through hell, were not about to get their tongues anywhere near the rest of the breakfast. In due course, with the oatmeal pushed about and squashed to its limit, they one by one set their chopsticks on the table, returning, outwardly at least, to meditation. The ensuing stillness, however, made me cognizant of a final continuing motion, of more worth to me today than that entire week's meditation, long since faded into nothing. At the far corner of the dining hall, posture erect, dignified, sat Tokiwa-san, oblivious of the others, gobbling in total absorption what his every expression said was one of the greatest meals of his life. At length he finished. Quietly, looking straight ahead, he lay down his bowl. Then, breaking the silence of the meal customary to the Zen tradition, silence now total with the rattling of every utensil quelled, there came from his lips—soft, yet with unmistakable conviction—"Delicious!"

———————•———————

My heart as if crushed in a vise, I sat by the garden through the break between the evening meal and the onset of the evening meditation. As I stood, I saw Tokiwa-san, who without my realizing it, too, had emerged onto the veranda.

"My sitting is entirely without tranquility. I feel only agony," I told him.

"The calm of the 'Vow of Humankind'[53] is ontological, not psychological," he replied. "The true realization of that calm is, I believe, intimately related to noise and disturbance." The consoling beauty of his voice broke me, and an avalanche of longing to relinquish the burden of myself propelled me into his arms. I wept and I wept. Beneath the darkening sky, he held me in silence.

———————•———————

At the conclusion of one *sesshin*, I ran into Tokiwa as we gathered our things in preparation for the return home: "I am too attached to the feeling of meditation," he said.

———————•———————

One evening midway through a winter *sesshin*, as we huddled in the tearoom on the electric carpet provided us by Chotoku-in Temple, Y, a Japanese American, recounted a recent conversation he had had with the chief priest of the temple wherein he, I gather, had been renting his living quarters. "If you truly want to enter the Way, you will have to become a monk," the priest had told him. "Still, this is not a decision you have to make now. When you are ready." It was clear from Y's tone that he held these words in high regard and that he was impressed even more with the patient generosity of his benefactor.

Knowing that he'd rejected his priest father's wishes and forsworn the obligation to enter the priesthood and become heir to the family temple, knowing he'd written that the only possible "refuge" for human existence was not the Buddhist *sangha*[54] but the awakened Self, I was curious as to how Tokiwa-san would react. He was silent, looking markedly unconcerned. In his face I could read nothing.

Three days later, when the *sesshin* had ended and we had only to chant the Heart Sutra to close the occasion, Tokiwa-san offered, atop his sitting cushions as meditation hall chief, some parting remarks. Throughout these he made no reference whatsoever to Y's tale, but suddenly, his voice full of passion, he ended: "I do not yield to any monk."

———————◆———————

Professor H, riding the crest of a wave of renown in American academic religious circles, had come to Kyoto to offer two lectures. Tokiwa-san was to interpret. Not content with the inevitable imperfections of an on-the-spot translation, he threw himself into a whirlwind of activity. In the seventy-two hours before the lectures were to occur, he produced completed Japanese versions of the texts for both. What impressed me was that this immense labor had been invested in lectures that could not have been more transient. They were given and they were gone—never to be published in Japanese—to an audience consisting largely of Japanese scholars who seemed to share little of Professor H's concerns. The preparation for the translated manuscripts must have taken twenty times longer than the combined total of the two events.

The second of the talks, two days after the opening presentation at Hanazono University, took place at Rakuyu Kaikan on the grounds of Kyoto University. The small room was filled. Professor H sat center stage, Tokiwa-san next to him. At one point the American lit up a cigarette, and while his sentences were being rendered into Japanese, Professor H, looking very philosophical, for some minutes blew the exhaled smoke directly into Tokiwa-san's face. With the smoke permeating his breathing channels as he spoke, Tokiwa-san fell into a severe spasm of coughing. He forced himself onward, his duty as interpreter overriding the mere demand of the human organism for air, but in the end, the sentences would no longer form. Professor H, cigarette in hand, gazed at the struggling Tokiwa-san. He seemed to be wondering what might be the cause of his affliction, all the while continuing to attack him with smoke in the thoroughly unventilated room. At length the professor inquired if Tokiwa-san might not like a cup of tea. Tokiwa gasped out in reply: "Could someone open a window?" and then hastened to the onrush of air as this was done. In a moment, having regained an equilibrium of breathing, he resumed his seat and proceeded with his translation.

The next time I saw Tokiwa-san, I could not resist asking how it was possible that Professor H, who had opened his lecture with the observation that as a theologian he was "paid to think," had been so busy thinking that he'd been oblivious to the fact that he was the cause of Tokiwa's distress. Tokiwa-san tilted his head, gave it a second's thought, and said: "Perhaps he was tired."

———————◆———————

In the years when I was writing my doctoral thesis, Tokiwa-san, with rare generosity, made himself ever available in my attempts to understand Hisamatsu's Japanese. I would come to his office at Hanazono University every so often in the afternoon. We'd drink tea and talk, and then for the next two or three hours he would answer questions and check my understanding of the text. What makes a man a man is often small things: When he produced two oranges to go with our tea and I confessed that my body reacted badly to citrus, he left his orange untouched.

I arrived early one Friday afternoon at the hour that had been previously arranged. Tokiwa-san, with great calm, told me that he'd have to leave immediately at the close of our session: His father had suffered a stroke, had fallen into a coma, and was not expected to survive the weekend. I cannot easily explain my feeling; it was one of those moments when you find reflected in the inner beauty of another the meaning of your own true being by seeing how terribly far from it you are. I had no telephone and could not be reached, and Tokiwa-san, who'd received this news the night before, had delayed his departure to be at his father's last rather than break a promise.

The following week, when I returned to Hanazono, I was struck again by the quiet of his movement. His father had somehow pulled out of the coma. They had conversed, and he was much improved. "My father, in my youth," he said, "had expected me to succeed him as a priest and to take over the family temple. When I was adamant in my refusal, he was extremely displeased. He is now in his middle nineties, but I am quite confident he will persist in the strength to live for quite a long time so that he may continue on with his criticisms."

———◆———

The week before the *sesshin,* in the mountains north of Kyoto, I'd heard of an episode that had occurred there the previous year. An American had been severely reprimanded by K, the owner of the premises, for using two flat cushions placed side by side to support his knees, citing the monastic rule that neither knees nor sitting cushion are permitted to extend beyond the width of one tatami mat. Tokiwa-san, I was told, had not sympathized with the reprimand but had felt, as a guest, that he was not in a position to countermand K's prohibition.

This episode was in the back of my mind the days before the *sesshin,* as at that time I sat with cushions piled unusually high. (At the monastery where I trained, someone chided that I sat on the third floor.) In consequence, the full lotus posture placed severe pressure on my knees. If they hung over the bottom cushion, my knees dug into the tatami—okay for a couple of hours—but for a *sesshin* of an entire week, it was quite painful and, to my mind, quite pointless.

Once in the meditation hall, therefore, exactly as the American had done the year previous, I proceeded to set up my pillows on a base of two adjacent flat cushions. I was crouched as I sought a suitable arrangement, but out of the corner of my eye I saw K storming toward me, eyeing me carefully to see if I was going to violate the rule. I knew what was coming but played dumb. K was standing over me, and soon Tokiwa-san was standing behind him. Suddenly, in a moment of devilish inspiration, I discerned that if I turned the two flat cushions lengthwise, they would fit exactly within the confines of a single tatami mat. I rapidly made the move. K, thwarted, was speechless. He stared at the cushions, hunting for a reason to ban what I'd done, then walked away, leaving me a direct view of Tokiwa-san. He was smiling. That rascal Tokiwa, the kindest, most sincere of men—for me the epitome of an increasingly diminishing breed of what for centuries has been called the Confucian gentleman—had within him a strong touch of the anarchist after all. His smile was the sanction. By the second day, more than half of the participants had two cushions, turned lengthwise, neatly placed within the black stripes bordering their tatamis.

———————◆———————

At the closing moments of a *sesshin* at Tokai-an, the ancient priest who had kindly offered the use of his temple came to the meditation hall to bid us farewell. In turn, seventy-year-old Sekiun Koretsune recalled the potato broth that this same priest had unexpectedly fed the sitters during a freezing *sesshin* decades before. Rendering this into English, Tokiwa-san began to smack his lips gently, cutting across time, salivating lightly at the invisible steaming bowl apparently now before him. At a 1986 *sesshin,* interpreting a talk I was asked to give into Japanese, he seemed to bask in the words, no longer simply translating but re-creating the lecture. The poet Philip Whalen, himself a Zen priest, has written: "I'll sing. You do the translations." But with Tokiwa-san, the translation is the song.

The only exponent of "interpreter *samadhi*" in the history of the world?

———————◆———————

Tokiwa-san called me to his office to go over the English of some "response papers" he was preparing for a conference in America. There were three of them. At the top of each was the name of a professor (one bore two names), followed by the title of the paper each professor was slated to present. We met often over the next few weeks, Tokiwa-san in high gear making his writings ready.

On the final reworking before he was to leave for the United States, I remarked on the difficulty of being obliged to present a public response to three separate papers.

"Oh, I'm not presenting anything at the conference."

I was puzzled. "You are scheduled to offer a response to Professors Cook, Kaufman, Cobb, and Hopkins, no?"

"No. I'm not on any of the panels."

"But what about all the work you've been doing? . . . Your essays?"

"A mere private expression. One by one, as I discern a moment convenient for them, I'll hand over the related response to each of the professors."

"Hiring the idiot-sage to fill the well with snow," the Zen master Hsueh-tou calls it.

———————◆———————

Regarding Hisamatsu's fundamental koan "Whatever you do will not do. What do you do?" Tokiwa-san has often said, "'Will not do' likewise will not do." But he has also written: "The mere raising of a single hand, insofar as it is rooted in the irretrievable discrimination of self and world, is just so much contamination of history."

———◆———

After one *sesshin,* Tokiwa-san told me: "I spent the whole week thinking about history." Having spent—because I viewed *sesshin* as the primary occasion to wrest free from myself—the entire week preoccupied with myself, this was an inconceivable utterance.

———◆———

Striking the wood blocks to end the evening sitting on Christmas Eve of the winter *sesshin* of 1978, Tokiwa-san in his beautiful voice said: "That among humans, whose true way of being is to be nothing, there existed a man who could be worshipped for nearly two thousand years, is *something*. And so, though I am not a Christian, I wish those who are: Merry Christmas."

———◆———

In Alberta, Canada, trying to get an extended visa for my third stay in Japan, I had written a letter to Tokiwa-san asking him to serve as my guarantor. I had enclosed a copy of a document I'd submitted to the Japanese embassy in Alberta in which I'd described him as a professor of Buddhism, an assumption I'd made as a matter of course since he'd been offering classes in Buddhism at Hanazono University during my previous stint in Japan. He sent back the needed document, attaching to it a personal letter for me. He would do everything in his power to help me, he wrote, but he was deeply concerned that his letter to the embassy would be ineffective. For he was not a professor of Buddhism, only a teacher of English. Thus it was that a status he would never have regretted for himself became a source of regret in that it might fail me.

His letter to the embassy procured for me the visa. When I arrived in Kyoto, he brought me to the Institute for Zen Studies, where he'd arranged a place for me to research my dissertation. When I expressed the next day my worry that I would come to be an intrusion on the workers in such a small space, he sought permission for me to study in the Hanazono University library. When this was denied, he offered me his office.

I tore the meniscus in my right knee at the June *sesshin* of the monastery where I trained. Unable to cross my legs, barely able to walk, I missed the Saturday evening meditation of the FAS group.

The following day, tired of lying in bed, I hobbled out to the Kamo River to exercise my knee. As I limped back toward the temple in which I lived, I saw someone sitting unconcerned on a low stone wall outside the temple gate. It was Tokiwa-san. Hearing of my injury at the meeting the preceding evening, he had made the trip from Osaka. He'd been waiting an hour and a half.

The pain from the full lotus sometimes caused me to groan when the bell rang and I released myself from the posture. A friend, considering this an indulgence, said to me in criticism, "Look at Tokiwa-san. You don't even know he's there."

When I said something Tokiwa-san could affirm, he never said: "You're right" but rather: "I agree with you."

———◆———

Once at his office, when we worked into the evening, Tokiwa-san called his wife to say that he'd be late. From the gentle tone of his opening words: "Watashi desu" (It's me), I knew everything I'd ever have to about his marriage.

———◆———

At a friend's house I came upon a catalog in English describing the academic programs of various Japanese universities. Turning to the entry for Hanazono, I was surprised to see that the description, in a publication whose raison d'être was to promote the schools, contained a subtle criticism of the college, one intended as an encouragement for Hanazono to rise to its full potential, but a criticism nonetheless. I laughed, quite sure I could guess who had written it. Later on I received confirmation that I had not been mistaken. For who else on earth would be thrust by his sincerity beyond the commonsense purposes of advertising and turn the blurb into an occasion for his university to engage in self-reflection, even, if read carefully, it might actually decrease enrollment?

———◆———

At the funeral of Professor J, who while problematic had been a member of Hisamatsu's group for more than forty years, I was told that among the long-standing members, Tokiwa-san alone had been in attendance.

———◆———

Watching Tokiwa-san prepare for meditation, I know he is a careful man. When he first enters the Zen hall after an absence from sitting, he sits with legs loosely crossed so as not to injure the knees. After a moment he assumes the half lotus; a moment later, the full lotus posture. It seems that only when he is sure of his flexibility does he go into the full lotus at the outset.

———————◆———————

Tokiwa-san's posture in meditation is one of the two most beautiful I have seen. The Thief, former head monk at my monastery, bursts from the lower torso like a tree erupting from the earth, his shoulders, in astonishing contrast, an evaporating mist. His form is explosive and forbidding. Tokiwa-san is at the opposite remove. Though perfectly erect, his frame, and a barely perceptible forward movement of the head, is inviting and soft. At an art exhibition, Masao Abe remarked to me about the slight bend at the hip in the statues of bodhisattvas—a sign of intimacy with sentient beings. Likewise to me is Tokiwa-san's meditation.

———————◆———————

When I observed to Tokiwa-san that Hisamatsu's fundamental koan "Whatever you do will not do. What do you do?" must include that meditation, too, "will not do," he said: "Yes. And yet I have great faith in this position of two buttocks and two knees touching the cushions, the back straight."

———————◆———————

I commented on Tokiwa-san's continual exertion of having to come, after a full workweek demanding a similar commute, all the way from Osaka to the Saturday evening FAS meeting in Kyoto and its two hours of meditation. "It's a good chance to sit," he said. That he could have meditated the same two hours at his home in less time than it would take to ride the train, take a bus to the temple, and ride back, and that he came primarily for the practice of the other members, he forgot to mention.

———————◆———————

When I asked his advice about meditation, Tokiwa-san said to me: "For years I failed completely—until recently."

———————◆———————

That three women, the first ever to do so in my understanding, gave lectures at the *sesshin* of 1977–1978 was due to the efforts of Tokiwa-san. He was also behind the failed attempt to amend the "Vow of Humankind," the bodhisattva vow of the FAS, to include—in addition to the rejection of distinctions of race, nation, or class originally written into the 1951 document—rejection of distinction of gender. When the change came to a vote, he was clobbered; he told me the ballot went against him something like thirty-seven to three. He informed me of this episode on my return to Japan, adding simply: "I was very depressed."

I remembered hearing that because of the enthusiasm he had shown for her work, one of these lecturers, the author Yasuko Mizoue, had offered to make a gift to Tokiwa-san of the entirety of her publications. He refused, insisting he would buy them instead.

The story charmed me, but I did not know how to politely substantiate its veracity. The last time I saw him, however, Tokiwa-san unknowingly confirmed it. I had asked him to corroborate my recollection of Mizoue-san's description of her meeting with Hisamatsu. My question must have triggered his memory, for augmenting his response, he added: "When Mizoue-san died, I asked six members of the FAS, five of them women, to write a remembrance. None of them was willing; they said she's not the kind of woman they like. So I wrote it myself. To prepare for this, I read her collected works, twenty volumes."

The piece appeared in an obscure journal of negligible circulation. Surely it was hardly read. For a woman but once briefly married, with no child to tend her grave, unworthy in some eyes of a eulogy, Tokiwa-san had read twenty volumes, his interview with the dead. "As we go to part," says Hsi-king in a verse, "a tall bamboo stands by the gate; its leaves stir the clear breeze for you in farewell."

———◆———

Tokiwa-san once said to me, in answer to a question: "These days, between 'before awakening' and 'after awakening,' there seems to be little difference."

———◆———

The last chapter of my dissertation on Hisamatsu was largely an attack on the naïveté of his political thought. Tokiwa-san's reaction to what I had written—"You—I mean all of us—must think through the matter further"—was disappointing, for I could not help regard it as a mere formal dismissal without any attempt at specific refutation of any of the components of an argument that world events make, it seems to me, increasingly irrefutable.

One of my main contentions was that a sheer *ahimsa*, or nonviolence, is untenable if Zen is to have a relevant social ethic. When Camus writes "All contemporary action leads to murder, direct or indirect," he is posing the koan: "Is it really more morally defensible or compassionate to allow the relatively innocent to be killed than it is to stop—through violent force if necessary—the more guilty from killing them?" Hisamatsu himself held that history is tragic; I argued among other things that there are tragic moments in history when you cannot simply allow people to be butchered or brutalized so that you can remain unstained.

Two years later I received a card from Tokiwa-san. It read:

A Happy New Year to you.

I have been reading ABRAHAM LINCOLN—A Biography by Benjamin P. Thomas, The Modern Library. New York. (I bought a copy at Huntington Library Bookstore, San Marino, California, last March). There I read how history moves in the direction in which Union is to be actualized, how many people had to die, and how great a president the American people had.

Sincerely yours,
Gishin Tokiwa

I was deeply touched as I read this. Not only for the tragic beauty of Lincoln, who in his second inaugural address, in the middle of America's bloodiest conflict, embraced his enemies in the words "With malice to none, with charity for all" and yet waged war to save the Union, in full knowledge that although "Both sides read the same Bible and pray to the same God. . . . The prayers of both could not be answered." Not only for the tragic death of Lincoln, despised unto assassination because, while fully conscious of the sin and evils of his own side, he found no recourse but to pursue "the right as God gives us to see the right."

I was moved because of a man who would not allow deeply held convictions and lifelong loyalty to his Zen teacher to block the continuance of his thinking and because of the honor in his sentence "There I read how history moves in the direction in which Union is to be actualized, [and] how many people had to die."

History moves toward union—and disunion. Many people will have to die. From the moment Hisamatsu tried to broaden the scope of Buddhist compassion, the vow of the bodhisattva is the tragedy of the bodhisattva.

———————◆———————

During a *sesshin* break, I asked Tokiwa-san why the incidences of awakening in meditation are so rare among the many Zen records. "It is true," he said, "though Hakuin awakened in meditation when he heard the sound of falling snow. But in meditation the external world is cut off, and so it is rather in having emerged from meditation, when the mind is struck by some outside stimulus, that one realizes it is not outside at all."

———————◆———————

At the *sesshin* north of Kyoto, because of the intense July heat, walking meditation—of far longer duration than usual—occurred along a main road of the village. Tokiwa-san would appear at the gate in Japanese wood clogs called *geta,* a straw fedora on his head. On the fifth night, we rose from our cushions amid an ominous thunder. I hoped, consequently, that the walking would take place indoors, but Ochi-san, chief of the meditation hall, led us briskly out the gate and five minutes later into a downpour. We retraced the path we came and Ochi-san, turning as we emerged again into the courtyard, acknowledged, lovably: "Lousy judgment!"

My lung X-rays at the time made doctors cringe, and I had been warned to avoid further weakening. On top of this I'd been plagued by nausea the entire *sesshin*. Soaked, absorbed in apprehensions of health, of time running out, I dried myself, changed, and left my room, pulled toward the meditation hall by an unrelenting need to get out from the succession of semi-adequate moments I call my life.

Near the end of the corridor, at the foot of the stairs leading to the meditation hall, I caught sight, from the corner of my eye, of Tokiwa-san. Profile turned toward me and hence unaware of my witness, he stood in his room, still in his wet clothes, white straw fedora on his head. He was fanning himself, leisurely, moving yet utterly stopped, dispassionate, without effort, without need of a future.

In this cascading discharge of unintended grace, I saw, I think, the true meditation of Tokiwa-san, the "basic posture to which," when no one is in need of him, he "always returns." He will live there and he will die there, probably unknown. Without ambition and hence unheralded, overlooked by the quickly bedazzled, he is the mirror without reflection in the left sleeve of the kimono of Hakuin's enlightenment dream: nothing next to the penetrating brilliance of the mirror in the right sleeve, until, with a second breakthrough glance (so Hakuin records), "I became aware that the luster of the mirror from the left sleeve was innumerable times brighter than the other."

Never with Wisdom . . .

M R. YI ARRIVED at my university with unsteady English. His lectures were often indecipherable, yet he laughed and laughed. Once, at the height of a reasonably clear exposition of enlightenment, a student burst out in distress: "But is Nirvana possible?"

Mr. Yi answered enthusiastically: "Oh, yes, very comfortable."

———————◆———————

Mr. Yi loved the story of the ancient Chinese who wore a Taoist robe, Buddhist sandals, and a Confucian hat. When questioned if he was a Taoist, the man pointed to his sandals. So the questioner asked the man if he was Buddhist. The man pointed to his hat. "I see," said the questioner. "You're a Confucian." The man pointed to his robe.

That was Mr. Yi. Once during a downpour during Thomas Dean's evening class on existentialism and Marxism, there was a tap on the door. Professor Dean opened it; there stood tiny Mr. Yi, an umbrella in each hand, one soaked, one dry. A student had forgotten his umbrella in the cafeteria where the three of us had eaten lunch together earlier that day. Mr. Yi had gone to the registrar, learned the times and room numbers of the student's classes, and tracked him down. He bowed to the professor in apology for the interruption, set the wet umbrella in the corridor by the door, walked to the young man's desk, and, without uttering a word, bowed and handed him the dry umbrella. The student burst into tears.

I later asked Mr. Yi why he had gone to so much effort when he would meet the student in class the following morning. He said: "It was my Confucian duty."

———————◆———————

Six students in the Religion Department, bearded hippies to the last, asked Mr. Yi to offer an independent study course in Chinese philosophy. In the name of the destruction of hierarchy, we proposed that we all receive an A grade. Mr. Yi replied, channeling Chuang Tzu: "You want to hide a universe in a universe instead of hiding a man in a man." He graded us as we requested.

My lasting memory of that class: A student brought in a section of Gary Snyder's *Mountains and Rivers Without End,* which includes these lines:

> Ko-san and I stood on a point by a cliff, over a rock-walled canyon. Ko said: "Now we have come to where we die." . . . [I] couldn't see why we should have to die. Ko grabbed me and pulled me over the cliff—both of us falling. I hit and I was dead. I saw my body for a while, then it was gone. Ko was there too.[55]

Mr. Yi said, when the student had finished reading: "The question is: Is there such a thing as death? If there is, you must fear it. Therefore, you must change the answer to that question."

———————◆———————

Mr. Yi liked to say that he had a very short memory, his way of stating that he lived in the eternal now.

A well-known American Zen master, an old friend of DeMartino, had come to our university to speak. In the midst of the lecture, Mr. Yi, having finished teaching his class, walked into the packed classroom, hopped onto a back table pushed against a window to make space for added chairs, and in his suit and necktie folded his legs into the full lotus posture, his little black shoes pulled up onto his thighs. When the talk was finished DeMartino, the Zen master, Mr. Yi, and I went to the student cafeteria for supper.

"How long have you been in America?" the Zen master asked Mr. Yi.

"I don't remember. My memory is very short."

"That's still too long!" snapped DeMartino.

"Each day I try to cut, cut," said Mr. Yi.

I was newly twenty and ignorant, but it seemed to me that the exchange went completely over the Zen master's head.

———————◆———————

My girlfriend Katherine invited Mr. Yi to a New Year's Eve party at her friend's house. He agreed, though apart from work he rarely left his campus apartment.

For two hours he sat in silence on the sofa, fingers intertwined at the back of his head, a many-toothed grin of contentment across his face. His sole remark, when I took off my winter coat to reveal bright red suspenders I was sure made me cool, was a quote from the *Blue Cliff Record*: "A dragon howling behind a withered tree." Mr. Yi's way of letting me know that my true Self was not to be found in any objectified image of myself. I went off to mingle and to flirt with Katherine. Each time I glanced at the sofa, he was smiling away. Around 11 p.m. I headed over to the sofa. Mr. Yi—beaming in the identical posture, interlocked hands still cradling his head—said: "Let us return home." My first glimpse of his detachment: complete enjoyment of a New Year's Eve from which he wanted nothing and that meant nothing.

———————◆———————

My first class in Buddhism began at 8:30 in the morning. DeMartino introduced the instructor, Keiji Nishitani, as "the world's greatest living Buddhist philosopher." Keiji Nishitani, however, was not in the room, for he was also an insomniac who, as I later heard in Japan, "went to sleep with the birds (when birds awoke and started singing)."

When he walked through the door at 9:10, he lit a cigarette, and in long, complex clauses that you lost all faith would ever conclude in a sentence until they always did, Nishitani proceeded to warrant his reputation. While doing so, the ash from the cigarette increased in size. When it finally dropped, a Chinese man as small as Nishitani, in an acrobatic dive with a campus newspaper improvised into an ashtray, intercepted it inches from the floor. My first sight of Mr. Yi.

He was forty-one then. He had fled China for Taiwan after the communist revolution. In hundreds of conversations, he mentioned his parents only once, for half a sentence—stopped in the middle after the words "what happened to them was *too* bad." In Taiwan he served in the army and attained the rank of major or colonel. He studied philosophy (Indian, Chinese, Western), taught philosophy, and for two years lived in a Buddhist monastery under a master who never lay in a bed but sat through the night in the high seat used for lectures. In 1962 Mr. Yi set out for Japan "to make direct contact with the living spirit of Zen." He arrived in Kyoto with $50 and stayed seven years, at first teaching Chinese to students he recruited by inserting flyers in neighborhood newspapers, teaching at Hanazono College by the end. DeMartino mentioned visiting his tiny room in the back of a public bath to find him reading the philosopher John Dewey. The visit could not have been reciprocated, since Mr. Yi told me: "We can say Dr. DeMartino is a man of some mystery. No one knew where he lived."

Invited to teach at my school for a semester, Nishitani brought his student Mr. Yi with him. When Professor Nishitani returned to Japan, Mr. Yi stayed on to teach courses in Chinese religion. It was a year too soon; had he delayed two semesters, his English—which though always thickly accented soon became rather good—would have caught up sufficiently to what was remarkable in him. Instead, he was fired. "I failed," he said when I went to his apartment. "I shall return to myself." When I expressed to DeMartino my displeasure that the Religion Department could be so blind to a treasure, he said: "How many people in the world are going to appreciate Yi's deeper dimension?"

A few days later, Mr. Yi moved to the Bronx with his wife and four-year-old son and found a job working for a Chinese language newspaper. He invited me to come and live with him until my first departure for Japan. There, I learned of his great idea: "The Man-Society Institute," which would offer courses in Buddhist and Taoist philosophy, meditation, and the art form in which I have not once seen his beauty equaled: tai chi. The snag: Mr. Yi insisted that these courses cost nothing. Whatever they have become for their teachers in America, meditation and tai chi were for him gifts, not products. He would support his institute solely from profits made in business. And Mr. Yi was among the worst businessmen who ever lived.

Thus, while he would have been a star in New York had he set up a tai chi studio (as I urged him to do), with time to devote to his scholarly projects, he slaved at work that made little money, or lost money, for years. Apart from one brief translation of Pai-chang, his other work on the Tang Zen masters who "jump from the page and into my life" fell past his reach. He shrugged it off. "To be only an academic is not enough. You have to do something practical for people."

"Your mastery of meditation and tai chi are of more practical help than doing drudge work," I countered.

"Maybe. But they are not for sale."

———————◆———————

He seemed to live without worry about money or the future. Locations changed, he needed work, found a job and did his best; the thought that one kind of work was less dignified than another seemed not to cross his mind. What did matter was to earn his way himself. "A dentist in Japan—far more beautiful than my wife—offered to support me if I married her," he said. "It isn't good to live on someone else's money." In New York he never sought an academic position. Professor Nishitani wrote that his doctorate degree—hard to achieve from a Japanese university at that time—would be awarded upon completion of his half-finished dissertation. Mr. Yi let it slide. Offers to return to university teaching and an easier life in Taiwan he ignored. *Detachment* is a word that gets thrown around a lot in Buddhism. Mr. Yi's detachment always struck me as different from what Buddhists think they mean by this word—not a matter of relinquishing an object or a desire but the relinquisher relinquished. I was sure of this in the way he lent me his car to drive from New York to Philadelphia; it wasn't the car but himself he wasn't concerned with. He never knocked on anyone's door, not out of some Gandhian criticism of friendship as an attachment to be averted but because it never occurred to him. He needed no friends. And befriended anyone who came his way, with a child's lack of discrimination.

———◆———

Two of these pals were Mr. Liu and Mr. Pan, like me living in his Bronx apartment. Mr. Liu was a student, no longer young, a man of exceptional warmth who would sing in English, I assume for my benefit: "Give Taiwan back to the Taiwanese." How Mr. Pan spent his days in New York was never clear to me. In Philadelphia he had been a cab driver, an expert in martial arts who was once arrested for scuffling with some police officers, then acquitted when he arrived at court, ponytail shorn and spruced up, and offered as his defense: "Can your honor really believe a little fellow like me could beat up these strong officers of the law?" His hero seemed to be a Taiwanese chi gong master who made an income as a street performer, controlling his body temperature and going shirtless in the winter and piling on wool garments in the summer with equal poise. The three laughed together every evening, on game nights while watching Mr. Pan's beloved New York Knicks—in whom Mr. Yi had not the slightest interest—on TV. In the cracks between work and hospitality, Mr. Yi studied, and while his guests and family slept, he meditated. A friend of mine who came to visit found the place so quiet that he looked through the keyhole before knocking. He saw Mr. Yi with eyes closed, full lotus on the sofa. Mr. Yi could sit in that position in complete comfort for two hours at a stretch. That work and family kept him so busy that he often had no time for meditation didn't faze him. "There are two approaches," he said. "One is meditation. The other is the pickup method." When I asked what the pickup method entailed, he said: "You pick up the moment as it comes and penetrate reality there."

His bookshelves—he was proud to have constructed them himself—sagged beneath the weight of hundreds of books on philosophy and religion in Chinese, Japanese, English, and German. On days when he didn't have to work, he could sit at his desk reading and translating from 6 a.m. until midnight in total contentment. The need to get out for an evening—to a movie, to anything—did not exist. I did rope him into seeing Jodorowsky's religious western *El Topo* though. At its finish, after the bodhisattva leads the sentient beings he has vowed to save to their mass murder, Mr. Yi's sole comment on the film was: "Many false gods." He never turned on the television of his own accord. It was there for his son, though he acknowledged that it improved his English. Once while he read C. G. Jung, when a thug from a Saturday afternoon B movie asked a plainclothes cop: "Who are you?" Mr. Yi lifted his eyes from his book and said to the actor: "The question is not 'Who are you?' The question is 'Who am I?'"

———◆———

It was Mr. Yi who wrote a Kyoto Zen master he knew and arranged for me to move into his monastery. The amount of meditation I'd have to undergo there terrified me, and I tried to accustom myself to lengthening stints of sitting in the months before I was to depart. Whenever I told him of my difficulties while sitting, he said: "You will experience many phenomena." When I excitedly told him of its pleasures, he said: "You will experience many phenomena." When I asked his advice as to how to achieve mastery in meditation, he said: "There are no shortcuts." When I asked him about breathing, he pulled up his shirt, dropped his trousers to his thighs to bare his lower abdomen, and with a long exhalation produced below the navel an astounding oblong protrusion the exact shape and firmness of a brick. "If you cannot execute the breathing well, it's better to forget it and just breathe naturally," he said. I asked about achieving no-mind. "While sitting, even in *samadhi,* there's usually some slight trace of thought. In tai chi, by contrast, I find all thought removed and experience something eternal." He squatted slightly—bent arms raised above his head—and proceeded to remain motionless for fifty minutes.[56] I lasted five.

From then on, each morning in his cheap white sneakers he taught me tai chi. He moved with a trained dancer's grace and a rare man's ecstasy, explosive and unmoving at the same time. His eyes became beautiful. I imitated. He would tap my fingers ever so gently and chastise my movements: "*You* are action. Tai chi is nonaction." He always referred to it as play. When a six-foot-six hulk cut in front of Mr. Yi in the park and challenged: "You think you can beat *me*?"—the five-foot Chinese laughed "Just exercising" with such delight that all hostility dropped from the man. Mr. Yi resumed moving in even slower motion. The man grew bored and walked away.

"Are you unaware the guy was threatening you?" I asked.

Mr. Yi quoted the *Ten Oxherding Pictures*: "Ox and Man both forgotten."

Katherine adored Mr. Yi's simplicity and in letters she wrote to him referred to herself with a lowercase *i*. She went her own way, and neither he nor I heard from her again. I never told him of the breakup, nor did he mention her. Months later, as we waited on the platform for the 1 train, I was invaded by my love for her. When I walked over to the bench where Mr. Yi sat, he said: "Have you heard from i with no capital?"

Two weeks later, during my tai chi lesson, I said: "Can you hold onto the koan while approaching a woman?"

Mr. Yi said: "Impossible."

———◆———

Mr. Yi never judged me. But he would delicately thwart me when I wrote checks for more money than I had in the bank. In Philadelphia, after my greenhorn's advocacy of the possibility of enlightenment failed to dent the skepticism of a friend visiting my apartment, Mr. Yi broke his long silence with: "Let us end our discussion." When from the backseat of his used Volvo I answered his wife's remark that I would someday be rewarded for helping her husband by claiming: "I already have my reward," Mr. Yi said from behind the wheel: "Not yet, not yet." One night in Chinatown, he introduced me to a pretentious Chinese monk who produced a business card so large that he had to carry it in a special pouch fastened to his robe. Reading down the long list of credentials front and back, I said to Mr. Yi out of the monk's hearing: "Didn't Lin-chi say the True Man is *without* title?" Mr. Yi said quietly, "You mustn't say that." Years later, explaining my plan to write a book about the difficulties of the Zen quest, he said: "You can give it up." I countered that the topic was important; Zen masters mostly expressed the awakening and spoke too little of the pitfalls and self-deceptions met trying to reach it. Mr. Yi said: "Yes, because to introduce such matters merely creates sources of attachment."

———◆———

My visa arrived and my departure date for Kyoto decided, Mr. Yi said to me: "Don't come back to America without something." He handed me an envelope with $200 he didn't have: "A Chinese custom for a journey, from my wife and I. Congratulations in advance." Before flying out from Philadelphia, I repeated Mr. Yi's admonition not to leave Japan "without something" to DeMartino. He said: "Don't put yourself under any ultimatums."

"You're letting me off the hook."

"What hook? I would think your task is to remove all the hooks."

I've described earlier my rapid and bungling monastic decline during my first stint in Japan. I must have written of it to Mr. Yi, for I received the sole photograph of the two of us in the mail with an inscription on the back: "I wish your health was as good as the day this photograph was taken." Some months later, after the nightly meditation, I was told I had a visitor, a Chinese with an astonishing Japanese vocabulary. Mr. Yi took one look at how scrawny I'd become and said: "You can go back home if you like."

When I did, I visited him. By then he had discovered Philadelphia Cream Cheese. It cracked him up to have packs of it waiting each time I arrived, often with friends from Philadelphia. Lunch would always be served, but before lunch: cream cheese, to be spread on loaves of super-market sliced bread that he would lift in one hand in their unopened cellophane package, the index finger of the other hand descending along the numerous slices as he invariably said: "There are *many*."

Two nights before one of our visits, I met a downtrodden old man on a Philadelphia street, bleeding from his hands and face with knife wounds. I took him to the hospital and waited with him in the emergency room until 2 a.m. When we left, the man asked me to take him home with me, as he had no place to live. It was one of the events that everyone must experience—even an atheist as myself—where the guilt of not living by the biblical injunction "Love thy neighbor as thyself" proves those words true. Since unexpected boarders in Mr. Yi's apartment were a common occurrence, I told him what had happened. He said: "If you have a home and someone needs a home, he or she has a home." I replied that I wasn't strong enough to have the man live with me in my one-room apartment, or even if I'd lived in a house. When we'd left the emergency room, I'd given him five dollars.

Mr. Yi said: "That's good enough."

———◆———

Suddenly Mr. Yi was co-owner of a Long Island supermarket, lined with shelves that from Wednesdays through Fridays I was paid $48 to organize and that by the following Wednesday were a chaos of thirty types of pasta mixed among cornflakes and canned peas. His Chinese first name proving too hard for patrons to remember, he decided his name was Sam. When at 11 p.m. we'd arrive at the sole remaining car in the parking lot, one mishap followed another. The front window was smashed. The tire was flat. Mr. Yi twice locked his keys in the car. I shivered at the bus stop, pleading for the bus that would take us into Queens, while Mr. Yi sat on the cement in the full lotus position in his shoes. Eighty minutes later, in Times Square Station, waiting for the 1 train bound for the Bronx, he was explaining Wittgenstein's later criticism of his *Tractatus Logico-Philosophicus* when mid-sentence he mistakenly boarded the train heading in the opposite direction. I let two trains and thirty minutes pass hoping for him to reappear, then gave up and boarded the Bronx train. Mr. Yi was seated by the door. The instant my butt hit the adjacent seat, without a hello, he resumed his lecture on Wittgenstein.

———◆———

Even while I lived under his roof, Mr. Yi was not a big talker about meditation or the Zen quest. He had no interest in the path, or intermediate steps, prior to enlightenment. He was pleased that I strove to awaken, yet if I didn't make the effort, or didn't attain, that was okay too. I asked him about meditation technique. He quoted Chuang Tzu: "Sitting and forgetting," and that was that. I asked him how grappling with the Mu koan differed from counting the breath. He said: "The same." I asked him—only once—about his own attainment. He said: "Falling through stars." I asked him what was the best way to proceed. He said: "Become a Buddha."

"I understand," I said, "but I'm asking about the best way to proceed to become a Buddha?"

He said: "I have no interest in becoming a Buddha. I only want to be a man."

———————◆———————

I once tried to reimburse Mr. Yi for a loan. He refused, saying casually: "What's mine is yours and what's yours is yours." I've known no other person who would have uttered these words, or who could back them up if he did. Twelve hours, six days per week were eaten up driving to and from and working at his supermarket. He performed his tasks with unconcern, caring not a whit for what he didn't have, or had not become, or that his scholarly pursuits were halted. He had no interest in being known to the world. No one at the supermarket knew he was a scholar. His spiritual attainment he of course kept to himself. This posed hardships for his family. His son's bed had a bath towel for a sheet and a small towel for a pillowcase. One Sunday afternoon, his kind, gentle wife sat on the arm of Mr. Yi's chair and in softest Chinese purred at him. His countenance got increasingly difficult to read. After twenty minutes, he answered her in English. "You are a chanting Buddha. Your mantra is: 'Money, money, money.'"

On rare nights after work we'd talk about Chinese philosophy. Of the *I Ching*, he said: "It's not a book of divination but of moral possibilities. The book must be internalized, not consulted." I showed him Ezra Pound's *Canto XIII*. We came to the lines

And Kung [Confucius] raised his cane against Yuan Jang,
Yuan Jang being his elder,
For Yuan Jang sat by the roadside pretending to
be receiving wisdom.
And Kung said "You old fool, come out of it,
"Get up and do something useful."[57]

Mr. Yi said: "Confucius would strike Pound with his cane if he could get his hands on him."

Another night I asked how Buddhist pacifism could stop a Hitler. Mr. Yi told me a story of an early incarnation of the Buddha. A group of five hundred had found gold. During the night, the Buddha preincarnate read the mind of a thief who planned to murder the whole lot of them and take all the gold for himself. The Buddha thought: "If the robber kills them, he goes to hell." So he killed the robber to go to hell in his place.

Before too long, the supermarket went under, of course. Nowhere to duck, then, from DeMartino's rebuke of a year earlier when I had predicted that Mr. Yi was going to lose his shirt: "Yeah, and you're going to help him do it."

———————◆———————

Five years earlier, in 1970, the amazing Keiji Nishitani—Mr. Yi's revered professor of Buddhist philosophy during his years in Kyoto—had returned to Philadelphia for a week en route to a conference in Syracuse. Mr. Yi pulled apart his bed frame, reconstructed it for Nishitani in his living room, and slept in his bedroom on a blanket on the floor. Mr. Yi invited me to his apartment. Nishitani was there, along with a Chinese who taught Confucian thought at Princeton, Professor Tu.

Like so many Americans I knew who were interested in Eastern religion, my passion was for Buddhism, Taoism, and Hinduism—whose cosmic enlightenment would automatically transform me into a compassionate, good person—while Confucianism, with its apparent emphasis on moral conduct in lieu of enlightenment, had been shunted to the side. Professor Tu said: "Any serious practitioner of any religion must go through an agonizing moral struggle." The white-hot intensity with which he uttered these words shocked me.

At one point Nishitani picked up from a coffee table a mimeo-graphed magazine sent to Mr. Yi from some American Zen center. Nishitani opened to a page that read in large letters: "How high is the sky?" Nishitani, with indescribable beauty and simplicity, cocked his head to think about this before saying, face full of wonder: "I don't know." Mr. Yi explained to him that I would be studying Zen in Japan. Nishitani said: "Write me. I will help."

It was a help I did not need for my first trip, as the monastery mas-ter's letters to the Japanese embassy on my behalf had procured for me a rare five-year visa. Robbed in Kentucky with a rifle at my head while hitchhiking east after flying in from Japan, I lost that visa along with my passport. The Japanese embassy refused to replace it. Mr. Yi suggested that I take up Professor Nishitani on his offer to help and ask if he would write the required letter of guarantee, generally regarded as a bureaucratic formality that imposed no actual liability on one's Japanese sponsor.

Three months later, my application for a new visa was turned down by the Japanese embassy. The first and last time I saw sadness in Mr. Yi's face was as he read the letter of rejection. "Sometimes enlighten-ment is not enough," he murmured. He knew that the guarantee letter had been weak, or the visa would not have been denied.

———————◆———————

From age twenty-one to thirty-seven, I did not live a single day without severe intestinal pain. When, after months of wrangling, a minimal visa finally was approved, the pain was so intense that I pondered delaying my departure. If I waited too long, however, the visa would expire.

I asked Mr. Yi what he would do in my place. Mr. Yi said: "Many ancient Zen masters suffered as much as you. I would go." A ridiculous remark. "Many ancient Zen masters have suffered far more than you" was the truth of the matter. The slight difference was Mr. Yi's great gift to me. A week later I was in Kyoto.

————◆————

I did not meet Mr. Yi again until 1980. He was owner of a hapless English language school in Chinatown that he did call the Man-Society Institute. Mr. Yi had a novel approach to language pedagogy: Level of proficiency was not taken into account; classes were exclusively based on when Chinese clientele were free. Morning classes were for restaurant workers whose shifts began in the afternoons. Evening classes convened for garment industry employees and others who got off at 5 p.m. Students who spoke English fluently and had lived in the United States for years sat next to immigrants who had arrived in New York ten days previous. I began teaching at the school, alternately boring longtime residents by teaching recent immigrants and improving veteran speakers by leaving beginners in the dust. When I discussed the untenability of this setup, Mr. Yi's solution was: "More meditation." My own solution was jitterbug lessons secretly interspersed with English instruction. Mr. Yi complimented me for knowing how to control a class.

I lived in the school in a closet-size room separated from a classroom by a curtain. Meals and a shower at his house, a promised salary of $150 per week for now and an apartment in the future. One lunchtime, watching Mr. Yi cook in his Chinatown apartment, I asked him about a phrase that Hisamatsu and Masao Abe made much of: "When deadlocked, there is a change. Where there is a change, one has broken through." He told me that Zen had lifted it from the *I Ching*. A minute later his month-old son started to cry. Mr. Yi went over to the crib, examined the diaper, and in great happiness boomed: "Change!"

Second week on the job, I found $100 on my pillow. We never discussed the pay cut; he didn't have more, so I shrugged it off. Mr. Yi was at the school from eight until eight except for lunch, working to the bone without tiring. I brought a melancholic sculptor I was in love with for a visit. Smiling away in his institute director's chair, head tilted back against intertwined palms, Mr. Yi replied, in response to her question as to what he did when he felt depressed: "It's impossible for me to be depressed. Buddhism and Taoism have made it impossible."

I accompanied him to storefronts run by his Chinatown friends—curtains down the middle of narrow shops, lamps sold left of the curtain, toys or household cleaning goods to the right—where he'd chat over tea in Chinese I couldn't grasp for as long as three hours. He took me to meet a former professor from Hong Kong or Taiwan, just emigrated, now living in his building. He hurried me along Canal Street in great excitement to a fancy restaurant that he excitedly promised "served the best Peking dog, the best Peking dog." Dog, to my joy, proved to be duck with a bad accent.

One morning a troop of five-year-olds barged past the curtain into my room to find it true that a skinny white guy sat cross-legged on cushions in his underwear. The institute, to stay afloat, had become a day-care center. When some months later we were suddenly in the business of selling videocassettes, I guessed the end was near. Mr. Yi's cheerfulness was undiminished.

I went back to Japan for eleven more years. I never saw Mr. Yi again. In the States for a visit when my father died, I tried to ring his bell. "Yi" was no longer on the mailbox. Two men in the management office seemed to know where he'd moved but wouldn't say. I told them I'd been his student and close friend for years. They grew hostile.

I'm thinking, as I write, of an ending to this portrait, of an ending to a book I've been writing for three decades. I had arrived one evening in Mr. Yi's second Bronx apartment across from Van Courtland Park. There was a cut across his forehead. A few days before, a police car had stopped him in his Volvo three blocks from his house. Worse, he had forgotten his license. The cops decided to take him to the station. Mr. Yi explained that his license was at home, two minutes away. The cops weren't interested. "I am Mr. Yi, I am Mr. Yi," he said again and again. The cops weren't interested in that either. Somehow he got into his car, U-turned, sped off, and stopped in the middle of the street in front of his house—to show he was he and where he lived. One of the cops yanked him from his car, banging his head against the steering wheel.

Some years after the institute closed, while I was in Japan, a dancer friend of mine living in Brooklyn went to buy a newspaper. The proprietor of the newsstand was Mr. Yi. Recognizing her, he energetically explained that he could sell the newsstand for $20,000.

Over Philadelphia Cream Cheese spread across many slices of bread, Mr. Yi once said to me in his Bronx kitchen: "I can't say I ever treat anyone with wisdom. I *can* say I never treat anyone without compassion."

Notes

1. Often esteemed as the greatest Zen master of modern Japan.
2. Elie Wiesel, *Souls on Fire: Portraits and Legends of Hasidic Masters*, trans. Marion Wiesel (New York: Random House, 1972), 61. Lieb refers to his teacher, the Maggid of Mezeritch, the greatest disciple of the founder of Hasidism, the Bal Shem Tov.
3. *The Record of Lin-Chi*, trans. Ruth Fuller Sasaki (Kyoto: Institute for Zen Studies, 1975), 53.
4. Shin'ichi Hisamatsu, *Zen and the Fine Arts* (Tokyo: Kodansha International, 1971), 16.
5. When I return for my second stay in Japan and inquire what happened to her, I am told that she's been placed in a nursing home. I ask: "After tending to the priest for all those years?" The monk imparting this news shrugs: "Who was going to take care of her? The priest?" When Mrs. K. brought fruit to the monastery monks, she would pray outside the main gate, head bowed and eyes closed, in awe of entering the space where the monks she so clearly loved trained.
6. D. T. Suzuki, *Essays in Buddhism: Second Series* (London: Rider and Company, 1970), 117.
7. D. T. Suzuki, *Manual of Zen Buddhism* (New York: Grove Press, 1960), 94.
8. Jiro Anzai, ed. and trans., "Two Cases of Zen Awakening (Kensho) Experiences: (1) Master Shibayama's Case," *Psychologia* 13 (1970): 141.
9. Shin'ichi Hisamatsu, "On the *Record of Rinzai* (1)," trans. Gishin Tokiwa and Christopher A. Ives, *Eastern Buddhist*, n.s., 14, no. 1 (Spring 1981): 9.
10. "Shōzan-Rōshi and Contemporary Zen," trans. Howard Curtis, *FAS Zen Society Newsletter* (Spring 1978): 2. See "Shōzan-Rōshi to Gendai no Zen," *Zen Bunka* 86 (September 1977): 28 for the Japanese text of this interview with Hisamatsu.
11. Hui-k'o, originally called Shen-kuang, according to the likely fabricated Zen account, stands through the night in a snowstorm outside the cave of the alleged first Zen patriarch, Bodhidharma. When the master warns him

that the Zen path is unendurably difficult, Hui-k'o pulls out a sword, cuts off his arm, and presents it to his chosen teacher.

12. DeMartino's apartment life when I met him was not without adventure. Once he was held captive, alone, inside the local Laundromat. On another occasion he was held up in his foyer at knifepoint. DeMartino told his attacker: "It's OK if you kill me. But I've got to get to class." The attacker insisted that DeMartino buy a watch for $5. When he declined, the stranger lifted DeMartino's wallet, extracted a $5 bill, returned the wallet, and handed over the watch.

13. The fact that Harada kept him in the *sanzen* room for so long—I was never in my own monastery teacher's room for more than a minute—indicated that something of significance had happened to him. For thirty years I never asked DeMartino why Harada had detained him at such length, since Hisamatsu's reaction was clearly what counted for him. But in one of our very last conversations, after the onset of his Parkinson's, I asked him about Hisamatsu's rejection of his Hosshinji experience and Harada's response. He said: "Harada tried to tell me the same thing." Then I said, "That was pretty audacious of you—to reject both of them." Shaking his head in disbelief at his confidence on that occasion, he said, softly: "I guess it *was*." He often warned: "A breakthrough must be tested against your weakest point."

14. That is, whether to actively try to break through the Zen koan or passively allow the koan to gnaw from within until a resolution comes of its own accord.

15. Literally, "seeking and contriving"—one's struggle on the Zen quest.

16. In a subsequent letter, when I despaired of my failure to muster supreme courage, DeMartino wrote in reply: "Courage doesn't sound right. Gautama sitting beneath the *bodhi* tree wasn't an act of courage. He had no choice."

17. Richard DeMartino, "The Human Situation and Zen Buddhism," in D. T. Suzuki, Erich Fromm, and Richard DeMartino, *Zen Buddhism and Psychoanalysis* (New York: Harper & Brothers, 1960), 153.

18. He could have easily not ended up teaching. Psychologist Carl Rogers, whom he met in Japan, had invited DeMartino to take a graduate degree with him at the University of Wisconsin. He accepted the invitation, but the funding fell through. In retrospect, he said he was "glad not to have gone into that line of work."

19. One of my earliest experiences of DeMartino was his ritual purchase of the *Philadelphia Inquirer* from a small newsstand across the street from his apartment. The proprietor would greet him: "What you got to say to the world, Professor?" "E!" DeMartino would bellow from his lower

abdomen, demanding the late edition that listed the day's closing stock returns. The shared pleasure and affection in this brief, nightly exchange, and DeMartino's exaggerated retort from the belly (or *hara*) in the Zen style suggested from the beginning of our acquaintance a past in Japan that would never be penetrated and a person, however much he revealed of himself in class, who would never be known.

20. A comical side of his meditation concentration: A Japanese aikido master who for a year taught free classes in ki (vital force) cultivation at Temple University could not budge DeMartino until he made him laugh. This invariably broke his concentration, whereupon Moriyama-sensei would give him a shove.

21. DeMartino always made a distinction between "zazen to" and "zazen from." The former involved the struggle to resolve the problem; the latter was anything an awakened person did. For him, neither was confined to "sitting."

22. Richard DeMartino, "On My First Coming to Meet Dr. Shin'ichi Hisamatsu," *Eastern Buddhist*, n.s., 14, no. 1 (Spring 1981): 113–116.

23. Hisamatsu refused to be referred to as a master and had, in consequence, no disciples. That didn't stop many of those who studied with him for decades from regarding themselves as such; hence my use of the term.

24. In Zen terminology, a synonym for the Great Awakening.

25. Richard DeMartino, "The Human Situation and Zen Buddhism," in D. T. Suzuki, Erich Fromm, and Richard DeMartino, *Zen Buddhism and Psychoanalysis* (New York: Harper & Brothers, 1960), 163.

26. At the monastery *yaza* was mandatory, usually for thirty minutes, though one was free to continue on one's own. With this lay group, it was entirely optional, though Toyoshima-san did more *yaza* than any monk I have known.

27. Abe here followed his teacher Hisamatsu, for whom "nothingness-*samadhi*" is a mere temporary realization of no-self-no-world. Thus Hisamatsu regarded it as a "particular *samadhi*"—a state of nonduality limited to a particular time and place—that fails to resolve the human predicament.

28. See "King of Whatever Universe," the opening essay of this book.

29. The letters F, A, and S are prounounced separately. *F* refers to the awakened or *Formless Self*, which, free of the forms of life and death, self and other, body and mind, can express itself freely in all forms. *A* refers to the reality that, having broken through the discrimination between self and other, the Formless Self stands on the standpoint of *all* humankind. *S* refers to *s*uprahistorical history, by which Hisamatsu means that the awakened Self, breaking through time, acts creatively in time with the aim of constructing an enlightened world.

30. In that same conversation, which occurred after the death of the last of the four mid-twentieth-century Zen masters DeMartino most admired (Shin'ichi Hisamatsu, Zenkei Shibayama, Shōnen Morimoto, and Mumon Yamada), he said of Kitahara: "He's probably the best Zen figure in Japan now."

31. Some years later I mentioned that his daughter shared a name with the great thirteenth-century Persian Sufi poet. He said: "The Formless Self can no doubt be found in Islam too. I'm not very familiar with Islam."

32. Nishida (1870–1945) is generally regarded as the greatest philosopher of modern Japan. He was Hisamatsu's most important teacher, along with the Zen master Shōzan Ikegami.

33. Ryūtarō Kithara, "Makujikikō," *Zen Bunka* 97 (June 1980). I wish to thank Dr. Hiromi Maeda for her deeply moving draft translation of Kitahara's essay, which served as the basis of my own renderings of the passages extracted for this book.

34. Kitahara is comparing Hisamatsu to the great Indian lay Buddhist Vimalakirti, whose abode was Vaisali City. Crumbling Vaisali City and toppling Vimalakirti would consist of "taking away both man and his surroundings," as *The Record of Lin-chi* would have it; that is, obliterating subject and object.

35. His interest in Indian yoga once prompted me to mentioned to Kitahara that the great nineteenth-century Hindu Ramakrishna, in the terminal stages of throat cancer, flinching at the terrible pain caused by the doctor's instruments as he explored the cancerous tissue, asked him to pause a moment, entered into meditative *samadhi,* and then invited the doctor to proceed. Kitahara said: "India really *is* full of surprises." In that same conversation on India, I asked: "Are you familiar with the sitar (*shitaru* in Japanese)?" "Shitaru shitara Kitahara," he said. (*Shitara* means "if I do" in Japanese, but the meaning is irrelevant. It was a glimpse of the speed of his sensitivity to sound.)

36. "Jinrui no chikai" in Japanese—composed by Hisamatsu in 1951 and recited at the end of each evening's meditation of the FAS Society.

37. The statement is by Huang Po (died 850) and appears in Case 11 of the *Blue Cliff Record.*

38. 1251–1284, regent of the Kamakura shogunate, de facto ruler of Japan, and an ardent practitioner and supporter of Zen.

39. The characters in Japanese read: "Hogejyaku." This utterance is from Chao-chou (798–897) in a well-known exchange. The oldest reference to this story is Case 57 of the 従容録 (*Shōyōroku*), which first appeared in 1224: Monk: "What if I come to you with nothing?" Chao-chou: "Cast it away!" Monk: "But I said I come to you with nothing!" Chao-chou: "Then carry it away."

40. The characters in Japanese read: "Hōshashoen kyūsokubanji."

41. The characters in Japanese read: "Shūrusetsudan."

42. 無位真人 ("Mui no Shinnin"), Lin-chi's (died 866) famous designation for an awakened Self.

43. Bunko's account differs from the version of the story in which Tanzan simply sent postcards announcing his death to his friends, assumed the meditation posture, and died.

44. There are several versions of this story. Most cite as the chief example of his stupidity Chūdapanthaka's inability to remember even a tiny verse of scripture. I've not yet found a reference to him being unable to remember his own name. In some versions, rather than having him sweep, the Buddha has him recite the mantra while rubbing a cloth with his palm. One anecdote describes his failure to recite the mantra "Sweeping broom" without forgetting one of the words.

45. In response to my recent letter inquiring into the identity of the monk, Bunko writes that more than one master has made such a claim, but believes the monk in question was the Chinese Zen master Wu-Yi Yuan-lai (1575–1630).

46. Somerset Maugham, *The Razor's Edge* (New York: Vintage International, 2003), 208.

47. Martin Lings, *A Sufi Saint of the Twentieth Century: Shaikh Ahmad al-'Alawi: His Spiritual Heritage and Legacy* (Berkeley: University of California Press, 1973), 26.

48. The repetition of the name of Amitâbha Buddha, "Namu Amida Butsu," is believed to be the saving chant in Pure Land Buddhism.

49. Kira Kōsuke no suke (1641–1703), an official of the Tokugawa shogunate, was assassinated by forty-seven samurai of the Akō clan in a celebrated episode of the *Forty-Seven Ronin*. At a reception for imperial messengers at Edo Castle in 1701, Kira, commonly disliked for his arrogance, received a slight wound in the forehead at the hands of Asano Takumi no kami (1667–1701), *daimyō* of Akō, who believed that Kira had intentionally withheld from him the fine points of court etiquette needed to avoid error in matters of protocol. For drawing his sword, he was immediately deprived of his domain and ordered to commit suicide. Kira escaped even reprimand, though later he was forced to leave office. Asano's retainers vowed vengeance, which they achieved in 1703, executing him in his own home.

50. Ryūtarō Kitahara, "Makujikikō [Straight Ahead]," *Zen Bunka* 97 (June 1980): 35–36.

51. His age in 1995, when this essay was written and published in Japanese translation. He was born in 1925. For the Japanese version of the essay, see *Zenbunkakenkyūjokiyo* (Annual Report from the Institute for Zen Studies) 21 (March 1995).

52. Fermented soybeans, slimy in texture and foul smelling to the uninitiated.

53. The "Vow of Humankind" begins with the words: "Keeping calm and composed, let us awaken to our true Self."

54. Traditionally, Buddhists believe there are "Three Refuges": in the Buddha; in the dharma, or teachings, of the Buddha; and in the *sangha,* the community of those who have attained enlightenment or, more generally, the community of Buddhist practitioners.

55. Gary Snyder, *Mountains and Rivers Without End* (Berkeley, CA: Counterpoint, 1996), 57–58.

56. Mr. Yi's thin thighs were so powerful that when hiking down a steep hill in the woods, they functioned as brakes, enabling him to descend at slow speed while I had to run.

57. Ezra Pound, *The Cantos (1–95)* (New York: New Directions Corporation, 1956), 58–59.

Acknowledgments

Having reached an age when neither time nor talent may afford a later opportunity, I wish to thank:

Jack Shoemaker, beyond speech and silence.

My great friend Naomi Maeda, former librarian of the Institute for Zen Studies in Kyoto and former editor of the journal *Zen Bunka*. Without her answers to my endless questions, this book would be greatly diminished. That parts of it have appeared previously in Japanese is also a consequence of her kindness.

The seven friends who have advised or assisted on all or parts of the manuscript: Jeff Cain, Lee Roser, Hiromi Maeda, Yui Matsuzaki, Nancy Davenport, Sis Mamolen, and the principal reader of all that I write, Marty Rosenfeld.

Peg Goldstein, my copy editor, and Matt Hoover, my production editor.

Finally, my unforgettable Kyoto friends of the 1970s: Urs App, Teddy Hyndman, Rick Hyndman (1944–2011), Howard Curtis, Tatsuo Tanemura, Jun Saburi, Bill Moseley, Erika Horn, Kenzō Toyoshima, Tim Pallis, Yuki Pallis, Michele Martin, Michiyo Ochi (1920–2010), Takeyo Maeda, Kazuyo Ōtani, Gishin Tokiwa, Priscilla Storandt, Yoke Chin Kham, Toshio Ōyabu, Kanko Murasaki, Wayne Yokoyama, and Yukie Dan—each of whom proves so very true the first sentence I learned in Japanese language school: "Tabi wa michizure yo wa nasake" ("In traveling, a companion; in life, sympathy").